THE TRINITY IN GERMAN THOUGHT

The Trinity in German Thought describes the three ideas that govern modern German Trinitarian thought: the ideas of reflective selfhood, of revelation, and of history. "Reflective selfhood" designates the attempt at finding an analogy between the Trinity and the structure of the human self. Such attempts, following the lead of Augustine, typically see the structure of self-consciousness as an especially apt analogy of the Trinity. "Revelation" points to two questions: what is the Word of God? and can the idea of the Trinity be derived from the Word? From Martin Luther to the present, Trinitarian thought has depended on the way in which theologians conceived of the Word. "History" designates the way in which historical modes of thinking have affected Trinitarian thought. For some, "history" has meant a critical approach to Scripture and creeds; for others, it has meant God's own participation in history.

SAMUEL M. POWELL is Professor of Philosophy and Religion at Point Loma Nazarene University. He is editor of *Embodied Holiness* (1999) and is a selected participant in the John Templeton Oxford Seminars on Science and Christianity (1999–2001). He is a member of the American Academy of Religion, the Society of Biblical Literature, and the Wesleyan Theological Society, and has received a fellowship from the Wesleyan Center for Twenty-First Century Studies.

THE TRINITY IN GERMAN THOUGHT

SAMUEL M. POWELL

Point Loma Nazarene University

CAMBRIDGE
UNIVERSITY PRESS

PUBLISHED BY THE PRESS SYNDICATE OF THE UNIVERSITY OF CAMBRIDGE
The Pitt Building, Trumpington Street, Cambridge, United Kingdom

CAMBRIDGE UNIVERSITY PRESS
The Edinburgh Building, Cambridge CB2 2RU, UK   www.cup.cam.ac.uk
40 West 20th Street, New York, NY 10011–4211, USA   www.cup.org
10 Stamford Road, Oakleigh, Melbourne 3166, Australia
Ruiz de Alarcón 13, 28014 Madrid, Spain

© Samuel M. Powell 2001

First published 2001

Printed in the United Kingdom at Redwood Books, Trowbridge

Typeface Monotype Baskerville 11/12.5 pt.   *System* QuarkXPress™   [SE]

A catalogue record for this book is available from the British Library

Library of Congress Cataloguing in Publication data

Powell, Samuel M.
The Trinity in German thought / Samuel M. Powell.
p.   cm.
Includes bibliographical references and index.
ISBN 0-521-78196-5 (hb)
1. Trinity.   2. Theology – Germany – History.   I. Title.

BT109.P69 2000
231′.044′0943–dc21
00-025316

ISBN 0 521 78196 5 hardback

Contents

Acknowledgments   *page* vii

Introduction   1

1 Martin Luther and Philip Melanchthon   12

2 Between scholastic theology and Enlightenment   31
   Introduction   31
   Nicolaus Ludwig von Zinzendorf   32
   Gottfried Wilhelm Leibniz   46
   Conclusion   58

3 The critical Enlightenment   60
   Introduction   60
   Hermann Samuel Reimarus   63
   Johann Salomo Semler   69
   Gotthold Lessing   80
   Friedrich Schleiermacher   87
   Conclusion   102

4 Georg Wilhelm Friedrich Hegel   104
   Introduction   104
   Preliminary orientation   104
   The nature of conceptual comprehension   111
   Questions of method   113
   The idea of revelation   116
   The ontological Trinity of eternity   120
   The Trinity of history   128
   The Spirit   134
   Conclusion   138

5   Liberal theology   142
      Introduction   142
      Albrecht Ritschl   142
      The spirit of Melanchthon   146
      History and criticism   160
      God's selfhood as person   166
      Conclusion   171

6   The twentieth century   173
      Introduction   173
      The Word and the Trinity   175
      God's selfhood and the Trinity   210
      The historicity of Bible and tradition   239
      The historicity of God   246
      Conclusion   258

Postscript to twentieth-century Trinitarian thought   260

Bibliography of works consulted   264
Index   276

Acknowledgments

I would like to thank those who helped me with this book along the way: the Wesleyan Center for Twenty-First Century Studies, for summer grants that made the writing possible; the faculty and staff of Nazarene Theological College (Manchester, UK) whose support while I was on sabbatical there was invaluable; Jack Verheyden, who reminded me of the importance of theology; Craig Keen, whose willingness to discuss ideas saved me many an hour of futile searching; my colleagues and staff at Point Loma Nazarene University, for their support and encouragement; and most of all to my wife, Terrie, and family, to whom I dedicate this book.

Introduction

The doctrine of the Trinity is once again on theology's front burner. Having languished under liberal theology, the doctrine is enjoying a resurgence of interest, as attested by the popularity of such works as Catherine Mowry LaCugna's *God for Us* and John D. Zizioulas' *Being as Communion*.[1] We may also point to the importance of the doctrine to the theologies of Jürgen Moltmann, Eberhard Jüngel and Wolfhart Pannenberg[2] as a testimony to its resurrection from obscurity.

Having taken note of this recent rise of interest in the doctrine, certain questions linger: Why has it lately sprung back to center stage? Why did theologians previously consign it to the irrelevant periphery? The easy answer to these questions – that only recently have theologians regained their senses and begun returning to theology's true source – not only begs numerous questions but also fails to explain the dynamics inherent in modern Trinitarian thought, dynamics that determine the fate of the doctrine in any given era. Such an explanation does not aid us in the task of understanding; understanding requires that we attend to the history of this thought.

My purpose in this book is to set forth the components of

---

[1] Catherine Mowry LaCugna, *God for Us: The Trinity and Christian Life* (San Francisco: Harper San Francisco, a division of HarperCollins Publishers, 1993); John D. Zizioulas, *Being as Communion: Studies in Personhood and the Church*, Contemporary Greek Theologians, no. 4 (Crestwood, NY: St. Vladimir's Seminary Press, 1997).

[2] Jürgen Moltmann, *The Trinity and the Kingdom: The Doctrine of God*, trs. Margaret Kohl (San Francisco: Harper & Row, 1981); Eberhard Jüngel, *God as the Mystery of the World: On the Foundation of the Theology of the Crucified One in the Dispute between Theism and Atheism*, trs. Darrell L. Guder (Grand Rapids: William B. Eerdmans Publishing Co., 1983); Wolfhart Pannenberg, *Systematic Theology*, trs. Geoffrey W. Bromiley, 3 vols. (Grand Rapids: William B. Eerdmans Publishing Co., 1991–1998).

modern Trinitarian thought in such a way that its history – both
distant and recent – becomes comprehensible. The thesis I propose
is that modern Trinitarian thought is driven by three engines: the
concept of the Word of God (i.e., revelation), the concept of
reflective selfhood, and the concept of history. The importance
and form that the doctrine of the Trinity assumes in any given
period depend on the ways in which the theologian or philosopher
understands these concepts and on the relative weight assigned to
them.

Since we are examining the ways in which these concepts –
Word, self and history – have changed in the last three centuries
and how these changes have affected thinking about the Trinity,
this book is necessarily concerned with history and in particular
with one slice from history, German Protestant theology and philosophy. Why *German* theology and philosophy? Whenever this
question is posed, one is tempted to adduce the opening lines of
Albert Schweitzer's book, *The Quest of the Historical Jesus*: "When, at
some future day, our period of civilisation shall lie, closed and completed, before the eyes of later generations, German theology will
stand out as a great, a unique phenomenon in the mental and spiritual life of our time."[3] Although a bit ostentatious by contemporary standards of prose, Schweitzer's statement is on the mark: it
was in Germany that an alternative to the medieval Roman
Catholic view of revelation was born, in Germany that modern
historical consciousness arose, and in Germany that the contemporary understanding of the self finds its roots. Like no other part
of the Christian tradition, German Protestant theology and philosophy of religion have consistently been on the forefront of
modern thought, functioning as a virtual idea-factory for the contemporary world.

In order to grasp the movement and inner logic of German
Trinitarian thought, it is necessary to understand the ways in which
the concepts of Word, self and history have developed and inter-
acted in this Germanic tradition. The concept of revelation has
been, even among Protestants, the subject of more disputation and
development than might be expected. In fact, as we will note, it was

---

[3] Albert Schweitzer, *The Quest of the Historical Jesus: A Critical Study of Its Progress from Reimarus
to Wrede*, trs. W. Montgomery (New York: Macmillan, 1948), 1.

the very first generation of Protestants who unwittingly sowed the seeds of later contentions with their ambivalent declarations on the subject. "Self" here refers to the way in which the doctrine of the Trinity is understood in relation to the fact that God is a subject; it raises the question of what it means to be a subject and in particular what it means to say that God is a subject. The dynamics of this concept are caused first by conflicting philosophical theories of subjectivity and second by the fact that the doctrine of the Trinity speaks of three Trinitarian persons. It has been a perplexing task to harmonize a belief in three persons with a belief that God is a single and personal subject. History is the third concept to be introduced because, historically, it was the third to become important for this tradition. Emerging in the eighteenth century, historical thinking first applied itself to a literary criticism of the Biblical text, then to a theological perspective on revelation, and finally, by the early nineteenth century, to a philosophical theory about the historicity of God's own being.

Since it is a daunting task to trace out the history of thought on so complex an issue, it may be helpful to sketch out in a preliminary fashion the general contours of the history of German Trinitarian thought, showing how these three concepts function as the engines that move the tradition along. From the beginning of this tradition in the Reformation until the early eighteenth century, only the first two of these concepts were operative; as noted above, "history" did not become an issue until the middle part of the eighteenth century. Early on, then, the main issues were two: first, whether revelation (i.e., the Bible) contains the doctrine of the Trinity and second, whether we can find an analogy to the Trinity in the nature of the human self, thus affording us an avenue for understanding the Trinity. The first issue (whether revelation contains the doctrine) might seem to admit of easy resolution, a matter of discerning whether the Bible does or does not contain the doctrine of the Trinity, or at least statements that imply the doctrine. However, as is so often true in theology, the matter is scarcely so simple. Involved here is the question of how one is to interpret the Bible and related questions about the role of the church and other authorities in coming to an adequate interpretation. We should also note that this was a peculiarly Protestant problem; no

Christian had ever questioned whether the doctrine of the Trinity could be drawn from the Bible until Luther and Melanchthon proposed a view of the Bible and of theological authority largely at odds with the medieval view. Luther and Melanchthon both dearly wanted to affirm the doctrine of the Trinity, yet neither could simply do so on the basis of its appearance in the ancient creeds – their understanding of authority compelled them to justify everything by means of a direct appeal to the Bible. But, as all could plainly see, the doctrine in its technical formulation is absent from the Bible; the most that could be accomplished would be to show that it is implied by Scripture. To this task Luther and Melanchthon set themselves assiduously and not without success.

However, complicating their work were their own public declarations to the effect that revelation is all about the way in which God relates to us, particularly in such vital matters as forgiveness of sin. Although initially innocuous sounding, such sentiments could be (and were later) taken to imply that revelation describes God only in a certain way, namely insofar as God appears to us in the events of salvation. Ensconced in this view is the suggestion that revelation does not disclose to us God's nature in its eternal essence. While it may seem that this distinction between God's appearance to us in revelation and God's eternal nature in itself is somewhat subtle, what is at stake is not subtle. The suggestion that God as revealed may differ from God's nature can lead to a Christian skepticism in which God's nature is set over against God's revelation and proclaimed to be something that is utterly unknowable. Theology, in this view, must restrict itself to expounding revelation and must consign God's nature to the realm of mystery. When this attitude is adopted, the doctrine of the Trinity becomes an ornament that, although admired and reverently adored, is generally regarded as useless and extravagant, belonging as it seems to the realm of mystery. Although Luther and Melanchthon each found this attitude abhorrent, their understanding of revelation had unwittingly established the conditions for it. From this time onward, there would always be representatives of this skeptical attitude within the Protestant tradition, claiming, perhaps with good reason, to find warrant for their views in the thought of the early reformers. Much of the energy devoted

to Trinitarian thought from the period of the Reformation until
the early eighteenth century was accordingly occupied with trying
to show that the doctrine of the Trinity is well grounded in the
Bible. However, there has been, in the last three centuries, a steady
stream of voices echoing Melanchthon's initial hesitation to accord
to the doctrine of the Trinity an important place in Protestant theology. These voices constitute the liberal wing of Protestant
thought, with its emphasis on what we may call the existential
dimension of the Christian faith and its disdaining of such recondite doctrines as the Trinity. Of course, whether the liberals have
been faithful to the breadth of Melanchthon's own theology may
be doubted; nonetheless, it cannot be denied that theologians such
as J. S. Semler in the eighteenth century, Albrecht Ritschl in the
nineteenth century and Rudolf Bultmann in the twentieth century
have laid claim to a vital aspect of early Reformation thought, a
fact that signifies a fundamental tension at the heart of Protestant
theology's understanding of revelation. At the same time, other
theologians (in the eighteenth century, notably Ludwig von
Zinzendorf; in the twentieth century, Barth, Moltmann and
Pannenberg are examples) have insisted just as adamantly that the
idea of the Trinity *can* be read off the surface of revelation;
however, their insistence is made possible by their having altered
the meaning of "revelation." No longer for these theologians is it
identical with the words of the Bible, as though the doctrine could
be deduced from a sufficient number of Biblical passages; instead
it refers to Jesus Christ – the person of Jesus Christ is the locus of
revelation and also the immediate source of the idea of the Trinity.
So, although we may represent the debate about revelation as an
internecine Protestant struggle between those who hold that
revelation does imply and those who believe that it does not imply
the doctrine of the Trinity, we must also observe that the conception of revelation itself is a moving target in the history of
Trinitarian thought. All hands agree on its centrality to theology;
however, accord on the meaning of revelation has not been forthcoming.

The second issue (whether we can find an analogy to the Trinity
in the nature of the human self) was of far less concern to the early
reformers because of their general antipathy toward speculative

approaches to the doctrine. Convinced that the Bible alone could provide a basis for the doctrine, they rather contemptuously eschewed the long medieval heritage of searching for analogies to the Trinity in the attempt at understanding the doctrine. Paradoxically, it was Melanchthon, who early in his life was most vehemently opposed to speculative and analogical approaches, who later in life proved most amenable to the speculative method among early reformers. Nonetheless, the medieval tradition of regarding the human mind as an analogy of the Trinity found few supporters in the Protestant theological tradition. There was, however, a tradition of philosophical thought (represented by G. W. Leibniz and Gotthold Lessing) that continued to find inspiration in this medieval and speculative approach. It found direct inspiration in the thought of Augustine and Thomas Aquinas, both of whom saw in the human mind an image of the Trinity. If we neglect subtle differences between Augustine and Thomas, we may summarize their view by stating that they discovered one analogy between the second person of the Trinity (the Son) and the human mind's *knowledge* of itself and a second analogy between the third person (the Spirit) and the mind's *love* of itself. Although these analogies may not seem intuitively obvious at first, they make sense if we focus on the mental processes involved. The easier of the two analogies to grasp is that between the Son and the mind's knowledge. According to the church's doctrine of the Trinity, the Son is eternally begotten from the Father. Although the notion of eternal generation has engendered considerable debate, at least the metaphor of begetting is established. The Augustinian-Thomistic approach finds an analogy between the begetting of the Son and the production of a concept in the mind when the subject reflects upon itself. That is, when in self-consciousness the subject thinks about itself, an idea or concept of the self is formed. Although we today refer to the result of this process as an idea or concept, in the medieval period it was called the "inner word." It helped immensely that one of the Biblical titles of the Son is "word" (John 1:1); "word" and "Son" in this view are interchangeable. Thus they discovered an analogy between the conception of the inner word and the begetting of the Son. The other analogy, that between the Spirit and the mind's self-love, is not as obvious. However, the Augustinian-Thomistic tradition noted that the mind is possessed of two faculties, intellect and will, and that, whereas the process of intellect issues forth in the conception of the word, the process of will culminates in love. They further noted that, just as in the doctrine of the Trinity the Spirit in a sense connects Father and Son together, so love in general unites lover and beloved.

Protestants were distinctively cool to this method of expounding the doctrine of the Trinity. Although Augustinians and Thomists did not claim that they could deduce this doctrine purely from the analogy between the Trinity and the structure of the self, they were enamored of this approach as a means of understanding the doctrine. Protestants, however, almost uniformly ignored this analogical method, preferring instead not only to infer but even to explain doctrines strictly by means of Biblical exposition. Nonetheless, there were a few in the Protestant camp who claimed the Augustinian heritage. Notable among these is the philosopher Leibniz, who among his other pursuits gave time to defending and expounding the doctrine of the Trinity by means of both Biblical and speculative arguments.

Yet the Augustinian-Thomistic tradition did not remain within the confines sketched above; it developed over time in response to changing conceptions of the self. Although the Augustinian understanding of the self had enormous longevity, by the early 1800s a different conception of the self had taken the field that, although having roots in the Augustinian tradition, effected substantial modifications to that tradition. The new conception was provided by idealist philosophers such as G. W. F. Hegel, for whom the leading concept for understanding the self was "spirit." The idealist conception of spirit had from the beginning a decidedly Trinitarian ring to it, for they understood spirit, whether in its finite or infinite form, as a threefold process of self-development. As a result, whereas Augustine had to labor mightily in order to accommodate the Holy Spirit into the analogy of the self-knowing and -loving mind, such accommodation was a comparatively easy matter for the idealists; their conception of the self readily lent itself to Trinitarian exposition.

No sooner had idealism come to fruition than its life as a movement came to an end, to be replaced, in the liberal theology of the late 1800s, by an understanding of the self built on the concept of "personality." At first, this change from "spirit" to "person" may seem beneficial for the idea of the Trinity, for it too utilizes the notion of person; however, what appears to be a boon turned out to be anything but, for "person" came to be applied, not to the Trinitarian persons, but to the single divine essence. As a result, when God is thought of as a person, it becomes difficult to make room for the Trinitarian persons without falling into a tritheism in which each Trinitarian person is a God. So, liberal theology, with a view of the self vastly different from that of idealism, had no significant interest in the idea of the Trinity.

Twentieth-century Trinitarian thought has witnessed, first, a resurgence of the Augustinian tradition in the theology of Karl Barth and, second, a renewal of the Hegelian view of the self in the thought of Jürgen Moltmann and Wolfhart Pannenberg. Barth rescued the doctrine of the Trinity from the oblivion facing it at the hands of liberal theology; he did so by reverting to the Augustinian account of subjectivity, with its emphasis on the unity of the self and its subordination of intellect and will to that unity. In its application to the Trinity, this meant in Barth's theology a heavy weight placed on the oneness of God and a tendency to understand the Trinity as the process of God's self-knowledge. Moltmann and Pannenberg, on the contrary, have truculently attacked Barth for his excessive zeal for monotheism and have reached back to Hegel for a view of the self that places greater emphasis on the inherent relationality of persons. In this interpretation, persons come to be what they are only in their mutual relations; persons are not independently existing entities, but instead are radically dependent on each other. Accordingly, Moltmann and Pannenberg have fashioned interpretations of the Trinity that emphasize the plurality inherent within God's subjectivity – the doctrine of the Trinity, they believe, implies the full subjectivity of each of the three persons. But does not the full subjectivity of each person raise the specter of tritheism? Only if subjectivity is thought to apply to individually subsisting entities; however in the Hegelian interpretation, persons do not exist apart from their relations with others – no "person" has subsistent reality in itself. Nonetheless, Moltmann and Pannenberg have definitely displaced the center of God's subjectivity from the divine unity to the Trinity of persons.

In summary, the changing conceptions of the Trinity in modern German thought have reflected the history of thinking about the self. In each era, the Trinity has been interpreted in light of some philosophical conception of the self.

The third issue is "history." The idea of history came to play a role in Trinitarian thinking only in the eighteenth century. Like the concept of subjectivity, it too went through several distinctive phases. At first, history was significant as a mode of critical thinking. We see this illustrated in the thought of Hermann Samuel Reimarus who came to the Bible with presuppositions dramatically different from those of Protestant scholastic theology. According to Reimarus, scholastic theology was guilty of a grossly anachronistic interpretation of the Bible – of interpreting the Bible in the light of later Christian doctrinal formulations. So, he argued, it is not surprising that Christians found doctrines such as the Trinity in the Bible, for they postulated complete historical continuity between the Bible and doctrines fashioned in the third, fourth and fifth centuries and read the Bible accordingly. Reimarus, on the contrary, postulated a vast gulf between the Bible and early Christianity, holding that the earliest Christians, indeed the apostles themselves, had either thoroughly misunderstood or even knowingly distorted the message of Jesus. Consequently, when the Gospels are interpreted against the background of first-century Judaism, instead of being interpreted anachronistically from the perspective of the later church, a great many traditional doctrines are found to be without Biblical support. So, at first history meant the use of historical criticism to question the validity of traditional modes of interpreting the Bible and its effects were utterly negative for the doctrine of the Trinity. If Reimarus' presuppositions were correct, then the doctrine of the Trinity would be nothing more than an enormous misconstrual of the words of Jesus. Although Reimarus' conclusions were generally repudiated by Protestant theologians, his overall conviction that the Bible must be read against the background of the ancient world – that the Bible is a thoroughly historical document – slowly began to become axiomatic for theologians.

A further application of the idea of historicity came at the hands of Friedrich Schleiermacher, who suggested that not only the Bible but also God's relation to the world develops historically. This historical development is due to the fact that God relates to the world through uniting with finite reality, first with human nature in the person of Jesus Christ, then with human nature more collectively in the community of the redeemed. Because these unions between God and the world are sequential, there is an element of historicity and a dynamic quality in God's relation to the world. Although this historicity does not, in Schleiermacher's opinion, vitiate God's eternity and impassivity, it does signify real changes in God's relation to the world, for in Jesus Christ and in the church something novel occurs in this relation. This dynamic and historical relation to the world is according to Schleiermacher the real meaning of the doctrine of the Trinity: the Son is the union of the divine essence with human nature individually in Jesus Christ and the Spirit is the union of the divine essence with human nature collectively in the church. For Schleiermacher, the doctrine of the Trinity is a way of representing the historicity and progressive nature of this relation; in history God becomes a Trinity.

However, Schleiermacher's sense of God's historicity left untouched the divine essence itself. The historicity he spoke of pertained only to the relation between God and the world, not to God; it was left to the idealist philosophers such as Hegel to extend the concept of historicity to the divine being itself. For Hegel the divine being is itself historical. This means not only that God enters into history, but also that God is essentially a process. For Hegel, the historical character of God was understood to mean that absolute spirit (Hegel's term for that which is metaphysically ultimate, the religious expression of which is "God") subsists in a logical process that is grasped by dialectical thinking. This logical process, consisting in three steps ("moments" is Hegel's favorite term), is observable both in pure thinking and in the phenomena of nature and history. Spirit has a history, according to Hegel, because it develops according to a rational pattern, whether that pattern occurs in logic, in the world of nature, or in the history of art, religion and philosophy. Since this pattern consists in three moments, God's history is a Trinitarian history.

Word, self and history: these are the concepts that underlie all the permutations of German Trinitarian thought. Like the persons of the Trinity, these concepts relate to one another in various ways; unlike the Trinitarian persons, the meaning of the concepts evolves over time, with the result that the complexity of modern Trinitarian thought is thereby exponentially increased. This book is an attempt at cutting through this complexity by demonstrating the contours of this history. It elaborates the themes adumbrated in this introduction, showing how in each period of modern German thought the changing fortunes of the doctrine of the Trinity can be explained by observing how these concepts developed and related to each other.

CHAPTER ONE

Martin Luther and Philip Melanchthon

It is one of the oddest facts of Christian history that Martin Luther and Philip Melanchthon have been claimed as precursors both by theologians and religious philosophers with no use for the doctrine of the Trinity and by those with a profound respect for the doctrine. This fact is all the more surprising when we recall that both Luther and Melanchthon repeatedly abjured the role of doctrinal innovators and protested without end their allegiance to the ancient creeds in which the doctrine of the Trinity is enshrined.

Germanic Trinitarian theologians who, like Luther and Melanchthon, subscribe to the creeds are legion; from theologians of the second Protestant generation such as Martin Chemnitz to contemporaries such as Jürgen Moltmann, the doctrine of the Trinity has in every generation been defended, expounded and developed. Yet there has also been, in the last two and a half centuries, a provocative minority report diverging from the orthodox mainstream. Unlike the sixteenth-century Socinians, who argued against the doctrine by refuting the orthodox position one scriptural passage at a time, this minority report has not so much expressly rejected the doctrine as consigned it to the trash-can of irrelevancy and has done so with what its members regard as perfectly sound Protestant reasons.

Consider, for example, Albrecht Ritschl's ruminations on Jesus Christ and faith in Christ.[1] It was Ritschl's belief that Luther achieved a major revolution in the Christian understanding of Christ, whereby, without excising the ancient credal formulations,

---

[1] Albrecht Ritschl, *The Christian Doctrine of Justification and Reconciliation: The Positive Development of the Doctrine*, ed. H. R. Mackintosh and A. B. Macaulay (New York: Charles Scribner's Sons, 1900), 391–399.

attention was shifted from belief in the predicates attributed to Christ to trust in Christ's lordship. Trust is the basis for our ascribing divinity to Christ, since, as Luther argued in his *Large Catechism*,[2] God is that in which we put our trust. The effect of this alteration was, in Ritschl's estimation, dramatic. With the emphasis on trust in Christ, the medieval attempts at reconciling faith and reason lost their motive. The credal doctrines of Christ and the Trinity become incomprehensible to human understanding and, in Ritschl's words, "worthless for the faith which consists in trust."[3] Melanchthon, whose thoughts were not uniformly liked by Ritschl, nevertheless pleased him by understanding Luther's theology to imply that doctrinal formulations of the two natures of Christ are unimportant as long as the benefits of Christ as redeemer are known.[4]

As another example of this tendency, let us look to Rudolf Bultmann. In spite of his manifest hostility toward certain fundamental aspects of nineteenth-century liberal theology exemplified by Ritschl, Bultmann like Ritschl eagerly and frequently employed statements by Melanchthon in a sustained effort to restrict theology to God's saving activities toward us.[5] While in itself a laudable and authentically Lutheran goal, Bultmann's aim resulted in a theology completely devoid of Trinitarian considerations. What must prove so infuriating to Trinitarian theologians is that Bultmann did not even bother to argue against the doctrine. He took its unimportance to be so obviously an implication of Luther's and Melanchthon's theology that inclusion of the doctrine of the Trinity never became a consideration for him, just as Ritschl's epic, *The Christian Doctrine of Justification and Reconciliation*, included only a perfunctory mention of the Trinity.

Against this use of Lutheran theology to downplay the significance of the doctrine, a host of able defenders has arisen, asserting that the doctrine in its credal form was of great

---

[2] Martin Luther, "The Large Catechism," in Theodore G. Tappert, ed. and trs., *The Book of Concord: The Confessions of the Evangelical Lutheran Church* (Philadelphia: Fortress Press, 1959), 365–371.   [3] Ritschl, *Justification and Reconciliation*, 395.   [4] Ibid., 396.
[5] Rudolf Bultmann, "Grace and Freedom," *Essays, Philosophical and Theological*, trs. James C. G. Greig (New York: Macmillan, 1955), 173; Rudolf Bultmann, "The Christology of the New Testament," *Faith and Understanding I*, ed. Robert W. Funk, trs. Louise Pettibone Smith (New York: Harper & Row, 1969), 263 and 279.

significance to Luther and Melanchthon and is an integral part of their theology.[6] By implication, Ritschl and Bultmann have removed a legitimate aspect of Luther's and Melanchthon's theology and thereby made that theology contradict itself. Beyond this historical defense, major theologians of the twentieth century[7] have argued for the centrality of the doctrine in Christian theology in explicit disagreement with the likes of Ritschl and Bultmann.

The issue, then, is how to understand Luther and Melanchthon in such a way that the divergent opinions noted above become intelligible and any latent tensions within the Germanic tradition become evident. While it is clear that one of the two sides in this debate must have the greater justification, it is also true that Luther and Melanchthon, quite apart from their intentions, may have released into this theological tradition certain ideas whose full implication they did not see and whose consequences they could not foresee.

The place to begin is with Martin Luther's understanding of the creeds, of the councils that composed them, and of their authority for the Christian faith. An initial point to note is that Luther's sentiments about creeds and councils varied according to the context in which he found himself. Consequently, it is possible to find Luther making statements that, if not contradictory, at least can support a range of views. With this disclaimer, we note Luther's opinion that church councils have no authority in themselves and that, as human assemblies, they are subject to error.[8] In the heat of battle, Luther was inclined to argue that points of doctrine and morality established by councils constituted something like the abomination of desolation mentioned in the Book of Daniel.[9] However, he protested that his intention was not to

---

[6] Notably Regin Prenter, *Spiritus Creator*, trs. John M. Jensen (Philadelphia: Muhlenberg Press, 1953) and Reiner Jansen, *Studien zu Luthers Trinitätslehre*, Basler und Berner Studien zur historischen und systematischen Theologie, eds. Max Geigner und Andreas Lindt, vol. XXVI (Bern: Herbert Lang/Frankfurt am Main: Peter Lang, 1976).

[7] Principally Karl Barth, Jürgen Moltmann and Wolfhart Pannenberg, each of whose views is discussed in chapter 6.

[8] For a brief summary and analysis of this issue, see Paul Althaus, *The Theology of Martin Luther*, trs. Robert C. Schultz (Philadelphia: Fortress Press, 1966), 338–341.

[9] Martin Luther, "Defense and Explanation of All the Articles" (1521), trs. Charles M. Jacobs, in *Luther's Works*, ed. Helmut T. Lehmann, vol. XXXII, *Career of the Reformer II*, ed. George W. Forell (Philadelphia: Muhlenberg Press, 1958), 77.

encourage casual rejection of conciliar decisions, but instead to subordinate them to Scripture.[10] Nonetheless, he was of the opinion, not only that councils could in principle err, but that certain identifiable conciliar declarations were erroneous and in fact contradictory to the gospel.[11] Luther singled out the first four ecumenical councils (A.D. 325–451) for special praise because, in favorable comparison to councils closer to Luther's day, they did not introduce any new articles of faith.[12] Since councils cannot guarantee their own veracity, we need some standard by which to judge their decrees; such a standard Luther found in the Bible. Luther could make no sense of the Roman Catholic argument that the Holy Spirit, acting through councils, could inspire the church to formulate new articles of faith, for in his view the Holy Spirit is not a source of new teaching; the Spirit's sole function is to teach us Jesus Christ, a topic that Luther believed had already been fully expounded in Scripture.[13] Accordingly, the purpose of councils, far from being the announcing of new articles of faith, was limited to defending the ancient Christian faith and practice using the Bible as the standard.[14]

With this attitude toward councils, Luther felt comfortable with subjecting the technical terminology of the creeds to scrutiny. Of direct pertinence are Luther's thoughts on a Trinitarian term such as *homoousion*, which, by asserting that Father and Son are of the "same substance," expresses the unity of God amid the diversity of Trinitarian persons. Luther was worried that the use of such terms contradicted the spirit of 1 Timothy 6:20, which warns against "profane novelties of words." Luther counseled using terms – the "old and sacred words" – found in the New Testament.[15] Confronted with the fact that *homoousion* was sanctioned by ancient and venerable creeds, Luther retorted that many otherwise orthodox ancient writers such as Jerome did not accept the term and that

[10] Ibid., 80–81.
[11] Ibid., 82–93 with reference to the Council of Constance and its condemnation of John Hus' theology.
[12] Martin Luther, "On the Councils and the Church" (1539), in *Luther's Works*, ed. Helmut T. Lehmann, vol. XLI, *Church and Ministry III*, ed. Eric W. Gritsch, trs. Charles M. Jacobs (Philadelphia: Fortress Press, 1966), 121.   [13] Ibid., 122.   [14] Ibid.
[15] Martin Luther, "Against Latomus" (1521), trs. George Lindbeck, in *Luther's Works*, ed. Helmut T. Lehmann, vol. XXXII, *Career of the Reformer II*, ed. George W. Forell (Philadelphia: Muhlenberg Press, 1958), 243.

the crucial thing was to affirm the scriptural truth that the creed asserts with this term. As long as one affirms the scriptural truth, Luther averred, one could not be considered a heretic even if reticent to employ *homoousion*. Luther went so far as to acknowledge the legitimacy of the Arians' complaint about non-scriptural terms being employed in dogmatic formulations. We should not, he believed, presume to speak more clearly than God spoke in the Bible.[16]

However, in spite of Luther's principled objection to the use of technical terms and his wanting to subordinate the authority of councils to that of the Bible, on the particular issue of the Trinity Luther could scarcely have been more orthodox. In "The Three Symbols or Creeds of the Christian Faith," he flatly affirmed his acceptance of the Apostles' Creed, the Athanasian Creed and the hymn *Te Deum*.[17] He accepted the Trinitarian teaching of these creeds because he found it to be based on the teaching of the Bible.[18]

John Eck, Luther's antagonist in the Leipzig debate in 1519, complained that Luther had, by questioning the technical terms of the Trinitarian creeds, effectively denied the doctrine of the Trinity.[19] Eck was on rather shaky ground in this accusation, but he would have been in a more tenable position had he chosen Philip Melanchthon as a target. In the first edition of *Loci Communes Rerum Theologicarum* (1521), Melanchthon made some statements that, in retrospect, must be regarded as incautious. He began the work by claiming that it covered "the principal topics of Christian teaching." The doctrine of the Trinity is notable by its absence.[20] The purpose is straightforward: to instruct youth in what to look for in the Bible and to expose the corrupt hallucinations of those

---

[16] Ibid., 243–244.

[17] Martin Luther, "The Three Symbols or Creeds of the Christian Faith" (1538), trs. Robert R. Heitner, in *Luther's Works*, ed. Helmut T. Lehmann, vol. XXXIV, *Career of the Reformer IV*, ed. Lewis W. Spitz (Philadelphia: Muhlenberg Press, 1960), 201.

[18] Ibid., 222. See also on these points Luther's own confession of faith appended to the end of "Confession Concerning Christ's Supper" (1528), in *Luther's Works*, ed. Helmut T. Lehmann, vol. XXXVII, *Word and Sacrament III*, ed. and trs. Robert H. Fischer (Philadelphia: Muhlenberg Press, 1961).

[19] Holsten Fagerberg, *Die Theologie der lutherischen Bekenntnisschriften von 1529 bis 1537* (Göttingen: Vandenhoeck & Ruprecht, 1965), 116.

[20] Philip Melanchthon, *Loci Communes Theologici*, in Wilhelm Pauck, ed., *Melanchthon and Bucer*, The Library of Christian Classics, ed. John Baillie, et al., vol. XIX (London: SCM Press, 1969). The following exposition is taken from pages 18 to 22.

who prefer the authority of Aristotle to Jesus Christ. He thus affirmed the by-now familiar Protestant anthem that the Bible is the sole norm and source of Christian theology.

Having briefly outlined the main topics of theology, Melanchthon stated that some of these are incomprehensible while others can be known with utter certainty. The incomprehensible topics turn out to be those often categorized as divine mysteries. There is, he professed, great danger in probing here and his counsel was finally to adore the mysteries and not to inquire into them. In itself, such advice may be considered a merely judicious recommendation; however, Melanchthon left no doubt about his meaning when he went on to state that there is no good reason to investigate mysteries such as the Trinity and the incarnation. On a charitable interpretation, we can understand that Melanchthon was attempting to steer students of theology away from speculative curiosity about matters not revealed in the Bible and not of direct importance to Christian faith. He was not rejecting these doctrines or claiming them to be unimportant, but instead only forestalling any needless philosophical analysis of them. Nonetheless, the anti-speculative tenor of his statements did implicitly raise the question of the exact role of the doctrine of the Trinity for Protestants. At the very least, the doctrine received a less than enthusiastic welcome in this first systematic statement of Protestant theology.

Not content to warn against speculation, Melanchthon went on to specify theology's center in an affirmative way. The fulcrum of the Christian faith rests in such doctrines as law and grace, because the knowledge of Christ consists in knowing his benefits to us. Any philosophical reflection on the natures of Christ and the "modes" of the incarnation would be subjects better left to the corrupt hallucinations of Roman Catholic scholastic theology.[21] To buttress this point, Melanchthon noted that the apostle Paul's compendium of Christian doctrine – the Book of Romans – does not so much as mention such doctrines as the Trinity.

---

[21] E. P. Meijering, *Melanchthon and Patristic Thought: The Doctrines of Christ and Grace, the Trinity and Creation*, Studies in the History of Christian Thought, ed. Heiko Oberman (Leiden: E. J. Brill, 1983), cautions against reading too much into Melanchthon's anti-speculative statements in the first edition of *Loci Communes* and finds the work to be expressly orthodox in its Christology (109).

Potential criticism from Roman Catholics and the rise of anti-Trinitarian thought[22] encouraged Luther and Melanchthon to be more forthcoming and careful in their pronouncements about the Trinity.[23] In addition to his statements of faith in "Confession Concerning Christ's Supper" and "The Three Symbols," Luther set forth a small creed in the Smalcald Articles. Although the opening section on the Trinity is brief, it indicates clearly enough Luther's orthodoxy. Interestingly, he appended the comment that Trinitarian issues needed no extensive exposition because they were not a matter of dispute in his controversy with Rome. This statement indicates the thoroughly contextual nature of Luther's thought; he was writing this formal confession of faith in response to a particular need, and so gave thorough attention only to the disputable matters; he simply did not see the need to reinvent the wheel, so to speak. The doctrine having been carefully defined in the ancient church, there was no need of or advantage in exploring the doctrine in the manner of medieval theologians such as St. Thomas. Still, Luther did occasionally insert into his works expositions of the Trinity that reveal his utter orthodoxy.[24]

However, there is another side to Luther's understanding of the Trinity, one that reveals a genuinely new insight in the history of Trinitarian thought. Here Luther was concerned, not so much to defend and expound the ancient doctrine, but to show why it is important.[25] Briefly put, our knowledge of the Trinity is, according to Luther, knowledge of God as God wishes to be

[22] See Peter Fraenkel, *Testimonia Patrum: The Function of the Patristic Argument in the Theology of Philip Melanchthon*, Travaux D'humanisme et Renaissance, no. 46 (Geneva: Librairie E. Droz, 1961), 46, n. 191 for a summary of the evidence for anti-Trinitarian activity in Germany possibly as early as 1529 and of Melanchthon's awareness of it.

[23] See Róbert Dán, "'Judaizare' – the Career of a Term," in Róbert Dán and Antal Pirnát, eds., *Antitrinitarianism in the Second Half of the 16th Century*, Studia Humanitatis, ed. T. Klaniczay, no. 5 (Leiden: E. J. Brill, 1982), 28–29 for an indication of the way in which the various sides in the Reformation debates hurled the accusation of Judaizer at each other in an attempt at discrediting the other sides.

[24] Martin Luther, "Treatise on the Last Words of David 2 Samuel 23:1–7," trs. Martin H. Bertram, in *Luther's Works*, vol. XV, ed. Jaroslav Pelikan (St. Louis: Concordia Publishing, 1972), 277–303.

[25] Fagerberg, "Die Theologie," argues, contrary to some interpretations, that Luther's appeal to the doctrine of the Trinity and to the creeds is not merely perfunctory or for political purposes, but relates directly to his understanding of justification by faith (116, 120). The same point is made by Prenter, *Spiritus Creator*, 176 and 180 and by Jansen, *Studien*, 84–85 and 223–224.

known. Whereas natural human reason can have a knowledge of
God the creator, we cannot know God as God truly is – the
essence of God – apart from the revelation of God as Trinity.[26]
The Trinity is, as it were, God's inwardness. Human reason can
only apprehend God's outwardness; by faith, however, we know
who and what God actually is.[27] But this essence of God is no
mere metaphysical aspect of God; it is instead God's "will and
counsel" by which God chooses to come to us in Jesus Christ and
the Holy Spirit and effect our salvation.[28] Consequently, the doctrine of the Trinity is not merely an addition to our knowledge of
God; it is in truth the only legitimate knowledge of God, for only
with our knowledge that God is Father, Son and Spirit do we
know God's actual essence and will. Apart from this revelation,
human reason goes astray and establishes gods of its own
imagination. In this revelation we see God giving God's own self
to us for our salvation.[29] Of course, even with revelation God the
Trinity remains an utter mystery to us. Revelation informs us *that*
God is a Trinity but it is still beyond our comprehension *how* God
is a Trinity.[30]

Melanchthon also publicly affirmed his support for the credal
doctrine of the Trinity. First, he noted in his *Apology of the Augsburg
Confession* that the Lutheran party had from the beginning accepted
the historical doctrine of the Trinity because of its attestation by
the Bible. As a result, those who reject this doctrine are idolaters,
which is a Lutheran way of saying that they do not accept God's
revelation but obstinately insist on allowing their own limited
human reason to set up false gods.[31] But Melanchthon went far
beyond this sort of formal declaration of orthodoxy. In particular,
he enlarged his *Loci Communes* many-fold and, in the 1533 edition,
included a substantial section on the Trinity and a separate section

---

[26] Martin Luther, *Sermons of Martin Luther*, ed. John Nicholas Lenker, trs. John Nicholas
Lenker, et al., vol. VIII: Sermons on Epistle Texts for Trinity Sunday to Advent (Grand
Rapids: Baker Book House, 1983), 7–8, 22 and 26.

[27] Ibid., 9. See also Althaus, *Theology*, 17–18.   [28] Luther, *Sermons*, 11 and 14–15.

[29] Luther, "Confession Concerning Christ's Supper," 365–366.

[30] Luther, *Sermons*, 21, 24 and 31–32.

[31] Philip Melanchthon, "Apology of the Augsburg Confession," in Theodore G. Tappert,
ed. and trs., *The Book of Concord: The Confessions of the Evangelical Lutheran Church*,
(Philadelphia: Fortress Press, 1959), 100.

on the Holy Spirit.[32] In this edition he justified using the term *homo-ousion* and clarified its meaning.[33] He also offered a defense of the doctrine on mainly Biblical grounds, drawing heavily on the Fourth Gospel's use of *logos*, and refuted various Trinitarian and Christological heresies.[34] In later editions, from 1543 onward, there was a separate section on the Son with a lengthy *Testimonia* (essentially proof-texts) from the Old and New Testaments.[35] Here we also find a greater use of patristic authorities to support and expound the doctrine.[36] Finally, we should note in a preliminary way that in the editions of the 1530s and beyond Melanchthon explained the Trinity in a way akin to Thomas Aquinas' specula-tive-analogical explanation. Thus Melanchthon, both out of conviction and in response to a growing anti-Trinitarian threat, offered increasingly more detailed and developed expositions of the Trinity in the *Loci Communes*.

What accounts for the dramatic about-face in Melanchthon's attitude? How could he have seemingly dismissed the doctrine in the earliest editions of *Loci Communes* and devoted substantial space to it in the later editions? The answer to this question per-tains to our understanding, not only of Melanchthon himself, but also of the later history of Trinitarian thinking. As previously noted, many notable theologians have appealed to Melanchthon's statements in the 1521 edition and drawn from them an indication that the doctrine of the Trinity is not of first importance in Christian theology.

The answer to this question is that the differences between the early and late editions of *Loci Communes* involve not a change of

---

[32] The two English translations of *Loci Communes* are *Loci Communes Theologici*, in *Melanchthon and Bucer* (see note 20) and *Melanchthon on Christian Doctrine: Loci Communes 1555*, ed. and trs. Clyde L. Manschreck, Library of Protestant Thought (New York: Oxford University Press, 1965). The former is based on the earliest editions, the latter on the latest editions. The various editions are available in Philippi Melanthonis, *Opera quae Supersunt Omnia*, ed. Henricus Ernestus Bindseil, *Corpus Reformatorum*, vol. XXI (New York: Johnson Reprint Corporation, 1963).

[33] "Cum igitur sit una tantum essentia divina, necesse est has personas communem et eandem essentiam habere, idque significat vox ὁμοούσιον . . . [Gregory] Nazianzenus scribit latinos pro hypostasi dixisse personam, quia non habuerint aliud commodius nomen," *Opera*, 258.   [34] Ibid., 259–267.   [35] Ibid., 615–629.

[36] On the subject of Melanchthon's use of patristic authorities, see Fraenkel, *Testimonia Patrum*.

mind but a transition, under pressure from various directions, from implicit declaration to explicit declaration. The strictures placed on the doctrine in the 1521 edition are, in this interpretation, not so much a rejection of the doctrine as an attempt at restricting the scope of inquiry into the doctrine. Doctrines such as the Trinity and the two natures of Christ were for Melanchthon presuppositions; as such they were not unimportant, but since they were not, at the time of the first edition, under attack, they needed neither exposition nor defense. In later editions, the doctrine had moved to the forefront of controversy and so Melanchthon felt the need to expand the *Loci Communes* appropriately.[37]

This judgment is confirmed by Melanchthon's response to Michael Servetus, published near the end of Melanchthon's life. In this work he began by confessing his acceptance of the Trinitarian creeds and claiming that acknowledgment of the creeds is a sign of the true church.[38] He went on in this work to give a variety of defenses of the Trinity against the criticisms of Servetus. He accused Servetus of reviving the ancient heresy of Paul of Samosata (essentially denying the two natures of Christ), thereby classifying him among the reprobate. He adduced Biblical testimony to the effect that the Bible attributes various divine properties to the Son. He argued that the New Testament affirms the pre-existence of the Logos. And he offered a recapitulation of the speculative-analogical explanation of the Trinity that he had been developing for some years.[39] While there is nothing new in this tract apart from its direct references to Servetus, it does provide us with an indication that Melanchthon believed himself to be thoroughly orthodox on the doctrine of the Trinity and that he believed this doctrine to be exceedingly important.

However, the fact that Melanchthon came finally to disclose in an express and unambiguous manner his adherence to the doctrine of the Trinity does not in itself settle all questions. Something had entered into the stream of Protestant Trinitarian thought that

---

[37] See Meijering, *Melanchthon and Patristic Thought*, 111 and 120 and Fraenkel, *Testimonia Patrum*, 36 and 45, for helpful interpretive comments.

[38] Philip Melanchthon, "Refutation of Servetus and the Anabaptists' Errors," in *A Melanchthon Reader*, trs. Ralph Keen, American University Studies, series VII: Theology and Religion, vol. XLI (New York: Peter Lang, 1988), 169–170.　　[39] Ibid., 171–174.

would prove difficult to control and unpredictable in its consequences. In spite of intentions to the contrary, an idea had been
introduced that would in future generations make the doctrine of
the Trinity a matter of suspicion. Luther and Melanchthon had
unwittingly driven a wedge between creeds and Bible by insisting
that the creeds are subject to inspection and criticism according to
their agreement with the Bible. Although honest in their conviction that the ancient Trinitarian creeds merely restated the teaching of the Bible in technical and defensive language and that the
subordination of the creeds to Scripture did not entail their rejection, they did open up the possibility of later theologians finding
tension and even contradiction between creed and Bible. The
reformers allowed such a contradiction in the case of medieval
creeds and decrees of councils; these they found to be quite contrary to Scripture. It would be for later Protestants to extend this
principle and claim that even the ancient creeds and councils had
gone awry by thoroughly misconstruing the Bible's teaching.
Implied in the reformers' theology is a view of the church and its
capacity for adhering to God's truth significantly different from the
Roman Catholic view. For the Protestants, there was a sense in
which the church infallibly maintained purity of doctrine and
practice; however, this quality was potentially limited to a mere
remnant of the church – there was for Luther and Melanchthon
no guarantee that the entire empirical church would adhere to the
whole truth. As a result, they and their progenies could not assume,
as Roman Catholics could, that councils, as representatives of the
entire church, were above the possibility of error. For the reformers, only the Bible contains no error – and even that judgment
received qualification, for the Old Testament was trustworthy only
as it agreed with the New.[40] Although the consequences of this dis-
joining of creed and Bible remained along the fringes of Protestant
thought for more than two centuries, in time the reformers' conviction that the Trinitarian creeds clearly and only expound the
Biblical message came under increasingly strong skepticism.

The fact that the reformers' own doctrine of the Trinity rested
on their interpretation of the Bible and not on their acceptance of

---

[40] Luther, "Treatise on the Last Words of David," 270 and 287.

the creeds conditioned their style of exposition. They simply used extensive scriptural proof. And it was good that they worked so industriously at this scriptural proof, because not only had they eliminated creeds as self-standing authorities, they had also intentionally deleted human reason as a potential source of knowledge about the Trinity. Although theologians had rarely embraced rational *proofs* of the Trinity, in the medieval period they had made extensive use of analogical reasoning to *explain* the doctrine and, implicitly, to defend it against attacks. The reformers did not hold a completely consistent view of this matter. Occasionally Luther would insert a bit of analogical reasoning in his scriptural expositions of the Trinity.[41] Nonetheless, the dominant refrain was that the doctrine of the Trinity is utterly inaccessible to human reason. The most charitable thing Luther could find to say was that the knowledge of the Trinity cannot in any way be derived from human reason. The Trinity can be neither comprehended nor explored by reason.[42] Reason may yield an accurate knowledge of God the creator and governor and of the majesty of God, but this really does not count as authentic knowledge of God, for it does not disclose God's mind and will to us.[43] Reason cannot grasp how three persons can be of one essence because it cannot even understand the ways of God's creatures.[44] Luther even hinted that the doctrine may be contradictory to reason.[45] The only appropriate attitude in the matter, Luther concluded, was a reverential self-confinement to revelation and the cessation of all inquiring into God's secrets.[46] If the boundary between reason and faith is transgressed, idolatry results as reason establishes a god of its own creation instead of accepting God's self-declaration in revelation.[47] Not

---

[41] For example, in "The Three Symbols," 219–222, he makes use of the image of the sun, its brilliance and its heat and reflects on the Trinitarian significance of calling Christ the image of God. John R. Loeschen, *The Divine Community: Trinity, Church, and Ethics in Reformation Theologies* (Kirksville, MO: The Sixteenth Century Journal Publishers, 1981), 16–17, asserts that although Luther rejected all thinking concerned with "God in himself" as the "vain speculations of Reason," he himself "speculated" rather boldly, for example in *The Bondage of the Will* and in the writings of 1527 and 1528 on the Lord's Supper. However, Luther did not consider this to be speculation, for it pertained to matters within the scope of God's revelation.   [42] Luther, *Sermons*, 7.

[43] Ibid., 10 and 14.   [44] Ibid., 24.

[45] Luther, "Treatise on the Last Words of David," 310–311.   [46] Luther, *Sermons*, 21–22.

[47] Ibid., 14.

surprisingly, those who reject Christ's divinity employ finite human reason in doing so and accuse those who accept his divinity of being senseless and irrational.[48] Even when, by faith, we come to know that God is a Trinity of persons, our language still falters and the terms we use, such as "Trinity," do not yield comprehension of the mystery. Such words amount to a "stammering" of the human tongue.[49]

From Luther onward Protestants were committed to proving, expounding and defending the doctrine of the Trinity strictly on the basis of Scripture. Creeds no longer counted as an independent source of knowledge; they merely restated the content of revelation. Reason could neither discover nor explain the Trinity. This total reliance on Scripture was not without consequence for the future of Protestant Trinitarian thought, for Luther's legacy of Biblical interpretation was ambivalent. On the one hand, he helped establish a certain way of using the Bible, according to which great doctrinal capital was derived from specific passages in Scripture and from particular expressions within the Bible. The result of this approach was to encourage future Protestants to look to individual statements in the Bible for support and for clues to resolving doctrinal perplexities. On the other hand, Luther urged a Christocentric interpretation of the Bible, according to which the Bible's preaching about Christ is its center and vital message. Although several generations of faithful Lutheran expositors would see no conflict between these two motifs, eventually some began to wonder whether there might be a critical principle latent within the Christocentric motif that would yield hermeneutical results contrary to the method of scrutinizing individual passages of Scripture.

With regard to the method of appealing to individual passages of Scripture, the first thing to be noted is Luther's overwhelming confidence that the Bible clearly attests the truth of the doctrine of the Trinity with words so plain that he depicted his conscience as "captured."[50] The doctrine of the Trinity, then, was no mere academic construal of the Bible, but the Bible's own message itself leaping up from the page and impressing itself on the reader with

---

[48] Luther, "The Three Symbols," 208 and 216.   [49] Luther, *Sermons*, 8 and 29.
[50] Luther, "The Three Symbols," 224.

irresistible force. Beyond this general attitude, Luther found support for the doctrine in the fact that the Bible clearly distinguishes the Trinitarian persons while attributing divinity to each.[51] For example, the Bible first declares that God will not share glory with anyone and then, in Psalm 8, proclaims that the Son of Man has been crowned by God with glory and honor. Luther also noted the Bible's method of asserting the divinity of Christ by assigning to him certain titles such as Lord (equivalent to *Yahweh*). For example, he noted that in Numbers the Israelites were reported to have tempted the Lord and that Paul (in 1 Corinthians) affirmed that they tempted Christ. By a sort of mathematical substitution, Luther inferred that "Lord" was here being predicated of Christ, confirming his divinity.[52] Luther also rested confidently on the observation that the plural form of "God," *Elohim*, denotes plurality while the verbs associated with *Elohim* are all in the singular, suggesting God's unity.[53] With these and many similar arguments Luther proposed that the doctrine of the Trinity is a true exposition of the meaning of the Bible.

However, there is another side to Luther's use and understanding of the Bible and that is his Christocentric interpretation. Having declared that Scripture is the norm by which we interpret the creeds, Luther grasped the need to have a principle to determine the meaning of the Bible. "Meaning" signifies not the literal sense of the words of Scripture but instead the central purpose of the Bible as the Word of God. This central purpose Luther found in the Bible's capacity to preach Christ to us. The message about Christ is the gospel. It is found throughout the Bible, but not equally in all parts. In particular, Luther was especially impressed with the Gospel according to John, Romans and First Peter, for these focus on the words of Christ and his benefits, whereas other Biblical books focus more on Christ's works.[54] Contrarily, certain books of the Bible are found wanting because of the paucity of gospel contained within them. Most noteworthy, the Letter of James, Luther judged, could not possibly have been written by an

---

[51] Ibid., 217.   [52] Luther, *Sermons*, 30.   [53] Luther, "The Three Symbols," 223–224.
[54] Luther, "Preface to the New Testament," in *Luther's Works*, ed. Helmut T. Lehmann, vol. XXXV, *Word and Sacrament I*, ed. E. Theodore Bachmann (Philadelphia: Muhlenberg Press, 1960), 362.

apostle, so little knowledge of the gospel does it disclose.[55] The importance of Luther's interpretive principle for future genera-tions is that, just as he had opened up a critical gap between Scripture and tradition, subordinating the latter to the former, so he also created a hiatus between one part of the Bible and the other – the part that preaches Christ and the part that does not. Although Luther himself continued, as we have seen, to use indi-vidual passages from the entire Bible as conveying inspired information about God, future generations of theologians would, for various reasons, hesitate to do so and would find solace in Luther's Christocentric interpretation, believing it to be a Protestant duty to regard the Bible as authoritative only in that part that is a genuine expression of the gospel. In other words, the question is about the concept of the Word of God. In spite of Luther's Christocentric interpretation, he continued to treat the Bible as a collection of inspired utterances, from which could be derived reliable information on a great variety of matters. Some later theologians, nervous with this approach, would limit the Word of God to those passages of the Bible that directly preach Christ; some of them, in turn, would fail to find the doctrine of the Trinity attested in those passages because of assumptions about the proper use of Scripture that differed greatly from Luther's. In short, certain streams of German Protestant theology in the modern era, already chastened by criticisms of the doctrine of the Trinity and uneasy with Luther's proof-text method, were hard pressed to support the doctrine and in fact constructed systems of theology that proved persuasive while avoiding all mention of the Trinity.

There is an interesting postscript regarding Luther's and Melanchthon's insistence on grounding the doctrine of the Trinity in Scripture and avoiding speculative approaches. Beginning in the 1527 *Loci Communes*, Melanchthon expounded the Trinity by means of the psychological analogy employed to such great effect in the Augustinian tradition. The second half of Augustine's *De Trinitate* presents a series of analogies by which Augustine sought to help

---

[55] Luther, "Prefaces to Jude and James," in *Luther's Works*, ed. Helmut T. Lehmann, vol. XXXV, *Word and Sacrament I*, ed. E. Theodore Bachmann (Philadelphia: Muhlenberg Press, 1960), 396–397.

the reader understand the Trinity in some measure.[56] Unlike the analogies employed by theologians prior to Augustine, which dwelt on images such as the sun, its light and its heat, the analogies that Augustine proposed were drawn from our human experience of knowledge and love. For example, in the phenomenon of love there are three components: the lover, the beloved, and the love itself, which unites lover and beloved.[57] Further on in his treatise, Augustine suggested an even better image of the Trinity – the mind that knows and loves itself. Here, in the mental acts of memory, understanding and will, there is a plurality of acts; yet, because this is a matter of self-knowledge and self-love, these acts must form a unity. Hence the mind is an image of the Trinity's unity and plurality.[58] A further appealing aspect of this latter analogy is that the act of self-knowledge is said by Augustine to beget within us a word – or, we would say today, a concept or idea – that expresses the self's knowledge of itself.[59] With this assertion, Augustine was able to show that the mind that knows and loves itself is an image not only of the Trinity's unity and plurality but also of the Father's eternal begetting of the Son – for the word or concept conceived by the human mind in the act of self-knowledge is analogous to the eternal Word and Son begotten by the Father. In this maneuver, Augustine connected his analogical reasoning to the Trinitarian theology of the creeds. Augustine's final word on this subject was to note that the closest analogy to the Trinity is found, not in the mind that knows and loves itself, but in the mind that knows and loves God.[60] Ultimately, analogical reasoning gives way in Augustine's thought to anagogy – the raising of our thoughts up to God.

Back to Melanchthon. Having first castigated all attempts at knowing God through natural reason,[61] Melanchthon observed that God is more clearly reflected in human selfhood than in

---

[56] Basic principles of Augustine's analogical reasoning in *De Trinitate* can be found in Philip Schaff, ed., *A Select Library of the Nicene and Post-Nicene Fathers of the Christian Church*, vol. III, *St. Augustin: On the Holy Trinity, Doctrinal Treatises, Moral Treatises* (Grand Rapids: Wm. B. Eerdmans Publishing Co., 1978), 103 (book 6, chapter 10, §12) and 113–114 (book 7, chapter 6, §12). [57] Ibid., 124 (book 8, chapter 10, §14).

[58] Ibid., 142–143 (book 8, chapters 11–12).

[59] Ibid., 130 (book 9, chapter 7, §12) and 209–210 (book 15, chapter 11, §20).

[60] Ibid., 191–192 (book 14, chapter 12, §16).

[61] Philipp Melanchthon, *Melanchthon on Christian Doctrine*, 4–6.

irrational creatures. In particular, there are within the human person three items: the soul itself, thought, and finally will or love. Thought is an image of what we contemplate; our love for what we contemplate follows the image we form of it in thought. All this, Melanchthon suggested, is similar to what we find in God: in the Father there is an act of contemplation and self-knowledge and from this act is born an image.[62] Drawing attention to the ancient problem of distinguishing the begetting of the Son from the procession of the Spirit, Melanchthon offered his opinion that the difference is easier to grasp if we attend to the various powers within our own souls – thoughts and images pertain to knowledge; love and motivation are found in the will and heart.[63] Of course, Melanchthon's presentation of the doctrine of the Trinity goes beyond this use of the psychological analogy. It includes exposition of significant Biblical passages and scholastic defining of technical terms. Nonetheless, it is interesting that Melanchthon, whose first edition of *Loci Communes* had militated so stridently against speculative approaches to the Trinity, rather quickly used such arguments as a method of exposition. Although the speculative approach based on the psychological analogy would never become a mainstay of Protestant theological argumentation, its bare presence in Melanchthon's thought testifies to its enduring fascination, even among those most resolutely opposed to it. As we will see, it recurs regularly in Protestant reflection on the Trinity.

By the mid-1500s, the general contours of the Protestant doctrine of the Trinity in Germany were established, following the lead of Luther and Melanchthon. We may look to the Formula of Concord as a convenient summary of the main points of this doctrine. First, the Bible was accepted as the only rule of doctrine; creeds and other writings were to be accepted only as they agreed with the Bible. Second, creeds such as the Nicene and the Athanasian creeds were recognized as necessary defensive strategies against false teachers and heretics; their content was regarded as a restatement of the Christian faith as set forth in Scripture.[64] In this way, although the creeds were not accorded any authority in

---

[62] Ibid., 13–14.   [63] Ibid., 30.

[64] Theodore G. Tappert, ed., *The Book of Concord: The Confessions of the Evangelical Lutheran Church* (Philadelphia: Fortress Press, 1959), 464–465.

their own right, in fact they functioned authoritatively as guides to the interpretation of the Bible. Protestants had gone on record affirming their belief that the Trinitarian creeds reproduced the message of the Bible in different words. Along with the insistence on the scriptural basis of the doctrine went an implied resistance to philosophical and speculative proofs and expositions of the Trinity.[65]

Yet there were also elements in the founding works of German Protestantism that in the future would provide opportunity for divergence from the confessional consensus. For one thing, the speculative mood evidenced by Melanchthon, although subdued, was never fully eradicated, even in the period of Protestant school-theology.[66] For another, as noted previously, Luther's and Melanchthon's innovative approach to interpreting the Bible, an approach in which the doctrines of salvation were preeminent and in which philosophy was mightily discouraged, was always a factor in Protestant theology.[67] As long as Protestant theologians assumed the congruity between the Trinitarian creeds and the Bible, Luther's approach to the Bible could pose no threat to the Trinity; however, when under the weight of historical criticism in the eighteenth century the proof-text approach to the Bible began to be discredited, Luther's salvation-centered theology could then be opposed to a scholastic use of the Bible. With this, the direct scriptural support for the Trinity would be weakened. The continued credence given to the doctrine of the Trinity would rest on its connection with salvation. If then Melanchthon's initial view that the doctrine of the Trinity possesses no close relation to salvation were adopted, the perceived lack of Biblical support would be fatal. But if theologians could argue convincingly that the doctrine is directly vital to salvation, then it might have a future.

---

[65] See Robert D. Preus, *The Theology of Post-Reformation Lutheranism*, vol. II, *God and His Creation* (St. Louis: Concordia Publishing, 1972), 118–121, for a statement about the overall attitude of theologians to rationalistic approaches.

[66] See ibid., 152 and 156 for examples in the scholastic period of analogical reasoning used to support the doctrine of the Trinity.

[67] In view of the important Reformed component of German Protestant thought, it is appropriate to note that the same insistence on the close connection between doctrine and salvation is prominent in the thought of John Calvin. See, for example, *Institutes* 1.2.2 and 1.5.9.

In summary, the future of the doctrine depended on the complex interactions between several intellectual commitments and on the ways in which later theologians would take the early statements by Luther and Melanchthon. To the extent that later theologians simply took the affirmations of Luther and Melanchthon at face value and accepted the Trinitarian creeds as faithful expositions of the Bible, the doctrine of the Trinity would be strenuously defended and perhaps employed in creative ways for the exposition of the Christian faith. However, to the extent that theologians accepted the modern historical critique of the Bible and became suspicious of the proof-text method, Luther's and Melanchthon's own approach to the doctrine would be weakened. If the doctrine was understood to be a theory of God's being, Melanchthon's stricture against speculation and Luther's Christocentric interpretation of Scripture could count as objections to the doctrine on the grounds that such theories lack the connection with salvation that is essential for theological doctrines.

In short, there were three potential lines of development for Protestant Trinitarian thought. First, it could perpetuate the catholic faith along the lines indicated in the Formula of Concord. That is, it could defend and expound the doctrine on the basis of Biblical interpretation and appeal to the ancient church. Second, it could question whether the doctrine is truly Biblical and closely connected with salvation. Although Socinian criticism of the doctrine was already prominent in the 1500s, extensive criticism of the Trinity as part of a revolution in thinking about the Bible dates from the rise of historical criticism in the 1700s. Third, it could develop the speculative and analogical approach to the doctrine as found in the Augustinian and Thomistic traditions.

Accordingly, although the doctrine had and continues to have many supporters, it faced trenchant criticism on three points: whether it is genuinely related to faith and salvation or is instead purely speculative and philosophical; whether it can legitimately be derived from the Word of God in the Bible; and whether, if it can be legitimately derived from Scripture, it can also be derived from, or at least helpfully expounded by, analogical and speculative reasoning, a move that would tend to undercut the evangelical character of the doctrine.

CHAPTER TWO

Between scholastic theology and Enlightenment

INTRODUCTION

The previous chapter's review of Luther and Melanchthon disclosed the fundamental tensions in Trinitarian thought in the modern period. First is the tension in the conception of the Word of God. On the one hand was the inclination to think of the Bible as a concatenation of revealed truths on a wide variety of subjects (including the Trinity); on the other hand was the Melanchthonian emphasis on the Christological and soteriological thrust of the Bible. As noted in the previous chapter, this tension briefly threatened to make the doctrine of the Trinity an unused if still venerated doctrine. At length, Luther and Melanchthon came to their senses and devoted some attention to the doctrine, finally discovering in it a direct connection to salvation that enabled them to incorporate the doctrine into their theology with good conscience. Second is the tension between understanding the Trinity by means of scriptural exposition and understanding it through metaphysical insight into the structure of the reflective self (the speculative-analogical approach). Lutheran invective against philosophy did not prevent Melanchthon and even Luther from occasionally using speculative motifs in their exposition and defense of the doctrine. In this way they bequeathed to later theologians and religious philosophers their uneasy accommodation between strictly Biblical arguments and speculative-analogical arguments. These two issues, then, constitute the terms of discussion for the period of the early Enlightenment, lying between the scholastic period of Protestant theology and the critical phase of the Enlightenment – roughly the first half of the eighteenth century.

Due to the limitations of space, we must pass over the scholastic theologians. This chapter will instead focus on the Melanchthonian tradition of Christological interpretation of the Word and on the speculative-analogical tradition.

In the early decades of the eighteenth century, the Melanchthonian approach was represented by pietism. Most pietists were adamant upholders of orthodox Protestant theology; however, they were suspicious of the scientific pretensions of this theology and were absorbed by the task of reforming the Christian life. Paradoxically, although pietists found the rationalistic approach of philosophers repugnant, their theological orientation had a revolutionary effect on the understanding of the Trinity similar to that of the rationalists. This is because, like the rationalists, they were not content simply to expound the Biblical text in keeping with the ancient creeds and tradition of the church. Instead they adopted an attitude much like that found in Melanchthon's early theology. They regarded the Bible as describing exclusively God's revelation and relation to us and not at all as describing the inner, eternal being of God. An example of this tendency is Nicolaus Ludwig von Zinzendorf (1700–1760), who expounded the doctrine of the Trinity in a way that was both highly original and also thoroughly unacceptable to the scholastic theologians.

The use of reflective selfhood to expound the Trinity is represented here by Gottfried Wilhelm Leibniz (1646–1716), who both preserved the medieval speculative-analogical approach to the Trinity and also subtly altered it by focusing much more directly on the idea of God's subjectivity than did theologians in the medieval period. In so doing he passed this heritage on to the idealist philosophers of the nineteenth century and ensured that future speculation along these lines would be most definitely an inquiry into God's own selfhood.

NICOLAUS LUDWIG VON ZINZENDORF: A MELANCHTHONIAN RESPONSE TO THE SPIRIT OF ORTHODOXY

Zinzendorf was a reversion of sorts to the spirit if not the letter of Melanchthon's early theology, with its emphasis on the practical benefits of religious knowledge. His Melanchthonian orientation is disclosed by his belief that the doctrine of the Trinity, and in fact all theology, begins with Jesus Christ. Unlike Leibniz and others in the speculative-analogical tradition, Zinzendorf had no interest in elaborating metaphysical concepts such as "being" and "spirit" or in explaining the Trinity by means of those concepts. What did interest him was salvation and the activity of God in salvation. Consequently, he paid comparatively little attention to what modern theologians have called the ontological or essential Trinity.

Zinzendorf also differed from the scholastic theologians who wanted to establish the doctrine on the basis of Scripture alone. For these theologians, the doctrine of the Trinity was essentially an exegetical matter of deciding whether or not the Bible teaches that the one God is three persons. Although Zinzendorf intended to remain within the bounds of orthodoxy and rejected speculative methods, his way of handling the doctrine marked a departure from the dogmatic and exegetical method of the scholastics. He narrowed the focus of Trinitarian thinking to one point – Jesus Christ. The guiding principle of his interpretation was the belief that Jesus Christ is the revelation of God and the principle of all our knowledge of God. His more Biblicist contemporaries sought to discern the Bible's meaning by solving problems of textual criticism and philology. Of course, Zinzendorf was not untouched by the prevailing methods of his day. He shared with other theologians the proof-text method and was not free from tendential exegesis. However, he was comparatively uninterested in these matters. This lack of interest was generated by his conviction that theology should confine itself to expounding revelation, eschewing all speculations into God's inner being. This conviction, although possessing a sound Protestant pedigree, drove him into Trinitarian directions that shocked the more soberly minded thinkers of Biblical orthodoxy who believed it was they who were bearing the Protestant heritage most faithfully. We see here an illustration of the ongoing tension in Protestant theology between radical and traditional tendencies in the interpretation of the Bible. Both tendencies were present in Luther and Melanchthon, the first in their critique of the credal tradition and their anti-speculative mood, the second in their ultimate affirmation of the ancient Trinitarian and

Christological creeds. It is also present in the difference between those who desire to restrict theology to the practical doctrines of salvation and those who desire to fashion a comprehensive and scientific dogmatics. The example of Melanchthon is instructive, for it is he who both iconoclastically limited theology to the practical doctrines and also formed the first attempt at a systematic theology for the Lutheran churches.

As a preface to Zinzendorf's view of the Trinity, we should note his allegiance to the Augsburg Confession. In *Twenty-One Discourses on the Augsburg Confession* he demonstrated his allegiance by emphasizing the equality and subsistence of the Trinitarian persons. He intended thereby to refute both Socinians and Arians: Socinians by affirming the distinction and subsistence of Father, Son and Spirit, Arians by affirming their equality.[1]

Zinzendorf's avowal of orthodoxy did not prevent him from making critical remarks about the Confession. He complained of the first article's lack of connection with the other, more soteriological articles. By beginning with the secret of the Trinity, he complained, the Confession contradicts the Holy Spirit's method of teaching, which is to begin with redemption and not with divine mysteries. This is an important point, for in the next century Friedrich Schleiermacher would likewise insist that knowledge of the Trinity presupposes the doctrines of redemption. Finally, Zinzendorf was convinced that the first article had been inserted into the creeds by the Lutheran theologians for one purpose only – to legitimate their political standing with the emperor by showing their agreement with the ancient church.[2] This conviction confirmed his suspicion about the article's soteriological deficiencies.

We have then a mixed picture of Zinzendorf's doctrinal inclinations. On the one hand he affirmed his agreement with the Confession, expressly with regard to its doctrine of the Trinity; on the other hand he attacked the article on the Trinity for its lack of

---

[1] Nikolaus Ludwig von Zinzendorf, "Ein und zwanzig Discurse über die augspurgische Confession," *Hauptschriften*, ed. Erich Beyreuther and Gerhard Meyer, vol. VI, *Verschiedene Schriften* (Hildesheim: Georg Olms Verlagsbuchhandlung, 1963), 4–5 and 67–68. See p. 7 for another assertion of his orthodoxy and p. 5 for an appeal to the Athanasian Creed to support his opinion that Jesus may legitimately be called father and creator.

[2] Ibid., 60–63.

religious importance and its suspicious political origins. The cause of this ambivalence lies in Zinzendorf's view of the knowledge of God.

Zinzendorf, in good Protestant fashion, swore abstinence from all forms of metaphysics, natural theology and the contamination of theology by philosophy.[3] Whether in his day other Protestant theologians uniformly abided by such a rule is questionable but Zinzendorf dutifully rejected all speculative prying into divine matters and insisted that Christian theology has to do only with God as God is revealed to us.[4] Nothing better signifies his affinity with Melanchthon's theology than this sentiment. Accordingly, Zinzendorf could claim Protestant warrant at least for this aspect of his theology.

However, Zinzendorf's rejection of speculation resulted in a doctrine of the Trinity far different from that of other Protestants. To see why this is so we must note that Zinzendorf joined to his suspicion of philosophy a theology of the Trinity based on the experience of redemption: "We attest to [one] another what the heart knows of the three persons, since we speak from the Bible and from our own blessed experience: The Father has begotten me, the Holy Spirit has borne me." Our knowledge of the Trinity, then, depends not only or even mainly on the correct exegesis of Scripture, but instead on the experience of redemption, which is the presupposition of all spiritual knowledge. For example, we learn of the fatherhood of God not mainly because the Bible speaks of God the Father, but because we have been begotten, which is an act of fatherhood.[5] Here the experience of redemption leads the way for theological reflection. For this reason, Zinzendorf declined to seek proof and to dispute – the proof of the Trinity was, he believed, to be found in the hearts of the faithful, not in arguments over Scripture.[6]

---

[3] Hans Ruh, *Die christologische Begründung des ersten Artikels bei Zinzendorf* (Zurich: EVZ-Verlag, 1963), 55–56 and Erich Beyreuther, "Christozentrismus und Trinitätsauffassung," *Studien zur Theologie Zinzendorfs: Gesammelte Aufsätze* ([Neukirchen-Vluyn:] Neukirchener Verlag, 1962), 23–24.

[4] Ruh, *Christologische Begründung*, 100; Beyreuther, "Christozentrismus und Trinitäts-auffassung," 22.   [5] Zinzendorf, "Ein und zwanzig Discurse," 69–74.

[6] Zinzendorf, "Sieben letzte Reden so er in der Gemeine, vor seiner am 7 Aug erfolgten abermahligen Abreise nach Amerika, gehalten," *Hauptschriften*, vol. II, *Reden in und von Amerika*, 4.

Zinzendorf differed from other Protestants also in his view of revelation. While agreeing with them that there is no general knowledge of God and that revelation really pertains to a particular history whose culmination was Jesus Christ,[7] Zinzendorf held that Jesus encompasses the totality of God's historical dealing with humanity and is the sole content of God's revelation.[8] So, when we encounter Jesus, we encounter God because Jesus is the creator, redeemer and sanctifier. He further held that we are related to the Father and Holy Spirit only in and through Jesus Christ – the Father is *Jesus'* Father and is *our* Father only in a derived sense.[9] Finally, it was Zinzendorf's belief that before the moment in history when Jesus revealed his own Father to the disciples, no one had worshiped or even known the Father. Accordingly, the God revealed in the Old Testament is Jesus, who is not only savior but also creator and the God of Abraham, Isaac and Jacob.[10]

What Zinzendorf was getting at was that Jesus performs all the functions of God in relation to the world. Although theologians have customarily associated the Father with creation and identified the Father with the object of any natural theology, Zinzendorf believed that it was the Son whom humanity had known through natural theology. In this way he reversed the common opinion that we know the Father through natural theology and the Son through revelation. He also rejected the teaching that, in Jesus Christ, the Father revealed the Son, arguing instead that it was Jesus the Son who revealed the Father.

What were the sources of Zinzendorf's conceptions of revelation and Jesus Christ? Beside the Bible and experience, one of his favorite supports was Martin Luther's hymn, "A Mighty Fortress Is Our God," especially the first stanza: "Do you know what that [one] is?/ Jesus Christ is his name./ The Lord Sabbaoth and there is no other God."[11] Here Zinzendorf found express warrant for his

---

[7] Ruh, *Christologische Begründung*, 62.

[8] Gary Steven Kinkel, *Our Dear Mother the Spirit: An Investigation of Count Zinzendorf's Theology and Praxis* (Lanham, MD: University Press of America, 1990), 92; Ruh, *Christologische Begründung*, 63; Beyreuther, "Christozentrismus und Trinitätsauffassung," 16.

[9] Nicholaus Ludwig Count von Zinzendorf, *Nine Public Lectures on Important Subjects in Religion*, trs. George W. Forell (Iowa City: University of Iowa Press, 1973), 98.

[10] Ibid., 12–13.

[11] Zinzendorf, "Eine Sammlung öffentlicher Reden," *Hauptschriften*, vol. II, 43 and 263; "Sieben lezte Reden," 25.

identifying Jesus with the one God known to humanity. What must have especially delighted Zinzendorf was his ability to call upon Luther himself in support of a Christocentric interpretation of things. Of course, whether Luther actually would have agreed with Zinzendorf's innovative Christology is debatable. Nevertheless, we may at least say that Zinzendorf took seriously Luther's emphasis on the centrality of Christ and consistently made it a systematic principle of his theology.

Zinzendorf's Christocentrism proved too much for some theologians of his day. Although Protestant theologians in the late seventeenth and early eighteenth centuries resisted the speculative-analogical approach to the Trinity that Philip Melanchthon had finally succumbed to in the last editions of *Loci Communes*, they nonetheless adopted a different sort of rationalistic method in tandem with their residual Biblicism. The willingness of Lutheran and Reformed theologians to embrace metaphysical categories as a means of buttressing confessional claims against each other is a testimony to this.[12] Likewise, scholars have drawn attention to a tendency in Protestant scholastic theology to accept the philosophical definitions and categories of Catholic theology and philosophy.[13] Zinzendorf in particular and pietists in general resisted this tendency and abhorred the kind of scientific theology that Protestants had developed. So Zinzendorf's Christocentric view was more than simply a faithful if eccentric adherence to Lutheran principles; it was also a conscious divergence from the mainstream rationalizing tendency of his day. By regarding Jesus Christ as the whole content of God's historical revelation, he registered a protest against any granting of autonomy to human reason with respect to the knowledge of God and insisted on taking Jesus Christ as the hermeneutical key to the understanding of Scripture and to the knowledge of God.

Which of these parties, Zinzendorf or the Protestant scholastics, may rightfully claim the mantle of the reformers? Each stood, perhaps one-sidedly, for an idea that the reformers espoused:

[12] Kristian Jensen, "Protestant Rivalry – Metaphysics and Rhetoric in Germany c. 1590–1620," *Journal of Ecclesiastical History* 41 (1990): 24–25 and 28.
[13] Richard A. Muller, "Scholasticism Protestant and Catholic: Francis Turretin on the Object and Principles of Theology," *Church History* 55 (1986): 204–205.

Zinzendorf, for the centrality of soteriology and Christocentrism; the scholastics, for the concern for apostolicity in the full range of catholic doctrine. We may simplify the issue by asserting that whereas the scholastics were intent on preserving the reformers' doctrines by finding a scientific form for those doctrines, Zinzendorf and other pietists took the doctrinal content for granted and emphasized what they believed to be the reformers' central soteriological insights.

From this emphasis on Christocentric revelation, Zinzendorf concluded that we can have no knowledge of the Trinity in itself (i.e., of the eternal divine life) and that all our knowledge is restricted to the Trinity as it is revealed in and through Jesus Christ. To support this contention, Zinzendorf had recourse to the theosophical notion of the divine abyss. According to this notion, the divine being is fathomless being, the *Ungrund*, and utterly incomprehensible. As a result, we can know only what is revealed to us; the abysmal being of God remains a mystery.[14] Of course, Zinzendorf did not make the mistake of separating God's being in itself from the revealed Trinity, as though the Trinity were something existing only in revelation as a mere appearance. On the contrary, he believed firmly in the eternal Trinity. It is just that his commitment to revelation was so great that he believed we should say nothing about God except what is given to us in revelation. He thereby excluded any thought of our discussing God in some merely objective fashion. His emphasis was on Jesus Christ's function as creator, redeemer and sanctifier – in short, on Jesus as God – rather than on the relation of the Trinitarian persons to one another in eternity.[15]

Was Zinzendorf saying anything new in these claims? Theologians of every confession have always insisted that the inner life of the Trinity is an incomprehensible mystery; however, this profession has not prevented them from discussing it according to whatever analogy they think fits. Zinzendorf's view of mystery, however, prohibited him from going beyond a mere

[14] Zinzendorf, "Eine Sammlung öffentlicher Reden," 44 and 77.
[15] Zinzendorf, "Sieben letzte Reden," 5–6. See also Zinzendorf, *Nine Public Lectures*, 5; Ruh, *Christologische Begründung*, 79–80, 103–105 and 118–119; Beyreuther, "Christozentrismus und Trinitätsauffassung," 19–21; and Kinkel, *Our Dear Mother*, 85–89.

mention of such an inner Trinity. In a way that looked backward to the early Melanchthon and forward, in a different way, to the critical philosophy of Kant, Zinzendorf strictly separated the revelation of God from God's own inner being. The former is all that we may know; the latter remains in the darkness. As we shall note in a later chapter, such a separation provoked the deepest anxiety in a theologian such as Karl Barth, who discerned in it a peril to salvation.

As stated above, Zinzendorf identified Jesus Christ as the creator of the world. By that he meant more than that Jesus is the agent through whom the Father created, which is the typical view. He meant that Jesus Christ is the only person of the Trinity that has a direct relation to the world.[16] Because it is Christ who is the creator, it is Christ, not the first person of the Trinity, who is our father.[17] The first person of the Trinity (i.e. Jesus' own Father) is not the father of humanity generally, for humanity in its natural condition stands under the authority of Christ, who created it. In order to indicate our indirect relation to the first person, we may call the Father of Jesus Christ our father-in-law or grandfather, but only if we are in Christ.[18] This line of argument, although consistent with Zinzendorf's theology, seems almost calculated to arouse opposition. While there is a certain logic to Zinzendorf's position, it is understandable that others, even astute theologians, objected to what they regarded as Zinzendorf's utter distortion of Scripture in this matter.

And there were yet more innovations to come. According to Zinzendorf, Jesus Christ may rightly be named as, and in fact *is*, God because he performs the functions of God in relation to the world. The principle that the divine functions in relation to the world are the key to our knowledge of God gave rise to a striking idea that has attracted attention from commentators – the use of metaphors drawn from family life to portray the Trinity. Theologians have often used analogies such as Father and Son to explain the relations between the persons in the *eternal* Trinity;

---

[16] Zinzendorf, *Nine Public Lectures*, 4; "Eine Sammlung öffentlicher Reden," 77–79; "Sieben letzte Reden," 8–9.

[17] Zinzendorf, "Eine Sammlung öffentlicher Reden," 181 and 262; Ruh, *Christologische Begründung*, 106 and 111. [18] Zinzendorf, "Sieben letzte Reden," 36–37.

however, Zinzendorf used certain metaphors to explain the activities of the Trinitarian persons in the economy of salvation.[19] He used these metaphors, which he pieced together from Biblical images, to signify the various relations that the Trinitarian persons have to the individual Christian: Jesus Christ is our husband, Jesus' own Father is our father-in-law, and the Holy Spirit is our mother.

The important thing is that Zinzendorf was using these metaphors to expound the ways in which the Trinitarian persons individually relate to us, not to explain how they relate to each other in eternity.[20] This prevents us from regarding the Father and Spirit as a married couple in some sort of heavenly marriage. Zinzendorf's use of these metaphors is in accordance with his insistence that theology is about God's relation to us in salvation. He was suspicious of attempts at depicting the relations of the Trinitarian persons one to another, because to do so meant attempting to know the abysmal mystery of God's being. Admittedly, even with this explanation of his motivation, his calling the first person of the Trinity our Father-in-law is peculiar; however, it is understandable once we remember that redemption includes our adoption by God, for we then see that the Father of Jesus is our Father only as we are redeemed in Christ. Just as one's own earthly father-in-law becomes such only upon marriage to one's spouse, so the Father of Jesus becomes our father only through our spousal relation to Jesus. Describing the first person as our Father-*in-law* reminds us that our relation to the first person is mediated by our relation to our husband in salvation, Jesus Christ.[21] Describing Jesus as Husband presents no problem, resting as it does on Biblical images of Christ and the church in Ephesians and Revelation. The potentially most controversial innovation lay in calling the Holy Spirit our Mother, lacking as it does explicit Biblical grounding. Apart from its lack of express Biblical warrant, it seemed to establish a marital relation between the Father and the Spirit. This image particularly appalled Johann Albrecht Bengel, the Biblical scholar, who attacked Zinzendorf for this and other doctrinal novelties.

---

[19] Ibid., 5–7; Ruh, *Christologische Begründung*, 103.
[20] Kinkel, *Our Dear Mother*, 87 and 101.   [21] Ruh, *Christologische Begründung*, 111.

Another idiosyncratic element of Zinzendorf's theology was his criticism of the traditional teaching about Trinitarian appropriations. By this teaching theologians have sought to show that particular divine acts such as creation are fitly attributed to one of the persons (in this case the Father) in spite of the generally accepted rule that the outward acts of the Trinity are acts of the whole Trinity. Because of the Roman Catholic tradition's concern to safeguard the unity of God, it tended to restrict divine plurality to the inward life of God and to regard God's outward acts (such as creation) as common to the Trinitarian persons. In spite of this tendency, certain divine acts have come to be attributed to one of the persons exclusively and not, as might be expected, to all the persons collectively. For example, the Father is routinely described as Creator, even though it is the whole Trinity that creates. Theologians used the word "appropriation" to explain that there is a certain order among the Trinitarian persons because of the inner-Trinitarian relations. Because the Son and Spirit have their origin in the Father, the origin of the world (i.e. creation) is attributed or appropriated to the Father in creeds and worship.[22]

Zinzendorf's rejection of this idea of appropriation resulted from his view of revelation. If the Bible is truly intended to show forth Christ, he reasoned, then every reference to God in the Bible must really be a reference to Christ. It follows that Christ was the God revealed in the Old Testament, that he is Yahweh and that he is the creator.[23] Since the act of creation is an outward act of God and since all such outward acts are done by Christ, it follows that only Christ is directly revealed in the created order of the world.[24] Although this judgment is sound according to the principles of his theology, Zinzendorf caused trouble for himself by affirming something that runs counter to many creeds that assign creation to the Father. This divergence in turn raised questions about the orthodox character of Zinzendorf's other teachings.

Another concern of Zinzendorf's was subordinationism, the view that since the Father begets the Son, the Son is in some sense

---

[22] See Thomas Aquinas, *Summa Theologica*, 1.39.8 and 1.45.6.
[23] Ruh, *Christologische Begründung*, 115 and Beyreuther, "Christozentrismus und Trinitätsauffassung," 14. [24] Ruh, *Christologische Begründung*, 119.

subordinate to the Father. This problem has engendered long controversies in Christian history but Zinzendorf resolved it by an appeal to his concept of revelation. Eschewing all inquiry into the eternal Trinity and, contrary to tradition, denying that the Father begets the Son,[25] he could not fathom the Son's being subordinate to the Father.[26] If anything, commentators on Zinzendorf have spoken of a subordination of the Father and Spirit to the Son because the Father and Spirit come into theological consideration only in relation to salvation, the center of which is the Son.[27] The difficult thing for Zinzendorf was to balance the centrality of Christ in revelation with a recognition of the important role of Father and Spirit in redemption. He could write on the one hand that there is no danger that we will ascribe too much to Christ and on the other hand, somewhat inconsistently, that although all things are subjected to Christ, the Father and Spirit are equal to the Son and cooperate with the Son in redemption and sanctification.[28]

Zinzendorf's novel views did not find universal acceptance among his contemporaries, Bengel being one of his most trenchant critics. We may divide Bengel's comments into two parts, those touching Zinzendorf's hermeneutical principles and those directly touching his idea of the Trinity. His comments about hermeneutics can be summarized: first, Zinzendorf had a weak view of Scripture; second, his theology was overly dependent on subjective feelings.

As to the first: Bengel had decided views about the nature of Scripture, views that conflicted with Zinzendorf's. In a lengthy book directed at Zinzendorf's theories, Bengel identified the Bible as God's book, the entire content of which is holy and salutary, and as a totality, a collection of testimonies selected by God, containing a system of truth in which nothing is superfluous.[29] What par-

---

[25] Ibid., 127; Beyreuther, "Christozentrismus und Trinitätsauffassung," 26–27; Kinkel, *Our Dear Mother*, 135.   [26] Ruh, *Christologische Begründung*, 121.   [27] Ibid., 113.

[28] Zinzendorf, "Sieben letzte Reden," 11, 26 and 28.

[29] See Johann Albrecht Bengel, "Abriß der so genannten Brüdergemeine," *Nikolaus Ludwig von Zinzendorf: Materialen und Dokumente*, ed. Erich Beyreuther et al., 2nd series, *Nikolaus Ludwig Graf von Zinzendorf: Leben und Werke in Quellen und Darstellungen*, ed. Erich Beyreuther und Gerhard Meyer, vol. x (Hildesheim: Georg Olms Verlag, 1972), 20–21 and 26–27.

ticularly irritated Bengel was Zinzendorf's granting of errors in the Bible in matters of natural and historical fact.[30] Zinzendorf was willing to grant such errors because he had discerned a process of developing insight and faith in the New Testament period. The writers of Scripture were not infallible; their understanding had increased over time.[31] Besides, for Zinzendorf, it is Jesus Christ that is the content of revelation, not various truths located in the Bible. In contrast to Bengel, he did not treat the Bible as a collection of revealed doctrines and did not regard all parts of Scripture as having equal value. The point is that Zinzendorf did not regard the Bible as an infallible source of propositional truth; Bengel did so regard it.

As to the second: Bengel charged Zinzendorf with elevating the subjective conviction of the individual over the objective authority of the Bible. Bengel was willing to grant the importance of the testimony of the Spirit as the ground of our confidence in the Bible; however, he also believed that this testimony functioned only in relation to the Bible. Zinzendorf, he believed, had substituted human subjective feelings for the witness of the Spirit and then established them as an independent authority with no connection to the Bible. This was intolerable for Bengel, given his identification of Scripture and the Word of God. He accordingly contrasted the Bible with any claim to authority based on feeling. Whereas, he asserted, Zinzendorf staked all religious knowledge on the heart, the Bible declared the heart to be dark and something not to be trusted.[32]

These two complaints come together in the charge of fanaticism. Bengel believed Zinzendorf had so emphasized Christocentrism that his subjective impression of the crucified Christ had become the principle of his theology without need of instruction from the Bible. As a result, Zinzendorf's congregation had become its own Bible and its own standard of truth.[33] For Bengel, this constituted the essence of fanaticism.[34]

Whether Zinzendorf had truly replaced the authority of the Bible with individual experience may be doubted. While he did concede the presence of errors in the Bible and has been credited

---

[30] Ibid., 30.   [31] Zinzendorf, *Nine Public Lectures*, 39.   [32] Bengel, "Abriß," 26–29.
[33] Ibid., 30–31.   [34] Ibid., 37.

by recent expositors with being a pioneer of the modern critical attitude toward Scripture,[35] there is no reason to think he had a low view of Scripture. It is more likely that he had a genuinely Lutheran view of Scripture, or at least a view that Luther himself had sometimes expressed.[36] In truth, the debate between Zinzendorf and Bengel on the question of authority reflects a deep and perennial division within Protestant thought. On the one hand is the Melanchthonian affirmation that the Bible's purpose is to lead us to Christ; on the other hand is the interest Protestants have had in using the Bible as a source book for a fully rounded system of theology, an interest necessitated by the Protestant rejection of the Roman Catholic church's magisterial tradition as an authoritative source of theology.

Bengel's points were that Zinzendorf's doctrinal aberrations resulted from his confused ideas of authority and that without Bengel's view of Scripture anything could be proposed as Christian truth as long as it was supported by the subjective feelings of a dominant personality like Zinzendorf's. In response, Zinzendorf, like all pietists, could only point at the helplessness that mere texts of Scripture had for the engendering of true Christianity unless accompanied by subjective conviction from the Spirit's witness.

Regarding the Trinity, Bengel criticized Zinzendorf for departing both from the recognized confessions and from the Bible. In particular, he objected to the suggestions that Christ is the creator and our Father, and charged Zinzendorf with being a new sort of Unitarian,[37] evidently believing that Zinzendorf was in danger of collapsing the three Trinitarian persons into one. He thought Zinzendorf had named the Spirit Mother in a completely arbitrary, i.e. exegetically inadequate, way and detected an insufficient guarding of the divine unity in Zinzendorf's analogy of the heavenly family.[38]

Many of Bengel's arguments were drawn from the familiar orthodox arsenal of proof-texts. Nevertheless, one cannot help sympathizing with his overall concern that Zinzendorf had engaged in some tendential exegesis. In fact, Zinzendorf and

---

[35] Ruh, *Christologische Begründung*, 22–29.   [36] Kinkel, *Our Dear Mother*, 137.
[37] Bengel, "Abriß," 55.   [38] Ibid., 22–23.

Bengel had each imposed a forced unity on the Bible, Zinzendorf's based on his Christocentric vision, Bengel's based on his identification of Scripture and the Word of God. The fundamental issue between them was whether the Bible is to be interpreted through a soteriological lens or in conformity with the ancient creeds. Is the Bible strictly about God's relation to us or is the Bible also informative, if indirectly, of the eternal Trinitarian life of God?

Zinzendorf's problem was that, having recovered an authentic Protestant idea – Christocentric revelation – he proceeded to fashion a complete interpretation of the Bible from that idea. He receives high marks for consistency. Nevertheless, there are serious weaknesses in his representation of the Trinity, even when viewed on its own terms as an account of the Trinity of revelation. We can sympathize with Bengel's uneasiness about Zinzendorf's insistence that it was Jesus and not God the Father that was known in the Old Testament.[39] At the same time, Zinzendorf has the backing of the Fourth Gospel, which supports his opinion that there is no knowledge of the Father except through revelation by the Son.

What are we to make of Zinzendorf? When we keep in mind his protests that he fully accepted the church's doctrine of the Trinity and that he was only expounding the Trinity found in revelation, then, guided by the principle of charity, we may judge that his main problem was eccentricity of expression and over-zealousness in applying his Christocentrism to the interpretation of Scripture. Bengel's comments, however, remind us that more was at stake. Zinzendorf had the luxury of assuming the credal doctrine of the Trinity. Only Socinians had hitherto seriously called into question the validity of the creeds and confessions; Biblical criticism was not yet a threat to orthodox theology. The question left over for the nineteenth century was how to fashion an idea of the Trinity based on Christocentrism when the reality of the eternal Trinity could no longer be assured by creed and Bible. Progressive theologians of the nineteenth century took up the pietist insistence on the witness of the Spirit, i.e. subjective

---

[39] Ibid., 45 and 48.

conviction, but did so because there seemed no other way of saving the content of Scripture from the ravages of criticism. The resulting theologies were adapted to the results of criticism; whether such a theology was up to the task of establishing the doctrine of the Trinity was another question, one that Zinzendorf did not have to ask.

GOTTFRIED WILHELM LEIBNIZ: THE SPECULATIVE-ANALOGICAL TRADITION

In turning to Leibniz' speculative articulation of the Trinity, we leave behind Protestant theological concerns and take up the tradition extending back to Melanchthon and beyond him to Augustine and ultimately to Aristotle. Here there is no inquiry into Biblical texts or ecclesiastical authorities, but only philosophical insight into the nature of God's reflective selfhood for whatever light it may shed on the Trinity. The first thing to note is that Leibniz' writings devoted to the Trinity are minuscule in comparison with his entire corpus of writings. However, although Leibniz was mainly concerned about philosophical issues, his interest in the doctrine of the Trinity was not perfunctory. He brought to bear the full weight of his philosophical acumen in the interest of better understanding the Trinity. Further, he sought to rehabilitate medieval philosophy's employment of Aristotelian thought in the wake of the criticism of René Descartes and Benedict Spinoza and to put that philosophy to use in the service of his religious beliefs.

In addition to his metaphysical orientation, Leibniz' affinity for scholastic philosophy is seen also in his adherence to the tradition whose slogan is "faith seeking understanding." The hallmark of this tradition is the desire to comprehend revealed truths rationally. Members of this tradition have satisfied this desire sometimes by relating revealed truth to a larger, often philosophical scheme of thought, as is customary in arguments for the existence of God, and sometimes by discerning the inner logic of a doctrine, as Anselm did with the doctrine of atonement in *Cur Deus Homo?* Leibniz used both of these two forms. On the one hand, he related the idea of the Trinity to his metaphysics, where it appears as the archetypal instance of the metaphysical category of substance; on the other hand he sought to grasp the inner logic of the idea of God as a Trinity by means of the concept of reflective selfhood.[40]

For these two concepts, substance and reflective selfhood, Leibniz called upon the resources of the Augustinian-Thomistic tradition. As I have already noted, Augustine had called attention to several ways in which the human self is analogous to the Trinity. Although he stated clearly that the closest analogy between human self and Trinity is the mind that remembers, knows and loves God,[41] theologians have usually focused attention on another aspect, the mind's memory, intellect and will. Thomas Aquinas gave greater precision to Augustine's ideas by portraying the Trinity as analogous to a mind with two internal movements, intellect and will, and by shifting the emphasis of the analogy so that it was no longer (as in Augustine's thinking) a more or less helpful means of speaking about God but was instead an analysis of God's being, resting on an analogical-metaphysical foundation.[42] There was, then, some variability in this tradition as to the most adequate analogy for the Trinity. Leibniz added to the diversity, for his point of departure was not the psychological analogy of memory, intellect and will but instead two related yet different analogies, one based on his analysis of substance, the other gathered expressly from reflective selfhood.

In the idea of substance Leibniz believed he had found the gateway to significant truths about all reality, including God. What was particularly important for him and constituted his innovation was the idea of force (Latin, *posse*; German, *Kraft*; French, *force*). To elucidate the meaning of force, Leibniz took pains to dissociate this notion from the Aristotelian-scholastic concept of power, i.e., *potentia* or *energeia*. Instead he equated force with the Aristotelian *entelecheia*, the activity of life and self-development.[43]

---

[40] See Jan Rohls, "Subjekt, Trinität und Persönlichkeit Gottes: Von der Reformation zur Weimarer Klassik," *Neue Zeitschrift für systematische Theologie* 30 (1988): 59–63 for an exposition of this theme in the thought of Leibniz and several theologians influenced by him.

[41] Philip Schaff, ed., *A Select Library of the Nicene and Post-Nicene Fathers of the Christian Church*, vol. III, *St. Augustin: On the Holy Trinity, Doctrinal Treatises, Moral Treatises* (Grand Rapids: Wm. B. Eerdmans Publishing Co., 1978), 191 (book 14, chapter 12, §15).

[42] Thomas Aquinas, *Summa Theologica*, 1.27.1–3.

[43] Leibniz, "On the Correction of Metaphysics and the Concept of Substance," *Philosophical Papers and Letters*, 2nd edn., ed. and trs. Leroy E. Loemker (Dordrecht: D. Reidel Publishing Co., 1969), 433.

In every being, he observed, force exists alongside perception and appetite. As a result, every being is in some sense a living soul.[44] Spirits are souls that possess intellect and self-reflection.[45] Spirits, then, are rational souls and have a level of clear perception denied to lesser souls whose perceptions are confused. Thus spirits resemble God. They are images of God; Leibniz called them little gods possessing a ray of divinity. They mirror God especially in their ability to understand the sciences by which God regulates the world and in the freedom of their actions.[46]

Although every substance shares these metaphysical attributes with God and although spirits are images of God, there is also a clear demarcation between them and God. The greatest difference is that the attributes of created substances – notably power, perception and appetite – exist in God in a preeminent way and are effects of those attributes in God.[47] So created substances both correspond to but also differ from God. God, then, is the archetype, i.e., the perfect instance, of substance. According to this portrait, there are certain features of substance that are universal, although variously manifested according to the kind of being in which they are found.

The connection between Leibniz' metaphysics and his view of the Trinity is now easily made, for he simply correlated the three aspects of substance with the Trinitarian persons. He related God's perception (knowledge) to wisdom, which is a traditional characteristic of the second person, and related God's appetition (will) to love, the characteristic of the third person.[48] So far, his understanding of the Trinity was in keeping with the Augustinian-Thomistic tradition, in which the connections among knowledge, wisdom and the Son and among will, love and the Holy Spirit were

---

[44] Leibniz, "Letter to John Bernoulli" (1698), *Philosophical Papers and Letters*, 512 and "Considerations on Vital Principles and Plastic Natures, by the Author of the System of Pre-Established Harmony" (1705), *Philosophical Papers and Letters*, 586.

[45] Leibniz, "Considerations on Vital Principles," *Philosophical Papers and Letters*, 588.

[46] Leibniz, "A New System of Nature and the Communication of Substances, As Well As the Union between the Soul and the Body," *Philosophical Papers and Letters*, 454–455; "The Principles of Nature and of Grace, Based on Reason," *Philosophical Papers and Letters*, 640; and "The Monadology," *Philosophical Papers and Letters*, 651.

[47] Leibniz, "The Principles of Nature," 639.

[48] Leibniz, *Textes inédits d'après les manuscrits de la Bibliothèque provinciale de Hanovre*, ed. Gaston Grua (Paris: Presses Universitaires de France), 139.

well established. In an apparent departure from the scholastic tradition, however, he correlated force with the Father. While this last correlation may not seem intuitively obvious, since force is not customarily used in theology to name the first person of the Trinity, it makes more sense in the context of Leibniz' philosophy, in which force, in the divine being, takes the form of creative power. Since the act of creation is normally appropriated to the Father, Leibniz' correlation of force with the Father is not as outlandish as it first appears.

In summary, Leibniz' analogy both resembles and differs from the Augustinian-Thomistic analogy. For Thomas, the principal features are the divine being itself and its intellect and will; Leibniz essentially took over from Thomas intellect and will and added the idea of substance, understood as power. Thomas and Leibniz each interpreted the Trinity in terms of a similar view of reflective selfhood and in so doing expressly related the Trinity to a larger metaphysical vision of reality. For each, the components of the human mind correspond to the persons of the Trinity because God is our creator and because created rational spirit mirrors God. Admittedly, Thomas was more clear than was Leibniz about the causal connections between the Trinity and finite spirit because he expressly grounded analogical language in the idea of God as first cause.[49] Nevertheless, there is great continuity between the two views, a similarity we expect because of Leibniz' manifest partiality for scholastic philosophy.

One thing that distinguishes Leibniz' view from Thomas' is the former's greater philosophical interest in the metaphysical correlate of the Father. According to Thomas' analogy, the Father is the divine subject itself, the source of intellect and will. Thomas felt no need to expatiate on the person of the Father because, for theologians, the first person is unproblematic – it is the divinity of the Son and Holy Spirit that is questionable, not the Father's. Leibniz, however, had an absorbing interest in the Father, because the Father corresponds to force, Leibniz' central metaphysical principle.

The explanation for this difference from Thomas is not difficult to surmise. Just as Thomas simplified Augustine's approach by

---

[49] Thomas Aquinas, *Summa Theologica*, 1.13.6.

concentrating on one analogy and by advancing the doctrine of the Trinity in a more self-consciously metaphysical direction, so Leibniz modified the Thomistic view by grafting on to it what he regarded as his distinctive metaphysical insight – force as the essence of substance.

The Trinity of force, intellect and will is part of Leibniz' metaphysics and functions as the archetype of spirits. This representation of the Trinity corresponds to the first form of "faith seeking understanding" – relating a doctrine to a larger philosophical scheme of thought. But Leibniz had another way of understanding the Trinity, a way with only a loose connection to his metaphysical vision but with a far greater connection to his religious concerns. This is the Trinity of knower and known – the Trinity of reflective selfhood. Leibniz drew this Trinity from what we ourselves experience in self-knowledge: "The Word, or that which is understood, is the image of the Father, because the Father, in conceiving [*percipiens*] the Word, conceives [*percipit*] the very thing that he himself is, namely the mind that understands itself." Furthermore, whereas the Word is the object of God the Father's perception, the perception itself is Love, the Holy Spirit, since God's act of self-perception is identical to self-love. Leibniz believed this analogy of self-knowledge to be the fittest possible for explaining the Trinity, since it accounted for the oneness of the divine substance and the plurality of the persons.[50]

Leibniz had a twofold purpose in representing the Trinity as knower, object known and the act of knowledge. First, it reinforced the notion of God as archetypal subject, although its connection with the Trinity of force, intellect and will remains far from clear; second, it permitted Leibniz to engage in his favorite diversion – defending orthodox doctrine. In particular, Leibniz used the Trinity of self-knowledge to refute two perpetual tendencies of Trinitarian theology, modalism (making the Trinitarian persons mere phenomenal aspects of the single divine subject) and tritheism. With regard to modalism, Leibniz had to show that the three persons are not mere appearances or names and that they are in

---

[50] Leibniz, *Textes inédits*, 178–179.

fact real in themselves. His strategy here was to argue that the conceptual distinction between knower, known and knowledge must indicate real distinctions in God, for the conceptual distinctions must have a foundation in reality itself. From this he concluded that in God there are three foundations [*fundamenta*, *Grundlagen*] that are really distinct (though not separable, since separability implies imperfection).[51]

With regard to tritheism, Leibniz was compelled to demonstrate the unity of God. He did so by means of the Augustinian-Thomistic concept of inner-Trinitarian relations, which relies on the fact that the Trinitarian names (Father, Son and Spirit) signify not entities but relations. For example, "Father" denotes paternity (the act of begetting) within God and "Son" denotes filiation (being begotten). "Spirit" signifies spiration (being breathed). Theologians employ the notion of relations to explain the distinctions among the persons (e.g. why the Spirit is not another Son) while not making the distinctions so firm that Father, Son and Holy Spirit are thought of as three beings. Instead they are intrinsically related, so that, for example, paternity unites Father with Son and spiration unites both Father and Son (as those who breathe) with the Spirit (as the one that is breathed out). God's unity is, he claimed, evident from the Trinitarian persons' essential relatedness: there is a relation between Father and Son just as there is between knower and known. Neither can be without the other. The Spirit is knowledge itself. Further, these relations must be eternal, for God the knower must eternally have an object of knowledge.[52] Leibniz thus represented God as a process of self-knowing, a reflection: the subject of knowledge, the object and that which both knows and is known.[53] The argument is that just as the presence of distinct components in the human mind does not imply that there are three minds, so the presence of three truly distinct foundations in God does not imply that there are three gods. What Leibniz did not seem to grasp is that his Trinity of self-knowledge seems to make the Spirit the principal member of the

[51] Leibniz, "Des Andreas Wissowatius Einwürfe wider die Dreieinigkeit," in Gotthold Ephraim Lessing, *Gesammelte Werke*, ed. Paul Rilla, vol. VII, *Das Epigram; Beiträge zu einem deutschen Glossarium; Philosophische und theologische Schriften I* (Berlin: Aufbau-Verlag, 1957), 519–520.   [52] Ibid., 505 and 518–519.   [53] Ibid., 520.

Trinity, since the Spirit encompasses the other two persons as the act of knowledge encompasses both knower and object known. Although we might be tempted to give priority to the knower and regard the act of knowledge as a mere attribute, in fact the knower is not actualized as knower without the act of knowledge. Likewise, the object of knowledge is not actualized as such without the act of knowledge. So it is the act of knowledge that seems to be most significant. Later idealists such as G. W. F. Hegel would capitalize on this point and would represent the Spirit as the most comprehensive and embracing person of the Trinity. Leibniz, however, with his metaphysical commitment to the priority of force and his commitment to Christian tradition, would naturally grant priority to the first person.

I have noted previously that Leibniz differed from Thomas in having a greater philosophical interest in the first principle in the divine being, force, which was his central metaphysical category and which corresponds to the Father. A second way in which Leibniz differed from Thomas lies in their respective views of the act of divine understanding. According to Leibniz, the Word/Son is the direct object of the Father's act of knowledge. In fact, it is by knowing the Word/Son that the Father comes to self-knowledge. Elsewhere, he strengthens this view by likening Father and Son to knower and known. Thomas, however, regards the Word more as the *result* of the Father's act of self-knowledge than as the *means* of that self-knowledge, as Leibniz seemed to do. Thomas stated that "the Father, by understanding Himself, the Son, and the Holy Ghost, and all other things comprised in this knowledge, conceives the Word."[54] In Thomas' view, the direct object of God's knowledge is the divine intellect itself; the Word is the expression of this act of understanding.[55] Thomas was concerned to account for the origin of the second person. The expression (or generation) of a concept (or word) in the act of understanding provided him with an analogy of the generation of the eternal Word. Leibniz, however, expressed no great interest in explaining or defending the origin of the Word from the Father. He was content to state that neither can be without the other. As a result,

---

[54] Thomas Aquinas, *Summa Theologica*, 1.34.1 ad 3.   [55] Ibid., 1.14.2.

he correlated Father and Son with each other as subject and object of divine knowledge.[56]

The effect of this second difference is to alter the significance of the Word. For Thomas the Word is the expression of the Father's self-knowledge; for Leibniz the Word is the object of that self-knowledge. Accordingly, Leibniz' representation of the Trinity conforms more expressly to the structure of self-consciousness than does Thomas' representation, although it is more difficult for Leibniz to assimilate his representation to the Trinitarian concept of the generation of the Son. Leibniz' view relates the Trinity more clearly to self-consciousness than did Thomas' because it represents Father and Son as subject and object of knowledge instead of representing the Father as the act of self-knowledge and the Son as the by-product of that act. Leibniz' view is less able to incorporate the idea of generation than Thomas' because in it there is no reason to think that the known (the Son) is generated from the knower (the Father). In this analogy, the Father does not have a priority, whereas in Leibniz' *other* analogy (force, intellect, will) the Father does have priority.

The importance of this shift in the understanding of reflective selfhood is that subsequent German religious thinkers who favored the speculative-analogical approach to the Trinity increasingly understood the doctrine of the Trinity as the theological expression of God's reflective selfhood – God's self-consciousness. The roots of this understanding go back as far as Aristotle's view of God as self-thinking thought and were developed by Thomas' adaptation of Augustine's concept of analogy; however, what Leibniz contributed was an express linking of the Father and Son to the knower–known relation.

In summary, there is a disjunction in Leibniz' representation of the Trinity. According to his metaphysics of substance, God is a Trinity because God, like all spirits, is force, intellect and will. According to his theological sensitivities, God is a Trinity because God is an act of self-consciousness consisting of the subject of knowledge (knower), the object of knowledge (knowable) and the

---

[56] It should be noted that Thomas did sometimes represent the relation of Father to Word in a way very similar to Leibniz: the Father is God understanding, the Word is God understood. See *Summa Contra Gentiles*, 4.11.9.

act of knowledge itself. Both understandings represent God as a subject, but Leibniz uses one or the other representation according to the demands of his writing.

It may be helpful to conclude this section with a few remarks of assessment about Leibniz' complete view of the Trinity.

First, his rather facile presumptions about the possibility of metaphysical knowledge about God must be regarded as questionable in the wake of Kant's critical philosophy. While we cannot fault Leibniz for failing to be in advance of his time, we must note that the pillars of Biblical orthodoxy in this period rested on assumptions about the Bible and about metaphysical knowledge that we must today regard as doubtful.

Second, Leibniz devoted distressingly little attention, by today's standards, to the historical dimension of the Trinity, preferring as he does the metaphysical approach of the speculative-analogical method. Of course, part of the reason for Leibniz' preference for the metaphysical approach is that he took for granted the church's doctrine and its scriptural foundations. He felt no need to examine the historical foundations of the doctrine of the Trinity because he regarded it as sufficiently supported by the Bible and ancient Christian writers. Even apart from these reasons, however, Leibniz was not much interested in the historical dimension of the Trinity because his philosophical interests lay in other areas and he detected nothing troubling in the traditional doctrine of Christ. He was therefore free to merge the doctrine of the Trinity with his philosophical system.

Nevertheless, there are two problems with Leibniz' lack of interest in the historical question. For one thing, like Bengel he had assumptions about the Bible and its revelatory character that are today questionable. The next chapter will elaborate on the difficulties caused to Christian doctrine when the Bible's historicity was discovered. The other problem is that Leibniz apparently found no great puzzle in the idea of the incarnation and its implications for God's historicity. Chapter 4 will show the importance for the doctrine of the Trinity of God's own essential historicity. A few words about this point are in order.

Leibniz largely evaded an issue that must arise if certain implications of the idea of incarnation are drawn out. That issue concerns history within God. Theologians customarily acknowledge that God has entered historical time in the person of Jesus; the doctrine of the incarnation describes that entry. But the doctrine of the incarnation signifies not only that God entered historical time, but also that God's life must be historical – that there must be a history in God's being. This thesis, counter-intuitive to traditional theology, is the logical outcome of claiming that the Son was united to human nature and that this occurred at a particular moment in human history. If the incarnation occurred at a particular moment, then it must be an event in God's life, with a before and an after in the divine life. The point is that something occurs within God so that we may speak of a before and after in the Son's eternal being. Even a doctrine of divine impassibility cannot escape the conclusion that the eternal Son has a history.

Leibniz, and not he alone, subscribed to the traditional doctrines of the Trinity and of Christ but did not seriously consider the idea of history within God's life. By describing the Trinity by means of such analogies as force, knowledge, and will and knower, known, and knowledge, Leibniz gave a certain plausibility to his own metaphysical system and to the doctrine of the Trinity, and he certainly put himself in good company. But his speculative-analogical account of the Trinity prevented him from grasping the full implications of the ideas of the Trinity and incarnation and kept him from seeing the historical dimension of the Trinity. In other words, for Leibniz history was not yet a problem in theology. The problem he devoted himself to – understanding the church's doctrine in the light of modern metaphysics – was in its day an important one, but also one that distracted him from the question of God's historicity.

Another notable point that we must assess is Leibniz' adherence to the speculative-analogical approach to understanding the Trinity. According to this approach, the Trinity is expounded as God's reflective selfhood. As already mentioned, Leibniz here stood in a line stretching back to Augustine and forward to German idealists such as Hegel. Several questions suggest themselves in regard to Leibniz' particular formulation of the analogy between the Trinity and human subjectivity.

First we may question the propriety of understanding the Trinity as analogous to a single subject. The Western tradition of theology has frequently been criticized for leaning toward a modalistic view of the Trinity; using the analogy of a single person to understand the Trinity reinforces the suspicion that Western theologians are obsessively devoted to God's unity at the expense of the Trinitarian persons. Second, we may note that the more a theology represents God as a single subject the more uncertain it leaves the relation of the eternal Son to Jesus Christ. If the Trinitarian persons are different aspects of one divine subject, then all talk of incarnation in the man Jesus becomes problematic – what does it mean for one *aspect* of a single divine subject to become human or be united with human nature? In particular, how is the historical man Jesus Christ connected with God's intellect and with the object of God's self-knowledge? Such a view lacks soteriological importance. Accordingly, either this view of the Trinity or the idea of the incarnation must be amended. However, we must keep in mind that this same notion of divine self-knowledge was to become a powerful Trinitarian and Christological idea at the hands of Hegel – but only because of a more profound and historical understanding of selfhood. Leibniz contented himself with handing on and slightly modifying the received speculative-analogical tradition; however, he did not know the full value of what he was handing on to later generations.

Finally, we may question the advisability of setting the idea of the Trinity in the context of a metaphysics. Leibniz represented the Trinity as the archetypal instance of a universal phenomenon: substance consisting in force, with perception and appetite. The Trinity appears to be not entirely different from other beings. As Leibniz said, the Trinity differs from finite minds only as the infinite differs from the finite.[57] Although Leibniz allowed for a significant difference between infinite and finite, one gets the impression that he was more interested in pointing out the Trinity's similarities to finite substances than in dwelling on the distinctiveness of the Trinity. This interest was due, no doubt, to the fact that Leibniz was fashioning a metaphysics and so was concerned to show the continuity between finite and infinite substance.

---

[57] Leibniz, *Textes inédits*, 559.

Leibniz', along with every speculative-analogical theology, presents the theologian with a decision about the way in which the Trinity is to be portrayed. Certain theologians, notably Karl Barth, have rejected not only the speculative-analogical approach, but also the attempt to understand the idea of God in the context of a larger vision of reality. Such a procedure is, in Barth's view, a subsumption of God under a more universal category and as such is a compromise of God's freedom. According to Barth, the only legitimate way of approaching the idea of God is through a faithfull response to the singular revelation of God; it is not through a general view of the universe. Regardless of the advisability of Barth's particular understanding of the problem, caution must be urged on anyone who would today want to represent God by means of metaphysical analogies.

Leibniz may be partially exonerated from the charge of subsuming God under a universal category; after all, he contended that God is the archetype of subjectivity – not one instance among others, but the first case, the pattern, the model, which finite subjects can only approximate. This contention applies especially to the force–intellect–will analogy. Nevertheless, the fact remains that Leibniz has proceeded by analyzing the concept of spiritual substance and then declaring that God is the principal example of subjectivity and that the Trinity corresponds to the structure of spiritual subjectivity. He did not, as Barth would demand, begin with God's self-declaration and proceed to understand all other things accordingly.

The issue here between Barth and Leibniz pertains to the Word of God. Has God made a self-declaration to which the theologian is obliged to respond or can God be apprehended as the human mind grasps the character of being and extrapolates that character to infinity? One thing that is problematic about any attempt like Leibniz' to move from the finite to the infinite is the assumed continuity between them. Such a movement threatens to draw both finite and infinite being under the same descriptive categories with only a quantitative difference. Barth's method of beginning with God has problems of its own when it states that God has entered into the finite while not in any way compromising God's own divinity. It may be that an idealist philosopher such as Hegel represents an alternative to the choice between Leibniz and Barth by conceiving of the metaphysical ultimate not as a being but instead as the categories of being themselves. This avoids the need of making an epistemological leap over the gap between finite and infinite while preserving the difference between finite and infinite; however, at least in its nineteenth-century form, it also entails the claim that the human mind can attain an absolute standpoint, a claim that is today an object of derision.

CONCLUSION

In this chapter I have sought to show that Trinitarian thought in the early eighteenth century was driven by the same dynamics that governed the Trinitarian thought of the early reformers. On the one hand, theologians and religious philosophers struggled with the concept of the Word. What is revelation and where is it to be found? More precisely, how is the Bible to be used? Can doctrines be constructed by piecing together Biblical texts? Does the Bible even contain a doctrine of the Trinity? Can the doctrine of the Trinity be derived from a Christocentric interpretation of the Bible and if so what are the implications for such a doctrine? Is revelation strictly about God's relation to us or is it informative of the eternal Trinitarian life of God as well? On the other hand, at least in the case of Leibniz, there was the question of the possibility of discovering or at least understanding the doctrine of the Trinity by means of analogical and metaphysical reasoning.

In many ways, the inhabitants of this period were closer in thought to the first generation of reformers than to the next generation in the eighteenth century, for by the mid-eighteenth century dramatic changes were under way in theology and philosophy. These changes are the result of the growth of historical thinking, which first and destructively called into question the traditional basis of the doctrine – Bible and creeds – and then constructively opened up new possibilities for the doctrine by introducing the concept of God's own historicity. Chapter 3 is concerned with the critical phase of the Enlightenment, when the doctrine of the Trinity became nearly indefensible in light of the advances of Biblical criticism. Chapter 4 is concerned with

German idealism, a philosophical movement whose chief theological insight was the incorporation of history into God's eternal being. Straddling the two lies Friedrich Schleiermacher, who, with the critical Enlightenment, was one of the harshest critics of the traditional doctrine of the Trinity and who, with the idealists, expounded the idea of the Trinity by appealing to God's union with historical being.

As a result, it is evident that the essential components of the modern idea of the Trinity were in place at the end of the idealist era – about 1850. Since then there have been a great many permutations of the three motifs (Word, reflective selfhood, history), but they are just so many variations on the same three motifs.

CHAPTER THREE

The critical Enlightenment

INTRODUCTION

In the previous chapters I set forth the argument that, until the mid-eighteenth century, Trinitarian thinking was driven by two ideas, Word and reflective selfhood. Although most theologians identified Word with the Bible and derived the Trinity rather simply from their exegesis of Scripture, a few such as Zinzendorf took up Melanchthon's suggestion that theology is about the practical doctrines of salvation and not about God's eternal being. The idea of reflective selfhood was used by Leibniz as a speculative and analogical way of expounding the idea of the Trinity. In this chapter I introduce the third and final fundamental idea that determines the shape of modern Trinitarian thinking – history.

What distinguishes the early phase of the Enlightenment from the critical phase to be studied in this chapter? The difference lies in the fact that in the early phase theologians and philosophers such as Leibniz, although mildly rationalistic, put their rationalism to work in the service of orthodox theology. Not so those of the critical Enlightenment, whose rationalism was marked by a growing freedom from, and even hostility to, the official theology of the churches. While one may judge that the seeds of this hostility were latent in the rationalistic attitude of Leibniz, it was only later in the century that these latent seeds sprouted forth into actuality. Whereas in the early Enlightenment the use of human reason in theology was a divine service for the better understanding of revelation, the title of a book published at the end of the critical Enlightenment expresses the sentiments of this period exactly: *Religion within the Bounds of Reason Alone*. In the earlier period human reason was an instrument for the ordering of revealed truths and for their defense; in the period under consideration reason was both the instrument of religious thought and also the *content* of religion itself, the criterion by which theology was to be judged. Under these circumstances not only the church's doctrine of the Trinity but also the practice of Trinitarian thinking fell on hard times and escaped the eighteenth century ridiculed and rejected.

But why did this change come about? Although such matters are enormously complex, we can at least point to the birth of modern historical criticism as it was applied to the Bible. To be sure, there was serious and scholarly study of the Bible before this period. In particular, theologians fretted over the implications of textual criticism. However, what distinguishes this period from the early Enlightenment is its rejection of the presuppositions that guaranteed continuity between the Bible and Christian doctrine. In this period assumptions about revelation and inspiration and miracle and prophecy were flung aside by many as superstitious relics of an incomprehensible past. The implications for the doctrine of the Trinity are obvious, for the doctrine had hitherto rested securely on just those assumptions. Without these assumptions the doctrine was as baseless as it was senseless. Worse for Protestants was the fact that, having jettisoned the Catholic idea of an inspired and authoritative tradition and having gambled everything on the proof from Scripture, they were now left with no other way of establishing the doctrine's truth. At least Roman Catholics could continue to insist on the reliability of an unbroken apostolic tradition. The critical and at times skeptical study of the Bible, then, without orthodox presuppositions guiding the interpreter in a certain direction, proved troublesome for the doctrine of the Trinity. In this way, the concept of history became a dominant and destructive factor for the doctrine of the Trinity. But it would not always be so. In the early decades of the nineteenth century, the concept of history would play a more positive role in the doctrine of the Trinity, for it would no longer be merely a concept employed to study the Bible but would also become an attribute of God's being. If in the eighteenth century the Word of God was historicized, in the nineteenth century God's own being was historicized, with decided implications for Trinitarian thinking.

In summary, leading members of the critical Enlightenment felt various degrees of unease about the doctrine of the Trinity. Historical criticism had, in the judgment of many, undercut the customary appeal to revelation. Further, the Enlightenment's preference for practicality over speculation, an emphasis at least partly derived from Melanchthon, seemed to make the doctrine a pure flight of fancy. Under these intellectual conditions, there was a limited number of options that theologians and philosophers could adopt regarding the Trinity. Some took the results of the historical criticism of the Bible to be definitive, defined religion in strictly moral and practical terms, and consequently rejected both the doctrine of the Trinity and Trinitarian thinking as such. This position was typical of deists, represented in this chapter by Hermann Samuel Reimarus (1694–1768). Reimarus signifies the triumph of the idea of history (understood as historical criticism) over the idea of the Trinity. A second option lay in an appeal to Melanchthon's theology as a means of defining religion in moral terms, while nonetheless retaining some sympathy for the doctrine of the Trinity instead of, like the deists, reproaching orthodox theology for its imbecility. Johann Salomo Semler (1725–1791) represents this complex position, which rests on a distinction between inward religion, which is not primarily doctrinal, and outward public religion, which is primarily doctrinal. Semler, then, was a sort of ecumenical liberal who sought to make room for individual freedom and to account for the necessity of doctrines like the Trinity. A third option fell back upon the tradition of understanding the doctrine by means of the speculative analogy of reflective selfhood. This option was Gotthold Lessing's (1729–1781). Lessing accepted the principles of historical criticism and largely defined religion in moral terms like others of his generation. However, he managed to retain the idea, if not the ecclesiastical doctrine, of the Trinity, by reverting to Leibniz' philosophical view, according to which God is a Trinity because God is an eternal act of self-knowledge. By reverting to Leibniz' position, Lessing accomplished the feat of beating the Enlightenment at its own game, for while urging the importance of historical criticism and human reason, he also demonstrated the perfect rationality of the idea of the Trinity and fashioned the idea independently of the

Scriptures. Finally, Friedrich Schleiermacher (1768–1834) offered another alternative, far more complex than the others discussed here. It combined the spirit of Melanchthon with a thoroughly historicist perspective. Schleiermacher acknowledged the validity of the traditional doctrine of the Trinity *according to its intention* but rejected the final form of the doctrine because of its incompatibility with his version of what true religion is about. To this extent Schleiermacher was in full agreement with the Melanchthonian sentiments of his time. But he went beyond others in this period by applying the concept of history not only to the Bible and the creeds but to revelation and the Trinity as well. That is, just as Lessing employed reason not for destructive purposes (as Reimarus and the deists had done) but constructively as a means of rehabilitating the idea of the Trinity, so Schleiermacher used the idea of history, not to dismiss the doctrine, but to reform it and to develop it in ways never before conceived.

HERMANN SAMUEL REIMARUS: THE HISTORICIZING OF THE WORD

If one wishes to attack the church's doctrine of the Trinity, two main fronts are available. On the one hand, the critic may seek to prove the intrinsic irrationality of the doctrine. On the other hand, the critic may try to show that the doctrine has no foundation in Scripture.

Protestant theology is particularly threatened by the second front. In response to the rare critics who claim the doctrine is irrational, Protestants, like others in the Christian tradition, can appeal to the idea of mystery. Protestants have customarily and gladly acknowledged that the Trinity is beyond reason's powers of discernment and even that the doctrine may be an affront to human reason. Having acknowledged as much, Protestants then fall back on the appeal to Scripture, which is their strong suit. That is why the critics' second front is potentially so devastating; it attacks the roots of the Protestant doctrine and seeks to beat Protestant theology in its foundation. Roman Catholic theology has had a bit more resistance to this sort of criticism, first because of its confidence in the church's infallibly inspired teaching authority and second because of the elaboration of the philosophical rationale for the doctrine, rationale of the sort articulated by Thomas Aquinas. Protestants, having cast aside the idea of an inspired tradition and for the most part sitting uncomfortably with the philosophically speculative approach, have been compelled to fight the battle for the Trinity on Biblical grounds.

It was on precisely these grounds that Reimarus determined to do battle.[1] In brief, he proposed to question the meaning of the texts on which theology had erected the doctrine and to reject the entire approach to the Bible used by theologians for centuries. He intended to apply the principles of historical criticism to the Word, i.e., the Bible, on the assumption that the Word is utterly historical in character and not something miraculously inspired. With this plan he would attack the foundation of doctrines such as the Trinity as formulated by the reformers and elaborated by scholastic theologians. We may organize those of Reimarus' ideas that are relevant for our subject into three main points: first, that the New Testament must be interpreted as a historical document, i.e., against the background of first-century Judaism; second, that the intention of Jesus was neither to found a new religion nor to reveal new doctrines, but instead was to reform the Jewish religion of his day; third, that Jesus' disciples were not faithful to his intention and that their own demented agenda was at work in the creation of the New Testament.

The first point, that the New Testament must be interpreted against the background of ancient Judaism, implied that Christological hermeneutics must be rejected. In particular, certain theologically loaded terms that, over the centuries of the Christian tradition, had come to have significant and well-defined meanings represented, according to Reimarus, the church's misconstruing of the Bible's message. He based this judgment on the belief that such terms would have been incomprehensible to first-century Jews such as Jesus. Of course, there was a deeper issue, namely Reimarus' rejection of the notion that the New Testament's real author is the Holy Spirit. By insisting that it be

---

[1] Harald Schultze, "Religionskritik in der deutschen Aufklärung: Das Hauptwerk des Reimarus im 200. Jahre des Fragmentenstreites," *Theologische Literaturzeitung* 103 (1978): 707 and 711.

interpreted in the context of ancient Judaism, Reimarus was denying divine authorship and was thereby rejecting the miraculous character of the New Testament. While this assumption on his part need not prevent the interpreter from finding Biblical support for doctrines such as the Trinity, at the very least it would open up the possibility of an interpretation very different from that of the Trinitarian one.

One of the terms whose original meaning Reimarus fastened on was "mystery." Protestants and Roman Catholics alike regarded the Trinity as a mystery and by that they meant that it surpasses human powers of comprehension. Accordingly, they held, it is a pure article of faith, i.e., one whose truth can not be known except by revelation. There was, therefore, in orthodox theology a close connection between the concepts of revelation and mystery – the content of revelation consisted largely in mysteries. Reimarus, however, contested this definition of mystery by pointing to Jesus' use of the term. Here "mystery" referred to the subject matter of the parables, a subject that was mysterious not because it was abstruse but instead because the parabolic form of instruction was perplexing. In fact the subject itself was quite understandable. What Reimarus denied was that mysteries in the orthodox sense of the term – revealed truths beyond human comprehension – were to be found in the New Testament.[2]

Another term with whose orthodox use Reimarus was dissatisfied was "Son of God." Reimarus railed on those who assumed that this New Testament phrase originally had the meaning assigned to it in later confessions and dogmatics. He suggested that its ancient use was not to denote divinity but rather to characterize a human person as one who is especially loved by God or is unusually pious. In the New Testament, the phrase designated Jesus as the Messiah, i.e., someone who was Son of God in an exceptional sense.[3]

A third term to whose original meaning Reimarus was anxious to return was "Spirit." On the basis of his review of the Old Testament, Reimarus determined that the New Testament concept of Spirit was either simply a reference to God or a

---

[2] Hermann Samuel Reimarus, *Reimarus: Fragments*, ed. Charles Talbert, trs. Ralph S. Fraser, Lives of Jesus Series (Philadelphia: Fortress Press, 1970), 76.   [3] Ibid., 76–84.

designation for special gifts imparted by God or even merely pious feelings inspired by God.[4] What the term did not originally mean was what the orthodox creeds meant – an eternal person within the divine essence.

It should be noted that Reimarus' criticisms are not above improvement. Although even conservative Biblical scholarship today accepts his premise that the New Testament must be read against its first-century background, our greater knowledge today of the diversity of thought in first-century Palestine makes Reimarus' confidence about the Jewish meaning of terms such as Son of God seem a bit naive. At least certain strands of Jewish thinking may have been more continuous with later Christian thinking about divine hypostases than he acknowledged. Further, Reimarus' criticism rests on the premise that Jesus' disciples either failed to understand him or deliberately distorted his teaching. Yet, he felt confident about assuming that the New Testament's ascription of "Son of God" to Jesus was accurate. This puts him in the awkward position of asserting that the writers of the New Testament somehow distorted Jesus' teaching while faithfully reporting a term as important as "Son of God." Nonetheless, there can be no denying that, by suggesting that the ancient Trinitarian and Christological creeds may not exactly reproduce the message of the New Testament, Reimarus said something of great importance and forced theologians to attempt to prove the continuity between the Bible and the creeds.

This position provided Reimarus with a ready response to those who would adduce favorite proof-texts for the Trinity. Such passages included Matthew 28:19 ("In the name of the Father and of the Son and of the Holy Spirit") and the Gospel passages that narrated Jesus' baptism. Reimarus acknowledged that the baptismal passages speak of three (God, Jesus, and the Spirit), but denied that such texts constitute evidence for the Trinity. Although in the baptism narratives Jesus is designated "Son" by the voice from heaven, this title had, according to Reimarus, its ordinary Jewish meaning described above and not the dogmatic meaning given to it by the early Christian creeds. As for the Spirit that descended on

Jesus as a dove, Reimarus understood this term simply as denoting special gifts that God gave to Jesus the Messiah, and not the third person of the Trinity.[5] Reimarus was further suspicious of the baptismal formula "In the name of the Father and of the Son and of the Holy Spirit." He noted that no baptisms reported within the New Testament use this formula, employing instead some variation of "in the name of Jesus." His conclusion was that the formula could scarcely have been taught by Jesus to the apostles; if Jesus had taught them an indispensable truth about the Trinity, then we can be sure that they would have used it. His suspicions were further aroused by the fact that only one evangelist, Matthew, included the formula. He took this fact to imply that the formula was not a part of the earliest gospel traditions.[6]

Reimarus' interpretation of Matthew 28:19 leads us into the second point in our analysis of his ideas, the contention that Jesus' purpose was not to found a new religion or to reveal new doctrines, but instead to reform the Judaism of his day. In particular, he believed that Jesus intended no more than to announce the imminent kingdom and to bring about repentance.[7] Reimarus adamantly refused to concede that Jesus either did establish or intended to establish a new religion containing incomprehensible revealed truths.[8] Consequently, he suggested, Jesus understood faith to consist in trust in him, not in the acceptance of revealed mysteries.[9]

This noted, Reimarus drew attention to the lack of explicit teaching by Jesus about the Trinity. He presumed that if Jesus had intended to establish a new religion based on doctrines such as the Trinity, the Gospel texts would contain clear teaching to that effect. Since such teaching is lacking, Reimarus concluded that Jesus' true intention lay elsewhere.[10] Accordingly, Reimarus was suspicious of the claim that Matthew 28:19, with its overtly Trinitarian language, truly represented the teaching of Jesus. His suspicion was aroused by other problems as well. For one, he noted that the Gospels describe Jesus forbidding the disciples to evangelize the Gentiles; in Matthew 28:19, Jesus commands the disciples to baptize the Gentiles. For another, Jesus, during his ministry, neither baptized

---

[5] Ibid., 92–95.   [6] Ibid., 109–111.   [7] Ibid., 65–68.   [8] Ibid., 69–71.
[9] Ibid., 72.   [10] Ibid., 96.

nor commanded his disciples to baptize; yet here he is in Matthew 28:19 reversing course.[11] These sorts of intra-Biblical conflicts inclined Reimarus to conclude that this passage is a later addition to the Gospel according to Matthew that does not reflect the true teaching of Jesus.[12] We can see here one of Reimarus' assumptions, namely that the Gospel writers were historians and that the Gospels are generally, but not totally, reliable reports of Jesus' teaching. His method, then, consisted partly in exercising critical judgment concerning the authenticity of individual passages according to his own reconstruction of Jesus' ministry and message. While we can recognize a certain danger in this procedure, since it depends on using a possibly very subjective criterion, there can be no denying that Reimarus exploited the apparent contradictions in the Gospel narratives in a very fruitful way. He thereby forcefully made the point that we cannot assume that Jesus' teaching is identical to that of the post-apostolic church or even to that of his immediate followers.

This last consideration leads us to Reimarus' third point, that the intention of Jesus differed from that of his disciples. Modern theologians have reconciled themselves to the existence of doctrinal development in church history and even in the New Testament. Zinzendorf in the early part of the eighteenth century had already conceded as much. But Reimarus was not suggesting a smoothly evolving growth of insight as we move from Jesus to the apostles to the New Testament; he was insinuating a sharp rupture between Jesus and the apostles and did not stop short of attributing bad motives to them. In particular, he charged them with being motivated by greed and by a fear of shame following the death of Jesus.[13] Without saying so directly, he implied that, with the exception of the Gospels, the New Testament writings were products of dishonesty. In effect, he called into question both Protestant faith in the text of Scripture and Roman Catholic confidence in an inspired and unbroken tradition from Jesus to the apostles and beyond.

Although Reimarus' thoughts did not affect theology until their publication several decades after their writing, they give testimony

---

[11] Ibid., 109.   [12] Ibid., 111.   [13] Ibid., 240–248.

to a new and critical spirit. This new spirit was based on the conviction that the Bible, universally regarded as the Word of God, is a thoroughly historical document and must be studied as such. From this time on, proving the doctrine of the Trinity by the proof-text method would never again find universal approval. Historical considerations had made the theologian's task considerably more difficult.

JOHANN SALOMO SEMLER: THE SPIRIT OF MELANCHTHON IN THE CRITICAL ENLIGHTENMENT

Reimarus represented one option that one could take up toward the Trinity once the hermeneutical assumptions of theology had been challenged. This option was in fact the simplest, for it amounted to rejecting the church's doctrine of the Trinity as unfounded. J. S. Semler represents another option, one far more complex and sensitive to the subtleties of doctrinal development than that of Reimarus. The first point to note is that while he wrote a great deal about the doctrine, he introduced no innovations into it and was utterly uninterested in defending it as some sort of revealed doctrine. Instead Semler sought to make room for two ideas that he insisted were of great value but whose reconciliation was troublesome. They were, first, the freedom that must be accorded to the individual's conscience and to scholarly inquiry and, second, the need of social unity in church and state. Semler's doctrine of the Trinity, then, consists in adjusting theology in order to legitimate the church's attempt at formulating doctrines while arguing that such attempts should never be binding on individual consciences.

What is particularly interesting about Semler is that he believed that in accomplishing this adjustment he was reverting to the attitude of the reformers, principally Luther and Melanchthon. For this reason, we must draw a similarity between Semler and Zinzendorf, both of whom consciously attacked the scholastic theology of the church in the name of the reformers. Both were dismayed at the direction Protestant theology had taken after the reformers and sought a return to what each believed to be Luther's hermeneutical principles. Of course, each interpreted Luther

uniquely, Zinzendorf laying emphasis on a Christocentric
hermeneutics, Semler focusing on the idea of freedom and individual conviction of the truth. Nevertheless, it would not be correct
unthinkingly to class Semler among the deists and rationalists of
his day. While he did share their interest in the practical value of
religion, he was more sensitive than they to the specifically evangelical character of Christian faith.

As one who strove to be faithful to Lutheran theology, Semler
sought to portray the intellectual dilemma of his day (about which
he was extraordinarily concerned) in spiritual terms. In terms
recalling Paul's Letter to the Galatians, he depicted the scholastics
of his day as modern pharisees and portrayed the plight of well-
meaning (and, we may assume, free-thinking) Christians suffering
from unease and doubt, fearing condemnation by the orthodox.
Whereas in the middle ages, he complained, theologians were free
to disagree with those of other schools, the coercively enforced
unity of his day created only inner turmoil.[14] The anxiety of
modern students of the Bible could be alleviated only by an awareness of the perfect law of freedom, preventing them from being
caught by the narrow conscience of their orthodox neighbors.[15]
His point was that within scholastic theology the idea of the canon
had become virtually an article of faith and thereby an obstacle to
scientific investigation. He feared that the inflexible orthodox view
of the Bible would lead to conflict with other scientific disciplines
and that the idea of the canon would lead Christians to think of
every part of the Bible as equal to every other part – an idea he
regarded as spiritually dangerous.[16]

Whether Martin Luther would have approved of Semler's
application of the idea of freedom is questionable, since Luther
was a good bit more doctrinally conservative than Semler. What
cannot be questioned is that Semler regarded his theology as the
application to intellectual matters of the same principle of
freedom that Luther had used in spiritual matters. As Luther had

[14] Johann Salomo Semler, *Abhandlung von freier Untersuchung des Canon*, ed. Heinz Scheible,
  Texte zur Kirchen- und Theologiegeschichte (Gutersloh: Mohn, 1967), pp. 46–47.
[15] Ibid., 90.
[16] Gottfried Hornig, *Die Anfänge der historisch-kritischen Theologie: Johann Salomo Semlers
  Schriftverständnis und seine Stellung zu Luther*, Forschungen zur systematischen Theologie und
  Religionsphilosophie, vol. VIII (Göttingen: Vandenhoeck & Ruprecht, 1961), 63–64.

sought to preserve Christian freedom in the matter of ceremonies and customs, Semler searched for an intellectual freedom as an aid to the study of the Bible. Of course, this demand for freedom went beyond the sphere of scholarship. Semler had in mind intellectually inclined Christians who had grasped the historically conditioned and relative character of creeds and even of the Bible. They feared that the orthodox association of faith with acceptance of creeds and ideas like canon and inspiration must consign them to infidelity. More positively, he regarded freedom as the condition of that wholeness that we should enjoy, encompassing our free thinking and acting as we inquire into doctrines in obedience to the Word of God.[17]

So, it is not a coincidence that like Luther Semler attacked his orthodox opponents on their interpretation of Scripture. Semler used like a weapon the Protestant axiom that the Word of God is the church's only norm, and accordingly approached creeds and doctrines with the same vigor as that with which Luther had approached the issues of his day. For both the nature and reality of salvation were at stake.

Semler's conception of the Word of God had two immediate consequences. On the one hand he elevated the Bible above doctrinal confessions, citing the confessions' own testimony on this matter,[18] in the interests of what we might call a Biblical, as opposed to a dogmatic, theology. On the other hand, he insisted that the Bible is not a simple unity but that it is composed of parts of unequal value.[19]

The first consequence signaled Semler's criticism of credal theology. He had no patience for questions about the inspiration and inerrancy of creeds. He was convinced that those who propagate these ideas were seeking to impose a false form of authority and was of the opinion that some of the credal formulas could be improved.[20] We may think of Semler as a doctrinal minimalist: he

[17] Ibid., 172–175 and 182.
[18] Johann Salomo Semler, *Apparatus ad Libros Symbolicos Ecclesiae Lutheranae* (Halae Magdeburgicae, 1775), 11.
[19] Johann Salomo Semler, *Beantwortung der Fragmente eines Ungenanten* [sic] *insbesondere vom Zweck Jesu und seiner Jünger* (Halle, 1779), 354.
[20] Semler, *Apparatus*, 8–9; see also Hornig, *Die Anfänge der historisch-kritischen Theologie*, 187–190.

favored restricting creeds to the length required for the practice of Christianity and seemed to have no taste for their elaboration beyond that necessity.[21] Now in itself, this inveighing against the authority of creeds is not surprising of a Protestant theologian – in their polemics against Roman Catholic dogmatics Protestants do occasionally seem to belittle the creeds. What is novel in Semler's approach is that his opponent is Protestant – not Roman Catholic – orthodoxy. His purpose is not so much to criticize the creeds, for as we shall see he acknowledged their essential value, as it is to score a point against an assumption of scholastic theology. This assumption is that the creeds are faithful expositions of the Bible, which they identified with the Word of God. So, while the orthodox did not hold the creeds to be authoritative in themselves, they were treated as authoritative because they were believed to correctly elucidate the significance of Biblical teachings. Semler's attack, therefore, was not so much a criticism of the Protestant conception of authority (since Protestants had always stated that Scripture alone is the norm and authority for theology), as it was an assault on Protestant hermeneutics. That is, Semler was rejecting the belief that the creeds were sure guides to the meaning of Scripture. What Semler wanted to do was to return to the Bible for a fresh look, using his understanding of Reformation theology and also his convictions about the historical critical method.

The second consequence, Semler's insistence that the Bible is not a simple unity but is composed of unequal parts, signified an attack on the orthodox idea of the Bible. We may analyze the attack under two points: first, Semler distinguished the Bible from the Word of God. Second, he asserted that some parts of the Bible are not inspired.

The distinction between the Bible and the Word of God is of inestimable importance for Semler's theology. For one thing, it allowed him to escape the destructive consequences of Reimarus' Biblical criticism, by enabling him to distinguish properly Christian faith from mere belief about historical events narrated in the Bible.[22] He thereby to some extent separated faith from the results

---

[21] Semler, *Apparatus*, 46.

[22] Leopold Zscharnack, *Lessing und Semler: Ein Beitrag zur Entstehungsgeschichte des Rationalismus und der kritischen Theologie* (Gießen: Verlag von Alfred Töpelmann, 1905), 337–338.

of historical criticism. For another thing, this distinction grounds his attack on scholastic theology and its view of the Bible. He could, with this distinction, assail the Bible with every sort of historical question, while resting assured that the Word of God remained untouched.

The assertion that not all of the Bible is inspired follows. Semler believed that the idea of inspiration had little value for the ordinary Christian who, he believed, was prepared to use truths from any source as means of moral improvement without inquiring into the question of their inspiration. That is, he charged that the idea of inspiration had no practical value and was of interest only to theologians. In fact, he held that inspiration actually describes the moral change that God brought about in the Gospel writers, preparing them for living religious knowledge and giving them an honest temper.[23] His point is that it was the writers, not the words they wrote, that God inspired and that inspiration was a divine act not radically different from the sort of moral transformation that all genuine Christians experience.

The relevance of all this for Semler's view of the Trinity is difficult to state briefly. He did not deny the reality of revelation and in fact, like the scholastics, believed revelation to be a sort of communication of divine truths to human beings; however, he seems to have identified revelation with what Luther called the gospel – those saving truths that lead us to spiritual blessedness. He believed in inspiration, although he severely qualified its meaning to bring it into line with his overall conception of religion.[24] He railed against scholastic attempts at making the Bible itself an object of faith, yet he thought that the Bible did testify to God's Trinitarian being and he was in his own way as much a Biblicist as the scholastic theologians. Nevertheless, his conception of Scripture did affect his view of the doctrine of the Trinity. For one thing, Semler was not at all enthusiastic about supporting the doctrine with citations from the Old Testament. Although it would not be fair to charge Semler with despising the Old Testament, his love for it was strictly measured and limited to passages such as those in the Prophets that transcended the particularities of Israelite society

---

[23] Semler, *Canon*, 84–85.　　[24] Hornig, *Die Anfänge der historisch-kritischen Theologie*, 100.

and touched on matters of universal human importance.[25] The doctrine of the Trinity was, in his thinking, a strictly *Christian* doctrine and therefore to be drawn from the New Testament. And not from just any likely passage in the New Testament, for Semler believed that there were portions of the New Testament, even of Paul's letters, that were of no enduring importance for religion.[26] No, the doctrine must rest on the Word of God, that is, it must arise from the New Testament's moral and soteriological message. For another thing, Semler could never become enthusiastic about the doctrine of the Trinity in its historical and credal form, for his separating the Bible from the Word of God impelled him to distinguish more generally between divine truth and the historical forms in which each generation seeks to express those truths.[27] Semler could give full rein to the historical criticism of Scripture and creeds because they were, in his opinion, only the humanly produced forms in which truth was stated. So, although he had great respect for the doctrine of the Trinity, his allegiance was not to it, as though it were a revealed truth, but to the truth that it in some measure expressed.

In order to complete our survey of Semler's view of the Trinity, only one more distinction must be treated and that is the difference he drew between inner and outer religion. This distinction was not original with Semler. Indeed all the theologians and philosophers of the critical Enlightenment were obsessed with discerning the nature of true Christianity, or at least of true religion.[28] It was customary in that period to differentiate between true religion (variously described) and official or public religion, which was held to consist largely in more or less meaningless ceremonies and unbelievable doctrines. In Semler's use of the terms, the distinction between inner and outer religion amounts to the difference between, on the one hand, the practice of religion and the understanding of divine truths, and on the other hand, the politically regulated public religion of a people. The importance

---

[25] Semler, *Canon*, 63.   [26] Ibid., 86.

[27] Hornig, *Die Anfänge der historisch-kritischen Theologie*, 74.

[28] Gottfried Hornig, "Die Freiheit der christlichen Privatreligion: Semlers Begründung des religiösen Individualismus in der protestantischen Aufklärungstheologie," *Neue Zeitschrift für systematische Theologie* 21 (1979), argues that the idea of inner or private religion has roots in pietism and in the reformers themselves. See 199 and 207.

of this distinction for the doctrine of the Trinity is, in brief, that Semler thereby distinguished between the historical form of the doctrine and its basis in revelation. The historical form pertains to outer religion; its relation to revelation pertains to inner religion. The former is important for certain purposes, but is not binding on individual consciences, i.e., it is not an article of faith, assent to which is necessary for salvation. The latter is vital for true religion, although it can never be perfectly formulated in a doctrine.

What is inner religion? Semler found it attested in certain passages of the Old Testament prophets, namely when they rose above the narrow confines of Israelite society and spoke about matters of true religion: circumcision of the heart, spiritual (as opposed to animal) sacrifices, the just observance of our moral duties to others. To the extent that the prophets were concerned with these matters, Semler was prepared to acknowledge that they were possessed by the Spirit of Christ, for they prophesied of the true religion that Christ would bring.[29] In the New Testament, Semler was particularly impressed with the teaching sections of Paul's letters, which he distinguished sharply from the merely historical portions, which were valuable only inasmuch as they served the teaching of true religion.[30] He described it variously: in theological terms it comprises salvation from slavery to sin, becoming more like God, more full of virtue, knowledge and discipline;[31] in philosophical terms it encompasses those natural and universal truths that transcend regional and ethnic particularities and that serve for our moral improvement.[32] In short, Semler seems to have assumed an easy agreement between true Christianity, as Luther taught it, and the moral ideals of the critical Enlightenment. Whether he was justified in this assumption has been the subject of strenuous debate; what is not debatable is that the emphasis on the inward character of true religion must necessarily result in a diminished importance for dogmatic theology, for inner religion is to outer as the enduring is to the transitory. Identifying religion with moral and spiritual truths with universal relevance meant that

---

[29] Semler, *Canon*, 63.   [30] Ibid., 86–87.   [31] Ibid., 49–50 and 81.
[32] Ibid., 57–58.

doctrines such as the Trinity, with identifiable and historically conditioned origins, could have no ultimate significance for true religion.

Yet contrary to expectations, Semler did not dismiss outer religion as entirely valueless. Outer religion comprises everything that may be visibly identified with public religion: ceremonies, institutions, officially enforced doctrines. Its value lies, he judged, in its similarity to the function of law in civil society – both are instituted by rulers for the regulation of society.[33] There is nothing to suggest that Semler dismissed this function of outer religion as unimportant; indeed, he seems to have held it to be a condition of inner religion through its offices of preaching and education.[34] Further, such components of outer, public religion as the canon of Scripture and doctrines serve a purpose in maintaining external church order and providing a basis for the public exercise of religion.[35] Although Semler did not write extensively about the positive aspects of outer religion, there is no reason to think he denigrated such religion or even regarded it as something indifferent; however, given his intention to demonstrate the independence of inner from outer religion, he necessarily had to emphasize their differences and portray inner religion as favorably as possible. In short, he was concerned with two things: first, to preserve the rights of Christians inclined to scientific sophistication against the attempts by the church to stifle the historical study of the Bible; second, to make sure that no one confused the practice of outer religion (affirmation of creeds and so on) with the exercise of true, inner religion. In his own fashion, then, Semler was attempting to combine the concerns of pietism with those of the critical Enlightenment.

In addition to the two concerns mentioned above, Semler believed there was another regrettable result of outer religion, one that bears directly on the doctrine of the Trinity. This was the consequences of the doctrine. He regarded the doctrines of the eternal generation of the Son and the procession of the Spirit to be not only unnecessary for salvation and inner religion, but also to be divisive. They created parties by separating those of differing opinions into groups anathematizing each other.[36] Semler thought of

---

[33] Semler, *Apparatus*, 26.   [34] Hornig, "Freiheit," 205.   [35] Semler, *Canon*, 21.
[36] Semler, *Beantwortung*, 69.

this as particularly unfortunate because he thought of such Trinitarian heretics as Arians and Sabellians as Christians who happened to differ from other Christians only in their refusal to adhere to certain aspects of outer religion.[37] Accordingly, Semler conceded the possibility, if not the desirability, of a plurality of doctrinal forms within outer religion. He argued on historical grounds that certain forms of doctrine had proved useful for a time before being superseded by other forms.[38] He asserted the practical impossibility of Christians of all times and places agreeing on a single form of doctrine.[39] We can see, then, that Semler thought of doctrines not only as historically conditioned but also as historically relative to their times. We may characterize his view of doctrine as pragmatic: doctrines, he held, perform a certain function in their own day but have no enduring validity. Each is an attempt at expressing Christian truth, but none can be judged to be an adequate expression. Consequently, the history of doctrine is the history of change; further, since Semler believed that later eras might have better insight than earlier ones, he concluded that the history of doctrine is also a progressive history.[40] Apart from relativizing all doctrinal formulations, this theory resulted in a dramatic change in the way theologians might think of the early church. Customarily theologians have held that the early church, standing closest to Jesus, represented the golden age, not only of piety, but also of doctrinal purity and truth, an age succeeded by the corrupting influences of heretics. In Semler's opinion, however, the early church has no such privileged status. It was instead a beginning and therefore it could not be a stage of complete development and perfection.[41] Of course, all this depends on Semler's optimistic confidence that he in his day was in a better position to judge matters such as the doctrine of the Trinity than were the early church Fathers, a point he expressly made.[42] What Semler has here suggested is a complete reorientation of theological thinking, so that truth is better expressed at the end of a period of development than at its beginning, and so that this expression is

---

[37] Ibid., 163.   [38] Semler, *Apparatus*, 25.   [39] Ibid., 6–7.
[40] On this subject see Gottfried Hornig, "Die Perfektibilitätsgedanke bei J. S. Semler," *Zeitschrift für Theologie und Kirche* 72 (1975): 381–397.   [41] Semler, *Canon*, 89.
[42] Semler, *Apparatus*, 46.

dependent solely on the cultivation of human intellect. Of course, none of this touches on human possession of inner religion – piety and morality seem for Semler to be above all historical evolution. But the expression of this in doctrinal form in response to various historical challenges does admit of improvement. Further, along with the possibility of improvement goes a commitment to allowing a plurality of expressions. Since no expression can be regarded as the final or perfect one, all doctrinal forms have a certain degree of legitimacy.

Let us turn to the consequences of Semler's views for the doctrine of the Trinity. First, his use of the Bible to support the doctrine deserves comment. As we have seen, he steadfastly rejected the use of the Bible adopted by scholastic theology, with its tendency to place all scriptural passages on the same level and regard them all as inspired directly by God. Contrary to expectation, however, Semler was himself prepared to defend the doctrine of the Trinity by means of specific proof-texts that he took to indicate the Trinitarian being of God. This is seen in his written assessment of Reimarus' theories. Semler may have seen the limitations of the church's doctrine of the Trinity, but he was little disposed to accept Reimarus' interpretation of Jesus as an overzealous Jewish prophet and reformer. While agreeing with Reimarus' desire to interpret the New Testament against its ancient Jewish background, Semler insisted that Christological concepts such as Son of God and Logos that the New Testament writers ascribed to Jesus were in fact a part of first-century Jewish thinking. Further, he accused Reimarus of ignoring data that did not agree with his theory in order to accuse the disciples of inventing ideas and of assuming that first-century Jews thought just like eighteenth-century deists.[43] So, we may conclude that Semler took seriously the New Testament Christological vocabulary and accepted its significance for the doctrine of the Trinity.

Semler did agree with Reimarus that the doctrine has one insuperable stumbling block – the concept of three persons in one God. Semler did not judge this concept to be a Biblical teaching and he consigned it to the learned as a topic for their abstruse

---

[43] Semler, *Beantwortung*, 68, 73–75 and 84.

discussions. While acknowledging that Reimarus had uncovered a problem, Semler refused to allow it to be a problem for inner religion as such; instead, he assigned it to the realm of outer religion.[44] What is, according to Semler, of importance for inner religion is not this concept of three persons or even particular formulas such as Matthew 28:19; rather it is a complex of ideas that he considered the true ground and content of Christianity and that distinguishes it from other religions. They are the ideas of God the Father and creator, of Jesus as the Son of God and his vocation (*Bestimmung*), and of the gift of the Spirit, given to all members of this religion to unite them into a society.[45] Semler was careful not to define these ideas too closely; indeed, his method is built on the premise that such definitions are ultimately fruitless and may be damaging. Such precise technical definitions are, he held, unnecessary for inner religion, proof of which is that many such definitions, for example, the procession of the Spirit, were unknown in the first century. Even after they had been propounded, many of them, for example the *filioque*, attained only regional acceptance. The only reasonable conclusion, he suggested, was that such definitions and terms are optional for inner religion.[46] Consequently, he took up a conciliatory attitude toward such heretics as the Sabellians. It was not a careless latitudinarianism that motivated this attitude; rather it was a conviction that Sabellians and other Trinitarian heretics agreed with the orthodox on the Biblical teaching (as Semler understood it) and differed only on the more recondite and esoteric aspects of the Trinity.

In summary, we may say that Semler believed that the Bible genuinely reveals a Trinity. Whether this is an eternal and transcendent Trinity or a historical Trinity is unclear. Presumably, Semler's disinclination at drawing distinctions too tightly and his desire to allow maximum freedom in doctrinal matters would deter him from stating too specifically where he stood on this matter. At any rate, he represents the attempt to preserve the Christian idea of the Trinity, if not the ecclesiastical dogma of the Trinity, in the face of historical criticism. As such he was the forerunner of such

---

[44] Ibid., 94.   [45] Ibid., 144 and 163–164.
[46] Ibid., 59 and 69–70. See also Wolfgang Schmittner, *Kritik und Apologetik in der Theologie J. S. Semlers*, Theologische Existenz Heute (Munich: Chr. Kaiser Verlag, 1963), 48–50.

theologians as Schleiermacher and such philosophers as Lessing. He also appears as a messenger of a new sort of Protestantism that took the phrase *sola scriptura* literally, i.e., as signifying not merely that the Bible is theology's sole norm, but also that it is theology's sole source. Here we behold a theologian who believed that a leap over the centuries of dogmatic development was necessary if inner religion was to be supported by theology, and who, although he was a historian, believed that the Bible contains a truth that is transhistorical. Indeed, Semler employed historical criticism as a means of liberating this super-historical truth from the inadequate historical forms in which it had appeared and with which the church was constantly confusing it, to the detriment of inner religion. We may, then, characterize Semler as an ecumenical liberal – as a theologian whose chief guide was his conviction about the essential unity of Christian believers in spite of external differences and whose task was to open the way to freedom for scientific inquiry and to liberate human conscience from bondage to external authority.

GOTTHOLD LESSING: THE TRINITY OF REFLECTIVE SELFHOOD

As the number of books and extent of disagreement about Lessing indicate, he is an enigmatic figure in the history of theology. As a source of perplexity to commentators, he is paralleled by few. Interpreters debate whether he was a follower of Spinoza and if so whether he followed Spinoza's pantheistic inclinations.[47] They question whether he understood religion primarily in rational terms or mainly as a matter of heart and life.[48] It is questionable whether he may be fairly considered to be a Christian.[49] Beyond these questions of Lessing's religious convictions, there are queries

---

[47] See, for example, Reinhard Schwarz, "Lessings 'Spinozismus,'" *Zeitschrift für Theologie und Kirche* 65 (1968): 271–290 and Friedmann Regner, "Lessings Spinozismus," *Zeitschrift für Theologie und Kirche* 68 (1971): 351–375.

[48] See Regner, "Lessings Spinozismus," 365 and 375 and Peter Willmer, *Lessing und Zinzendorf: Eine vergleichende Studie zu Lessings Glauben*, American University Studies, Series I: Germanic Languages and Literature, vol. LXXII (New York: Peter Lang, 1989), 104–106.

[49] Leonard P. Wessel, *G. E. Lessing's Theology: A Reinterpretation. A Study in the Problematic Nature of the Enlightenment* (The Hague: Mouton & Co., 1977), 154.

about his purpose. Was it to defend orthodox Christianity? To rethink Christian doctrines and show wherein their truth lay? Was it to develop a rationalistic system of theology? Each of these alternatives has some claim on our attention. A further difficulty arises from the fact that Lessing occasionally expressed his thoughts in writings that remained unpublished during his lifetime, prompting us to ask whether these writings are mere exercises of thought and speculations or whether they represent Lessing's real sentiments, even when they differ from his published works. Inasmuch as one of these unpublished writings ("The Christianity of Reason") contains his most developed expressions on the idea of the Trinity, this question has special importance for our topic.

Given these questions about Lessing's religious beliefs and the suggestion that even the character of his Christian faith is suspect, he may seem a poor candidate for inclusion in a history of Trinitarian thinking. Nevertheless, there are certain facts that suggest that the idea of the Trinity was of great importance to Lessing. For one thing, he published a work by Leibniz in defense of the Trinity.[50] With all his other activities and interests, it seems peculiar that Lessing would take the time to translate, publish and comment on this otherwise obscure work by Leibniz if the doctrine of the Trinity were of no importance to him. Further, Lessing expounded the Trinity not only in the unpublished "The Christianity of Reason" but also in his published work, "The Education of the Human Race." Although his writings on the Trinity are brief, they are suggestive of the overall direction of his thought.

Moreover, even though Lessing did not elaborate a doctrine of the Trinity in systematic form, the significance of his treatment of the doctrine far outweighs the brevity of that treatment. Lessing was among the first intellectuals to attempt to transcend the impasse between Christian theology and Enlightenment theology. Although frequently critical of Christian theology, he nevertheless was as or more critical of Enlightenment theologians and their desire to restrict theology to what human reason could discover on

---

[50] "Des Andreas Wissowatius Einwürfe wider die Dreieinigkeit," in Gotthold Ephraim Lessing, *Gesammelte Werke*, ed. Paul Rilla, vol. VII, *Das Epigram; Beiträge zu einem deutschen Glossarium; Philosophische und theologische Schriften I* (Berlin: Aufbau-Verlag, 1957).

its own. Lessing took the attitude that what was needed was, first, a demonstration that Christian doctrines contain the truth in some important way, and, second, an argument to the effect that the truth ensconced in these doctrines could be shown to be fully rational. That is, Lessing's theology was driven by the conviction that orthodox doctrines, although not always true in the precise sense in which the church believed them to be true, are nevertheless deserving of attention because they express a truth that people on this side of the critical Enlightenment can grasp rationally. Lessing, in other words, is a forerunner of the approach to the Trinity that we find in such idealist philosophers as G. W. F. Hegel. Although he was not himself an idealist, there are substantive and significant points of continuity between him and the idealist philosophers of the next generation. One such point is their common interest in the idea of the Trinity and its utility for solving the thorny problem of how best to conceive God's relation to the world.

"The Christianity of Reason"[51] takes up a conception of God similar to Aristotle's notion of God as the act of thinking that is its own object. God, that is, the most perfect being, is eternally concerned only with the knowledge of what is most perfect (§1). Since only God is what is most perfect, the object of God's eternal contemplation is simply the divine being itself (§2). So far, Lessing was following the path set out by Aristotle and developed by Thomas Aquinas and Leibniz. Then, however, Lessing introduced another axiom: In God, conceiving, willing and creating are all one (§3). Without saying so directly, Lessing seems to have presupposed here the scholastic notion of God's simplicity, according to which God's nature is not divisible. So far, so good, but then the conclusion he drew from this axiom was potentially controversial: Whatever God conceives, God in the same act creates (§3). This conclusion suggests that God lacks the freedom to create any world except this one. This in turn implies that this world is in some sense necessary. Ideas of this sort suggest Lessing's affinity for Spinoza.[52] After the interlude in paragraph 3 about the unity of God's nature,

---

[51] "The Christianity of Reason," *Lessing's Theological Writings*, trs. Henry Chadwick (Stanford: Stanford University Press, 1957), 99–101.

[52] Regner, "Lessings Spinozismus," 358–359.

there follows a return to a consideration of the divine eternal act of thought: God can think of the divine perfections in only two ways, either collectively or individually (§4).

At this point, Lessing put all these thoughts to use for the idea of the Trinity by equating God's eternal contemplation of the totality of divine perfections with God's eternally creating a being with all these perfections (§5). In other words, because in God there is no distinction between thought and act, God's eternal contemplation of the totality of divine perfections is the same as God's eternal creating of a being with these perfections. Lessing then employed Trinitarian terminology to elucidate his point: This created being, the collective totality of the divine perfections, is the Son. Having all the divine perfections, this being is divine; being the object of thought, it is in a sense posterior to the divine act of thinking; therefore, as something in a sense brought forth, it is appropriate to name it "Son." Besides this philosophical rationale, Lessing adduced another reason why this being is called Son – Scripture uses this name (§6). So we can see that Lessing was concerned not only with a speculative doctrine but also with demonstrating the agreement of this speculative doctrine with revelation.

The next paragraph of "The Christianity of Reason" strengthens the notion that the Son is God. It asserts that one cannot think of God without immediately thinking also of this Son, since our thought about God necessarily includes thought of God's self-conception (§7). Of course, this all presupposes a scholastic idea of God, an idea that not all philosophers would accept. The theistic philosophers of the Enlightenment surely did not think of God in these terms. What we can see here is Lessing's affinity for a theological tradition with deep historical roots. Although he was, in this work, offering a speculative justification of the idea of the Trinity, it is also true that he is part of a tradition of Trinitarian thought that was self-consciously Christian. This is not to claim that Lessing was interested solely in a repristination of orthodox theology; the point is that Lessing was rejecting the Enlightenment conception of God and, as an alternative, using a Trinitarian conception of God that could boast a distinguished heritage.

The next several paragraphs are taken up with establishing the identity of God and God's self-conception and with setting the stage for the Holy Spirit. Lessing noted that we can also call the Son the image of God (§8), a term that the Bible employs and that Thomas Aquinas made use of. He then observed that, since the harmony between two things increases in proportion to their similarity, there must be the greatest harmony between God and God's self-conception, for they are one (§9). This harmony Lessing then declared to be the Spirit; he specifically alluded to John 15:26 ("The Spirit of truth who comes from the Father" [NRSV]) and casually amended this passage to support the Western doctrine of the *filioque*: "The Spirit which proceeds from the Father and Son" (§10). Pressing farther into theological territory, he affirmed the Spirit to be *homoousios* with the Father and the Son, for whatever is in them is also in the Spirit. On this basis he considered the Spirit to be God also (§11).

Having multiplied divine beings to a Trinity, Lessing then moved to establish their unity. It was not enough to show that each is God; that conclusion could be interpreted as tritheism. Rather, Lessing asserted that all three together are God. In a way that fore-shadowed the strategy of German idealist philosophers, Lessing argued that neither Father nor Son could be God without the harmony that is the Spirit (§12). Although this argument did not go as far as scholastic theology in acknowledging the subsistent being of the Trinitarian persons, it did prevent any possibility of under-standing Lessing in tritheistic terms.

Lessing's understanding of the Spirit is a bit peculiar. It is cer-tainly different from the scholastic tradition, in which Leibniz also participated, according to which the Spirit is associated with the divine will. It also differs from Leibniz' view that the Spirit is knowl-edge, in the Trinity of knower, object of knowledge and knowledge itself. Where Leibniz regarded the Spirit as hypostasized knowledge, Lessing represents the Spirit as the perfect harmony of knower and known. Also curious is Lessing's statement that the Bible calls this harmony the Spirit (§10). While it is true that the Bible makes exten-sive declarations about the Spirit, it nowhere connects the Spirit with the harmony between God and God's image. Lessing has obvi-ously assumed a congruity between the Biblical notion of Spirit and the idea of Spirit as a sort of bond between Father and Son that he took from the Christian Trinitarian tradition.[53]

But how close to Trinitarian thought is all this? Lessing made no attempt at connecting his view of the Trinity with Jesus Christ. In fact Jesus Christ is not even mentioned and there is no sense of a specifically religious understanding of the Spirit. Lessing has offered a purely speculative doctrine of the Trinity, derived from the idea of God as the being whose eternal act is one of self-contemplation. Of course, it is doubtful that without an awareness and appreciation of the Christian tradition of Trinitarian thought he would have deduced the Trinity from this idea of God. After all, Aristotle did not arrive at a Trinity, in spite of a similar view of God. So perhaps the claim that Lessing was offering a purely speculative doctrine needs qualification. He did make references to the Bible and clearly believed that he had given the true philosophical sense of the Biblical teaching about God. Further, we must keep in mind the fragmentary nature of this work. It was most likely not meant to be a fully developed exposition of the Trinity and was not even intended for public consumption. Then again, Lessing was not entirely unconcerned with the historical dimension of the Trinity. In his comments on Leibniz' *Defence* Lessing observed that Islam must be considered an improvement on Christianity *unless* Jesus Christ is truly God. Although this is a sort of backhand confession, we may take it that Lessing did indeed affirm the divinity of Christ in some sense. If so, there is at least an implied connection between Jesus Christ and the doctrine of the Trinity in his theology, even if he did not elaborate on the connection. Finally, we should keep in mind Lessing's belief, expressed in "On the Education of the Human Race" and here in paragraph 21, that all Christian doctrines will ultimately be known to be fully rational. In "Education" he claimed that the Bible will become progressively less necessary for religion, for truths revealed in it historically will eventually be demonstrable by reason alone. Lessing believed this had already occurred in the case of such Biblical ideas as monotheism and the immortality of the soul.[54] The lesson drawn with

---

[53] Schwarz, "Lessings 'Spinozismus,'" 282.
[54] Gotthold Ephraim Lessing, "On the Education of the Human Race," *Theological Writings*, 94 (§72).

regard to the Trinity is the likelihood that the doctrine will some day bring human reason to see that God's unity is of a unique sort, one that includes plurality.[55] What he offered in "The Christianity of Reason" is nothing other than a rational exposition of a doctrine he found expressly stated in the Christian tradition and in some way revealed in the Bible. It is not a speculative doctrine in the sense that it was deduced purely from an idea; rather, it is the rational reconstruction of a doctrine that Lessing believed to be revealed. In fact, according to the teaching of "Education," revealed truths such as that of the Trinity have a pedagogical function. Although their truth is purely rational, humanity could not have discovered their truth in a purely rational way. In the infancy of the human race, revelation was necessary in order for humanity to discern the truth about God.[56] Lessing was not presenting a truth for the first time, but instead giving the rational and purified version of an ancient doctrine.

A noteworthy aspect of Lessing's doctrine of the Trinity in this work is its role in defining the relation of God to the world. In fact, this work presents a strong correspondence between the origin of the Son and the creation of the world. The foundation of his argument was that the ideas of God's mind issue forth in being. The Son is those ideas expressed as a collective unity; the world is those ideas expressed in their diversity. With this premise, the only difference between the Son and the world is that the Son is all the divine perfections contemplated by the divine mind in a unified way and the world is all the divine perfections contemplated separately (§13–14). The implication is that the only significant difference between Son and world is the mode of divine contemplation. Put differently, both Son and world have ideal existence, for both are the thought that God thinks.[57] Further, the world in some way seems to be necessary, for, as the thought that God thinks, the world is one of two logically possible ways in which God may think. Such a view marks a clear departure from the orthodox theological view that the world is separate from God and that God's act of creation is sufficiently distinct from God's conceptions that God can

[55] Ibid., 94–95 (§73).   [56] Ibid., 95 (§§76–77).
[57] Gotthold Ephraim Lessing, "On the Reality of Things Outside God," *Theological Writings*, 102–103.

conceive of things without creating them. Here we again see a parallel between Lessing and the later idealistic philosophers, for whom there was a similar difficulty in distinguishing the eternal Son from the world.

In summary, Lessing is to the critical Enlightenment what Leibniz was to the early Enlightenment, namely someone who transmitted and modified the speculative-analogical heritage of Trinitarian thought. Although far more rationalistic in intent than his predecessors in this tradition and less concerned to defend the orthodox doctrine, Lessing nonetheless remains an outstanding representative of this tradition. Further, he must be regarded as a direct antecedent of and influence on the idealist philosophers. Accepting the results of historical criticism, Lessing sought to rescue the doctrine of the Trinity by recourse to an *a priori* argument that is nevertheless strongly in continuity with those offered by Leibniz, Melanchthon, Thomas Aquinas and others.

FRIEDRICH SCHLEIERMACHER

Introduction

The transition from Lessing to Schleiermacher is a dramatic one. Schleiermacher utterly abhorred speculative approaches to the Trinity; Lessing offered only speculative approaches. Schleiermacher's doctrine of the Trinity is based solidly on the historical realities of Jesus Christ and the Holy Spirit; Lessing went out of his way to avoid connecting the doctrine of the Trinity to history. Nevertheless, Schleiermacher must be classified as a thinker of the critical Enlightenment, for his attitude toward the ecclesiastical doctrine is typical of that period – and that is to say, utterly critical. Schleiermacher took the distinctive feature of the Enlightenment – its critical attitude – and combined it with an allegiance to the Christian faith. He thereby fashioned a doctrine of the Trinity that is simultaneously theological and critical.

We may summarize Schleiermacher's view of the Trinity by noting, first, that he sought to combine a critical outlook with a Christocentric method and, second, that his doctrine of the

Trinity represents a triumph of historical thinking over metaphysical thinking. As noted above, Schleiermacher was unstinting in his application of the critical methods and attitude of the Enlightenment. At the same time, he was above all a Christocentric thinker; his view of the Trinity is not understood until we grasp it as an attempt at making sense of the church's confession that God was in Christ. Further, his view of the Trinity is a complete rejection of all metaphysical doctrines of the Trinity. He attempted to establish the doctrine on the basis of historical revelation in Jesus Christ and the Holy Spirit. He strenuously objected to all attempts at stating anything about God apart from this revelation. In short, he fully accepted the critical Enlightenment's historicizing of the Word (revelation) and partook of its Melanchthonian spirit by sharply opposing true religion to speculative philosophy. Schleiermacher was a theologian of the Word (understood in Melanchthon's sense) and history, with utterly no interest in the Trinity of reflective selfhood.

Preliminary remarks

The first task in expounding Schleiermacher's view of the Trinity must be to clear away certain misunderstandings.[58] Chief among these is that made by a multitude of theological commentators, to the effect that Schleiermacher did not even have a constructive view of the Trinity. The critics cite three bases for their judgment: First, Schleiermacher's overemphasis on God's absoluteness; second, his excessively subjectivistic account of faith; third, his locating the doctrine at the conclusion of his system of theology.

First, some charge that Schleiermacher was so occupied with asserting the absoluteness of God that he overlooked God's relatedness and thus could see no value in the doctrine of the Trinity.[59]

---

[58] The following comments are based, in part, on Eckhard Lessing, "Zu Schleiermachers Verständnis der Trinitätslehre," *Zeitschrift für Theologie und Kirche* 76 (1979): 450–488; Robert Francis Streetman, "Friedrich Schleiermacher's Doctrine of the Trinity and Its Significance for Theology Today" (Ph.D. diss., Drew University, 1975); and Carol Jean Voisin, "A Reconsideration of Friedrich Schleiermacher's Treatment of the Doctrine of the Trinity" (Th.D. diss., Graduate Theological Union, 1981).

[59] Gerhard Spiegler, *The Eternal Covenant: Schleiermacher's Experiment in Cultural Theology* (New York: Harper & Row, 1967), 182–184; William J. Hill, *The Three-Personed God: The Trinity as a Mystery of Salvation* (Washington: The Catholic University Press of America, 1982), 87–89.

While acknowledging that, according to Schleiermacher, God is related to us, they criticize him for failing to carry the principle of relationality into the divine being itself. This amounts to the indictment that Schleiermacher's doctrine of God is fundamentally philosophical – that it is another version of the Absolute that philosophers extol. The problem with this line of criticism is that Schleiermacher did not, in his theology, regard God as something absolute. He did claim that we must think of God as simple, but as we shall see he means by this anything except metaphysical simplicity. Schleiermacher's objection to affirming a Trinity of persons within the divine being has nothing to do with any alleged affinity for a metaphysical doctrine of God; it has everything to do with his conviction that faith itself knows of no such Trinity and that means are lacking by which we could form words to discuss such a Trinity.

A second criticism is that Schleiermacher's excessively subjectivistic foundation of theology makes it impossible to discuss God as a Trinity.[60] This longstanding error rests on the critics' overvaluation of the word "feeling," admittedly central to Schleiermacher's thought, and on a studied neglect of certain important statements by Schleiermacher. It is true that Schleiermacher declared that "descriptions of human states of mind" compose the fundamental form of dogmatic propositions.[61] This unfortunate phrase, misunderstood since its first appearance, emphatically should not be taken to mean that theology is all about subjective human feelings. As the following exposition will show, the fulcrum on which his theology rests is not feeling, but divine causation. So far from preventing an objective knowledge of God, Schleiermacher's theology is a sustained proof of human knowledge of God.[62] What he feared was the reduction of theology to a merely objective knowledge that is indistinguishable from metaphysics. The charge of excessive subjectivity is misguided.

A third criticism is that Schleiermacher's locating the doctrine

---

[60] Jürgen Moltmann, *The Trinity and the Kingdom: The Doctrine of God*, trs. Margaret Kohl (San Francisco: Harper & Row, 1981), 3–4.

[61] Friedrich Schleiermacher, *The Christian Faith*, ed. H. R. Mackintosh and J. S. Stewart (Philadelphia: Fortress Press, 1976), 126 (§30.2). Hereafter abbreviated as *CF*.

[62] This is the point of Robert R. Williams' *Schleiermacher the Theologian: The Construction of the Doctrine of God* (Philadelphia: Fortress Press, 1978). See p. 11.

at the end of his system of theology, in what appears to be an appendix, is a testimony to the unimportance of the doctrine.[63] This may be the most popular charge cast against Schleiermacher's view of the Trinity. In fact, however, it is a perfectly absurd charge. Schleiermacher's *The Christian Faith* does indeed contain appendices to various chapters and to these appendices he does in fact relegate discussion of traditional doctrines for which he has little use.[64] The doctrine of the Trinity, however, is contained, not in an appendix (*Anhang*), but in the conclusion (*Schluß*). Further, he hints at its importance by calling the essential elements of the doctrine the coping-stone or keystone (*Schlußstein*) of Christian doctrine.[65] Of course, this is not to claim that Schleiermacher's version of the Trinity is fully satisfactory. He himself admitted that what he offered in *The Christian Faith* was only "a preliminary step toward" a reconstruction of the doctrine. He believed he wrote in a time when the critical task had not yet been completed, so that only an adumbration of a reconstituted doctrine could be proposed.[66] Nevertheless, it just will not do to dismiss Schleiermacher's account of the Trinity because of its location in his system of doctrine. Schleiermacher took great care in designing the architecture of *The Christian Faith*; the doctrine of the Trinity occupies the conclusion, not because it is unimportant, but because it is the logical culmination of his doctrine of God, which spans the entire second part of *The Christian Faith*.

Schleiermacher's criticism of the traditional doctrine

Any discussion of Schleiermacher's view of the Trinity must consist in two parts, one that addresses his criticism of the traditional doctrine and one that portrays his constructive thoughts. The former part is easily done, for Schleiermacher's reasons for

---

[63] W. Waite Willis, Jr., *Theism, Atheism and the Doctrine of the Trinity: The Trinitarian Theologies of Karl Barth and Jürgen Moltmann in Response to Protest Atheism*, American Academy of Religion Academy Series, no. 53 (Atlanta: Scholars Press, 1987), 20; Hill, *The Three-Personed God*, 84; Richard Roberts, "Karl Barth," *One God in Trinity*, ed. Peter Toon and James D. Spiceland (Westchester, IL: Cornerstone Books, 1980), 79.

[64] For example, supervenient upon the chapter setting forth the doctrine of creation are two appendices, one on angels, the other on the devil. *CF*, 156–170 (§§42–45).

[65] Ibid., 739 (§170.1).   [66] Ibid., 749 (§172.3).

rejecting the church's doctrine of the Trinity were utterly clear; however, the latter part is more challenging. This is the case not only, as noted above, because he did not consider the time ripe for a complete elaboration of the doctrine, but also because his thoughts on the Trinity are scattered throughout the second part of *The Christian Faith* and in his historical monograph about the ancient heretic, Sabellius.[67] Nevertheless, what Schleiermacher there had to say is sufficient to convey his thoughts on the subject.

Schleiermacher proposed three reasons why a criticism of the traditional doctrine of the Trinity is needed. First, the doctrine was fashioned in the midst of controversy. Schleiermacher was convinced that such circumstances fomented extreme statements whose validity must be lost when the historical conditions that called them forth were past.[68] Second, he believed that it is impossible for human language ever to portray definitively the being of God in Christ.[69] As a result, the traditional doctrine could not be regarded as sacrosanct and beyond challenge. Third, some professed anti-Trinitarians possess the same sort of piety that Trinitarian Christians do, a fact that suggests that the traditional doctrine itself is neither a requirement for nor an expression of Christian faith.[70] These reasons embody three of Schleiermacher's characteristic interests: in the historical development and conditioning of doctrines, in the nature of language and its relation to faith, and in the desirability of an irenic theology.

We may summarize Schleiermacher's actual criticism of the traditional doctrine of the Trinity under five points. First, the doctrine of the Trinity posits eternal distinctions (i.e., Father, Son, and Holy Spirit) in the divine essence, in spite of the fact that such distinctions are not "utterance[s] concerning the religious consciousness."[71] Since all knowledge of God arises from the religious consciousness, the point here is that this notion of eternal personal distinctions in the essence of God bears no relation to actual faith and can be derived only from speculation. The validity of

---

[67] Friedrich Schleiermacher, "On the Discrepancy Between the Sabellian and Athanasian Method of Representing the Doctrine of a Trinity in the Godhead," trs. Moses Stuart, *Biblical Repository and Quarterly Observer*, 1835. The German text is in *Friedrich Schleiermacher und die Trinitätslehre*, ed. Martin Tezt, Texte zur Kirchen- und Theologiegeschichte, vol. XI (Gütersloh: Gütersloher Verlagshaus Gerd Mohn, 1969).   [68] *CF*, 747 (§172.1).
[69] Ibid., 748 (§172.1).   [70] Ibid., 749 (§172.2).   [71] Ibid., 739 (§170.2).

Schleiermacher's observation depends entirely on whether he has, in the first part of *The Christian Faith*, accurately if abstractly described the human consciousness of God. His contention was that our consciousness of God results from the activity of God upon us. For this reason, the doctrinal language that expresses this consciousness pertains to God's causal relation to the human subject but not to any supposed being of God in itself.[72] We may contrast Schleiermacher's view of language with the more orthodox opinion that revelation is given to us (in the Bible) in a language that, because it derives ultimately from God, is a fit vehicle for portraying the divine being. Schleiermacher, however, held that revelation is a divine activity in the soul; since it works upon us not as cognitive beings but as beings in need of salvation, it is given to us not as doctrine but as the existence of God within us. As a result, revelation is not informative about the being of God in itself[73] and the orthodox conception of eternal distinctions within God cannot have arisen from revelation and genuine faith. Even if Christ and the apostles had expressly taught eternal personal distinctions in God, the resulting doctrine would still be nothing more than "testimonies regarding a supersensible fact."[74] Its being taught by Jesus would not in itself qualify it as a doctrine of faith, because it would not have arisen from revelation – from the saving activity of God in human consciousness.

Second, the eternal personal distinctions posited by the orthodox doctrine have no support in the Gospel according to John, where such support might be expected. In particular, Schleiermacher disputed the customary way of interpreting the opening verses of that Gospel, according to which the Logos is understood to be an eternal and personal being distinct from God the Father. Schleiermacher drew attention to the fact that both Trinitarians and Arians used these verses and construed them in their own way, a fact suggesting that both Trinitarian and Arian interpretations are anachronistic. He also commented on the absence of any mention of the Holy Spirit in the Gospel's prologue, an omission that likewise casts doubt on the supposition that the author believed what the later creeds would assert.[75] In short,

---

[72] Ibid., 198 (§50.3).   [73] Ibid., 50–52 (§10.3).   [74] Ibid., 740–741 (§170.3).
[75] Ibid., 739–740 (§170.2).

Schleiermacher found the Fourth Gospel to be concerned with something quite different from the concerns of later Trinitarian theology.

Third, the traditional doctrine is incoherent. It requires a twofold equality, first among Father, Son and Holy Spirit, then a second equality between the divine persons and the divine essence.[76] However, the doctrine also asserts that the persons are associated by relations of generation and procession. In fact, only these relations distinguish the persons: the Father begets and is not begotten; the Son is begotten and from the Son the Spirit proceeds; the Spirit neither begets nor is the source of any person – the Spirit merely proceeds. The problem that Schleiermacher saw here is that these relations vitiate the equality that the doctrine insists upon. "The term [generation] itself . . . must at least indicate a relationship of dependence . . . Undeniably the power of the Father is greater than that of the Son."[77] The result is either subordinationism (if the persons are not equal) or modalism or tritheism (if there is no equality between the persons and the essence). The doctrine, then, undermines the very assertion it regards as of crucial importance. Further, the doctrine's affirmation of the equality between the persons and the essence cannot be sustained. Schleiermacher suggested that the only way of conceiving the relation of the persons to the essence is by analogy with the relation between members of a species and the species itself. According to this analogy, the divine essence is a sort of species and the Father, Son and Spirit are individuals who embody it. The problem here is that within this analogy thought constantly vacillates between a realistic view (the species is more real than the individuals) and a nominalistic view (the persons alone are real; the species is an abstraction).[78] The former results in the modalistic view in which the persons are subordinated; the latter results in tritheism. Schleiermacher averred that no mean between these two could be discerned. Further, if this analogy is rejected, then "we really are not in a position to form any definite ideas on the subject, and hence [we] can have no interest in it."[79]

[76] Ibid., 742 (§171.1).   [77] Ibid., 743 (§171.2).   [78] Ibid., 744 (§171.3).
[79] Ibid., 744–745 (§171.3).

Fourth, Schleiermacher objected to the way in which orthodox theology treats the doctrine. For one thing, it was customary to begin systems of theology with an extended philosophical discussion of the essence and attributes of God far in advance of any mention of the Trinitarian persons. For another, the treatment of the persons was likewise conducted without first mentioning Jesus Christ and the Holy Spirit as historical revelations. The persons were considered strictly as eternal distinctions within the divine essence.[80] What annoyed Schleiermacher about this arrangement was its wholly speculative character – the fact that such a procedure bore no necessary relation to the Christian knowledge of God. Of course, what underlay Schleiermacher's censure was his conviction that God is known only in Christ and the Holy Spirit, that is, only through revelation. As noted above, this conviction implied an impatience with all talk of eternal distinctions within God; however, Schleiermacher also believed that this conviction should condition the arrangement of topics within the system of theology. That is why the doctrine of the Trinity comes last in *The Christian Faith*. Since Jesus Christ and the Holy Spirit are the principles of the knowledge of God, the doctrine of God cannot be completed until they have been treated. Further, since the knowledge of God rests exclusively on revelation, the Christian doctrine of God is identical with the doctrine of the Trinity.[81]

Finally, Schleiermacher detected in the traditional doctrine a subtle subordination of the Son and Holy Spirit to the Father. He noted that in most systems of theology the divine attributes are represented as pertaining to the Father, so that theologians must exert themselves to show that the attributes also pertain to the Son and Spirit. The conclusion he drew is that orthodox theology actually identified the Father and the divine essence in a special way, thus establishing a superiority of the Father to the Son and Spirit. He commented that this error had its beginning with Origen.[82] Of course, it may be that previous theologians were simply responding to the challenges of heretics who denied the divinity of the

[80] Ibid., 746 (§171.5).

[81] On the subject of the doctrine of God in *The Christian Faith*, see Gerhard Ebeling, "Schleiermacher's Doctrine of the Divine Attributes," trs. James W. Leitch, *Schleiermacher as Contemporary*, ed. Robert W. Funk, Journal for Theology and the Church, no. 7 (New York: Herder & Herder, 1970), 125–162.   [82] *CF*, 746–747 (§171.5).

Son and Spirit. That is, perhaps the orthodox systems of theology continued to reflect the Trinitarian controversies; perhaps their attempts at proving the divinity of the Son and Spirit and their belief that the Father needed no such proof were not as sinister as Schleiermacher represented. Nevertheless, there can be no denying that there has been a tendency in Christian theology to identify the Father with the divine essence in a way that distinguishes Father from Son and Spirit. This tendency, Schleiermacher feared, supported the inclination to treat God first philosophically and only then to consider the properly Christian knowledge of God based on revelation in Christ and the Spirit.

In summary, then, Schleiermacher condemned the traditional doctrine of the Trinity for lacking a relation to Christian faith and piety, for its lack of Biblical support, for its incoherence and for its speculative character. It was not truly, he charged, a doctrine of *faith*. The most salient Biblical passage adduced for its support (the prologue of John) did not justify it. It could not provide a solid conception of the divine essence and persons sufficient to avoid contradiction. Its customary position in the system of theology opposed the fundamental principle of Christian theology – the restriction of authentic knowledge of God to the revelation of Jesus Christ and the Holy Spirit.

It is difficult to pass by such a review of Schleiermacher's thoughts without comment; however, any substantive critique would have to take into account the totality of his theology. It must suffice here to note that the key to his views lies in his highly inno-vative understanding of God's activity within the human person. In essence, this is Schleiermacher's theory of revelation, although he does not expressly use the term "revelation" as such. This divine activity explains the uniqueness of Jesus Christ as the savior and also is the basis of his doctrines of the Holy Spirit and the church. While it is clearly a theocentric theory of revelation (and not an anthropocentric theory, as it is frequently misunderstood to be), resting as it does on the notion of divine activity and causation, his entire approach has been out of step with the dominant trends in twentieth-century theology. Theology in that century has been much more explicitly *Christo*centric in its doctrine of revelation. Which of the two theories is preferable depends on a great many theological and perhaps philosophical factors. At any rate, the least that can be said is that Schleiermacher's view deserves much greater sympathetic attention than it has received in recent years. Its use of causation as a central category for God's interaction with the world certainly has a sufficiently respectable history in Christian thought to warrant such attention.

Schleiermacher's constructive doctrine of the Trinity

Schleiermacher's constructive doctrine of the Trinity rests on a Christological basis, at least in the sense that it is an attempt at making sense of the church's confession that God was in Christ. This Christological basis in turn illumines for him the conception of the Father and Spirit.

The point of departure of Schleiermacher's doctrine of the Trinity is his insistence that activity must replace nature as the leading conception for understanding God. As is well known, theology represents the Trinity by means of the idea of nature. The one divine nature comprises three eternal persons. The person of Jesus Christ comprises two natures, divine and human. Schleiermacher objected strenuously to this use of "nature" both on general theological grounds and on specifically Trinitarian grounds. He complained on general grounds that its use implies a generic category – nature – of which human and divine nature are specific instances, thus compromising God's uniqueness. It is also confusing because it is desirable to distinguish God from the world of nature, "nature" denoting something limited and possessing a passive element, whereas God cannot be conceived as passive in any sense. Further, "nature" is tainted, he averred, because the ancient heathens employed it as a basis for polytheism.[83] Finally, he disapproved of this term because of the logical perplexities it raised: Is it only the second person that has a distinctive nature in addition to the common divine nature shared with the other Trinitarian persons? If the three persons are posited as eternal distinctions within the divine essence, how is it possible to avoid asserting that each of the persons has a distinctive nature?[84]

---

[83] Ibid., 392–393 (§96.1).   [84] Ibid., 395 (§96.1).

As a result, Schleiermacher proposed that the only appropriate way of conceiving God is by means of the idea of "activity."[85] However, this activity is neither impersonal nor general. It is instead "an activity which aims at and furthers the salvation of man."[86] It is the same divine activity that is both creative and preserving.[87] This conception of divine activity underlies Schleiermacher's Christology. Christ's divinity consisted in the existence of God within him. But this existence was not a union of two natures; it was instead "the innermost fundamental power within Him."[88] This power, or divine activity, brought about Christ's perfect and continuous God-consciousness[89] and in fact formed the person of Christ.[90] That is, Christ's existence cannot be explained as the result of normal human activity, for such activity would have brought about only another person with an imperfect God-consciousness; only the divine activity can explain the fact that Jesus' God-consciousness was perfect and continuous.

This being of God in Christ constitutes, according to Schleiermacher, one of the basal facts that any doctrine of the Trinity must encompass. We have already reviewed Schleiermacher's quarrel with the orthodox doctrine of the Trinity. He believed that a doctrine more in conformity with Christian faith could be fashioned that would do justice to the fundamental fact of Christology, the active and constitutive presence of God in Christ. To fashion such a doctrine Schleiermacher used this Christology as a foundation and then proceeded to construct a doctrine of the Holy Spirit. He did so by asserting that just as God was actively and constitutively present in Jesus Christ, so God is actively and constitutively present in the church. This being of God in the church is the Holy Spirit. A proper conception of Jesus Christ yields the doctrine of the Holy Spirit.

Unfortunately, some of Schleiermacher's statements about the Spirit seem calculated to inspire misunderstanding. He referred to the Spirit as the common spirit of the church,[91] a term that has conjured up all manner of misconceptions among his readers. His

---

[85] Ibid., 387 (§94.2). See 197–198 (§50.3) for the argument that causality furnishes the only sound way of understanding the divine attributes. [86] Ibid., 50 (§10, postscript).

[87] Ibid., 426 (§100.2). [88] Ibid., 397 (§96.3). [89] Ibid., 387 (§94.2).

[90] Ibid., 400 (§97.2). [91] Ibid., 535 (§116.3).

theology of the Spirit seems to reduce the Spirit to human subjectivity, just as his view of language appeared to reduce theology
to statements about feeling. In fact, however, his view of the Spirit
is largely conditioned by his Christology, and although it is possible to interpret his theology of Christ and the Spirit as implying a
thorough-going subjectivism, it is more plausible to interpret his
thoughts in such a way that the emphasis falls upon God's activity
and grace.

Schleiermacher began his doctrine of the Spirit with the
observations that everything godly in the regenerate derives from
Christ, and that Christ, no longer being a historical person, no
longer exercises any directly personal influence on the regenerate.
From this twofold observation he concluded that there must be
something divine within the church that is the source of spiritual
life and power. In fact, this something is the being of God in the
corporate church, just as God was in Christ individually; and it is
this being of God in the church that communicates to the regenerate the "perfection and blessedness of Christ."[92] This being of God
in the church is the Holy Spirit.

Like Jesus Christ, the Holy Spirit is the union of the divine
essence with human nature. The difference is that in the case of
Christ the union is a person-forming act – it results in an individual (i.e., Jesus Christ); in the case of the Holy Spirit the union is not
person-forming but instead results in a "common Spirit animating
the life in common of believers."[93] The similarity between Jesus
Christ and the Holy Spirit is established by the fact that each
Trinitarian person results from the union of human nature with
the divine essence, an essence that Schleiermacher regarded
axiomatically as being "one and everywhere self-identical." Both
Jesus Christ and the Holy Spirit come about in history as the divine
essence actively unites with human nature. Even though the mode
of God's being in Jesus Christ differs from its mode of being in the
church (the former being person-forming, the latter being com-
munity-forming), the activity itself must be the same: "The
impulses proceeding from it must be the same in both cases."[94]

Because the Holy Spirit *is* the being of God in the church, the

---

[92] Ibid., 535 (§116.3) and 568 (§122.3).   [93] Ibid., 569 (§123 theorem) and 573 (§123.3).
[94] Ibid., 579 (§125.1).

Spirit is fully divine just as the being of God in Christ was fully divine. Schleiermacher emphatically denied that the Spirit is merely a "supernatural and mysterious though not immediately divine [essence], a higher yet created essence." Nor is the Spirit some human capacity actualized.[95] Accordingly, the Spirit is associated with God's grace and revelation.[96] Further, it is the Spirit that mediates the life of Christ to believers. Since the divine essence is "no longer personally operative in any individual," the divine that was in Christ is now in the community as an impulse in believers as the Holy Spirit.[97]

God was in Jesus Christ. The same divine activity that determined the person of Jesus Christ (since the "innermost impulse" of Christ was his "absolute and continuous willing of the Kingdom of God"[98]) is present in the church as its corporate spirit. On this basis, Schleiermacher proposed to construct an adequate doctrine of the Trinity. However, Schleiermacher had hitherto demonstrated only that the divine essence had united with human nature twice, in the man Jesus Christ and in the church as a whole. Although stating that the divine essence could be conceived only as creative activity, he had also made statements to the effect that the essence of God in itself is unknowable and that our knowledge of God extends only to what God is in relation to humanity.[99] The problem is that such statements open the possibility of an epistemological gap between God's being in itself and God's being for us, a gap that undermines the importance of revelation. Further, these statements raise the specter of modalism, the view that the Trinitarian persons are mere names for the one divine being. Modalism threatens to render the Trinitarian persons and their revelation unimportant because the divine being remains behind them unchanged while they appear successively in history. To compound this problem, Schleiermacher made no secret of his admiration for Sabellius' view of the Trinity,[100] a view customarily associated with modalism. Schleiermacher's many critics have not been slow to charge him with adopting a modalistic view of the Trinity.

---

[95] Ibid., 571 (§123.2). [96] Ibid., 577–578 (§124.3) and 326–327 (§80.1).
[97] Ibid., 576–577 (§124.2). [98] Ibid., 535–536 (§116.3).
[99] Ibid., 198 (§50.3) and 52 (§10 postscript). [100] Ibid., 399 (§97.2) and 750 (§172.3).

What Schleiermacher had to do was to show not only that the divine essence had united with human nature, but also that this union was not external to God – that in some way these unions involve God intimately. Schleiermacher introduced the attributes of divine love and wisdom to accomplish this. The significance of love as a divine attribute is evident from Schleiermacher's statement that "love alone and no other attribute can be equated thus with God."[101] Until this point in *The Christian Faith*, Schleiermacher had said very little about the divine essence, occasionally insinuating that nothing could be said about it. He had noted that it could be understood only as creative activity, but this still left it a bit abstract. However, toward the end of *The Christian Faith*, Schleiermacher asserted that love alone can be identified with God. This procedure was in keeping with notices given here and there that the course of *The Christian Faith* was from the most abstract components of faith to the most concrete.[102] This means that the Christian understanding of God is not fully expounded until the doctrine of love and wisdom have been treated and their significance for the Trinity shown. What, according to Schleiermacher, is love? It is nothing other than "the impulse to unite self with neighbor and to will to be in [the] neighbor." So the union of God's essence with human nature is not an act peripheral to God; God's "underlying disposition" can be conceived only as this will to unite.[103] Likewise, the divine wisdom "is nothing but the Supreme Being viewed as engaged in this absolute . . . self-presentation and impartation."[104]

The Trinity is the result of this divine impartation. Because God's activity aims at redemption and because God is love, the divine essence unites with human nature in Jesus Christ and the church. As a result, God becomes a Trinity in the course of history. Although not altering or otherwise affecting the divine essence, which always remains purely active and is never passive, something of significance transpires within God's life and it is appropriate to speak of a historical development, not of God's being, but of the modes of God's being in relation to the created world.

However, the doctrine of the Trinity is still incomplete, for only

---

[101] Ibid., 730 (§167.1).   [102] See, for example, ibid., 131 (§32.1) and 736 (§169.3).
[103] Ibid., 726–727 (§165.1).   [104] Ibid., 733 (§168.1).

the second and third persons have been accounted for. How did he understand the person of the Father? It is one of the weaknesses of *The Christian Faith* that it contains no substantive discussion of the Father and not even a hint as to how the person of the Father might be analogous to Jesus Christ and the Holy Spirit. To discern Schleiermacher's view of the Father it is necessary to turn to his monograph on Sabellius. Here he noted that creation and preservation are, according to Sabellius, most properly appropriated to the Father, not to the divine being itself. In accordance with his general understanding of Trinitarian persons as unions of the divine essence with something else, Schleiermacher concluded that, in the Sabellian framework, the Father is constituted by the union of the divine essence, not with human nature, but with the created universe as a whole.[105] Schleiermacher did not elaborate upon this thought; however, at least it locates the Father in the scheme of divine self-impartation and thus allows Schleiermacher to lay the foundation for a doctrine of the Trinity that is comprehensive and coherent.[106] However, he did no more than lay the foundation. As he noted, he did not offer in *The Christian Faith* an elaborated doctrine of the Trinity. Although we cannot blame him for failing to accomplish something he did not intend to, the lack of a substantial doctrine of the Father is a glaring omission that mars the architectural balance of his work and fails to address one of the fundamental topics of theology.

[105] Schleiermacher, "On the Discrepancy," 144 and 148.
[106] Voisin, "A Reconsideration," 191 detects in Schleiermacher's theology a subordination of the Father to the Son and Spirit: Because the Father is not the source of the Son and Spirit, there is a sharp distinction between creation (the Father) and redemption (Son and Spirit). "This could imply an inequality wherein the Father is excluded from the designation of a self-impartation of the divine essence," the Father being a mere preparation for redemption. Streetman, "Friedrich Schleiermacher's Doctrine of the Trinity," 79–82, has a different view of the matter, asserting that according to Schleiermacher each of the divine persons contributes "a specific aspect to the actualization [in history] of the sole divine action." Streetman subsumes the doctrine of the Trinity under the category of the divine causality, so that each of the persons is understood in terms of that causality. This prevents, he believes, a subordination of one person to another. Streetman also believes that Schleiermacher's theology intends to associate the Father with our consciousness of sin and with the divine attributes of holiness and justice, just as the Son and Spirit are associated with our consciousness of redemption and the attributes of love and wisdom. As a result, the Father is regarded not only as the creator but also as the legislator, thus connecting the Father more firmly with redemption. Streetman's view is suggestive, but rests more on an analysis of the structure of *The Christian Faith* than on specific textual warrants.

CONCLUSION

Schleiermacher exemplifies the theological concerns of this period and brings to them a depth and clarity that both mark him as the culmination of the critical Enlightenment and also constitute him a bridge to the next period. Schleiermacher grasped the fact that religious thinking had entered upon a course characterized by a critical stance toward traditional doctrines and also by a greater sense for the development of and disruptions within history. Whereas in the early eighteenth century critics of orthodox doctrine were relegated to a tributary outside the mainstream of German thought, the principle of criticism abounded in adherents as the century wore on. Schleiermacher's goals were to come to terms with this critical spirit and its results and to employ this spirit for the purpose of purifying evangelical theology. Whether he accomplished this purpose is a judgment that depends on one's theological convictions about the desirability of acquiescing in the critical spirit of the age and about the adequacy of the traditional doctrine of the Trinity. Nevertheless, we may at least acknowledge that something of great importance occurs in the transition from Reimarus to Schleiermacher: criticism became an evangelical concern. Whereas Reimarus exercised his critical acumen in order to save true religion from the distortions of Christian dogma, Schleiermacher was convinced, and along the way convinced a great many others, that criticism was required in order to safeguard the Christian character of theology from speculative philosophy. From this time on, this opinion would be a contentious matter, one still unresolved today.

Schleiermacher also grasped another point, namely that the doctrine of the Trinity is about revelation – Jesus Christ. In itself this was no astonishing discovery; however, two points should be made: First, at the hands of idealists such as Lessing, there was no little danger that the Trinity might come to be regarded as a wholly speculative doctrine. Schleiermacher's insistence that in Jesus Christ the ideal had become historical prevented the doctrine of the Trinity from being interpreted as anything other than an explication of the church's confession about Jesus Christ. Second, Schleiermacher realized that the historical and critical attitude of the modern world necessitated a view of Jesus Christ different from the traditional conception of Jesus as the incarnate second person of the Trinity. Schleiermacher's doctrine of the Trinity was an attempt to account for the fact that there is redemption in Jesus while replacing traditional language about divine and human nature with what he thought was more adequate language of divine causation and human receptivity.

Schleiermacher, then, presents us with a doctrine of the Trinity that sought to be both critical and Christological. It was critical in its awareness of the intellectual gap between an ancient metaphysical approach and a modern historical approach and in its steadfast insistence that the character of true religion requires a thorough revision of the doctrine. It was Christological in its belief that the doctrine is about Jesus Christ, that its point of departure is redemption in Christ. Accordingly, Schleiermacher spared no effort in ensuring that the doctrine not be construed as a theory of the divine being in abstraction from the involvement of God in human history. In his trenchant criticism of the traditional doctrine Schleiermacher showed himself a complete devotee of historical thinking. His constant effort to separate Christian theology from the influence of speculative theology, especially with respect to the Trinity, shows him to be an important inheritor of Melanchthon's legacy. But Schleiermacher's theology also looks forward to the era of idealistic philosophy in its willingness to apply the category of history even to God. By arguing that the Trinitarian persons arise in history as the divine essence unites with human or finite nature, Schleiermacher introduced an element of historicity into God, even as his other theological commitments prevented him from representing this as some sort of divine becoming in history. In short, to repeat a point made previously, Schleiermacher was a theologian of the Word (understood in Melanchthon's sense) and of history.

CHAPTER FOUR

Georg Wilhelm Friedrich Hegel

INTRODUCTION

By about 1800, the future of the doctrine of the Trinity appeared bleak. Enlightenment theology either dismissed it altogether (Reimarus), downplayed its doctrinal significance (Semler), or sought to rationalize it (Lessing). Schleiermacher's theology, although favorable to the doctrine in an amended form, did no more than enumerate the problems with the traditional doctrine and suggest directions for future developments. Unfortunately for the doctrine, although Schleiermacher's theology as a whole proved enormously influential, his prescriptions for the doctrine of the Trinity fell on deaf ears. What was required to revivify the doctrine was an altered understanding of the three principal ideas – Word, history and reflective selfhood – that have governed its development in modern thought. The required alteration was provided, in various ways, by the philosophers of German idealism. Georg Wilhelm Friedrich Hegel (1770–1831) is here taken as the representative figure.

PRELIMINARY ORIENTATION TO THE INTERPRETATION OF HEGEL

The first thing to note about Hegel is that his philosophy of religion, including his view of the Trinity, has been the subject of vast disagreement among the interpreters. Hegel's philosophy was variously understood, even during his own lifetime. As is well known, upon his death his disciples drifted into at least three discernable interpretations, with the result that Hegel has been represented as an atheist, a pantheist and a theist, to say nothing of the divergent interpretations of his political thought and its implications. Given the multitude of conflicting interpretations and the voluminous bulk of supporting literature, I will in this chapter expound Hegel's doctrine of the Trinity according to the interpretation that I find most compelling and will refrain from offering either a complete justification of that interpretation or a full review of the alternative interpretations. The interpretation that seems most correct is that set forth by Peter C. Hodgson, Walter Jaeschke and Dale Schlitt.[1] I am not claiming that the views of these scholars form a homogeneous whole; however, each does take fully seriously Hegel's attempt at conceiving the idea of the Trinity and his genuinely religious interests. In other words, each treats Hegel as a religious philosopher in a convincing way.

As an introduction both to Hegel and his doctrine of the Trinity, it may be helpful to situate Hegel between his two most prominent theological partners in dialogue: the Enlightenment and pietism. The burning question that Hegel posed to these two traditions is whether humans can attain the knowledge of God.[2] In different ways, the theology of the Enlightenment and of pietism denied the possibility of such knowledge, at least on the terms that Hegel demanded. Hegel's ideal for the knowledge of God was rooted ultimately in the Aristotelian belief that the highest wisdom consists in participating in the self-knowledge that is constitutive of the divine being.[3] God is, according to Aristotle, the eternal act of self-knowledge.[4] The highest of all human activities is contemplation (*theoria*) by which we have a share in this divine activity and transcend mortal thoughts. Although Hegel's view of God differs from Aristotle's in important respects, they do share a confidence in humanity's capacity to know God through this participation. Hegel's opponents in this matter were of two

---

[1] Peter C. Hodgson, "Hegel's Christology: Shifting Nuances in the Berlin Lectures," *Journal of the American Academy of Religion* 53 (1985): 23–40; Walter Jaeschke, *Reason in Religion: The Foundations of Hegel's Philosophy of Religion*, trs. J. Michael Stewart and Peter C. Hodgson (Berkeley: University of California Press, 1990); and Dale Schlitt, *Hegel's Trinitarian Claim: A Critical Reflection* (Leiden: E. J. Brill, 1984).

[2] Throughout the exposition of Hegel, I will refer indifferently to "God" and "Spirit," even though a more complete interpretation of Hegel's thought would require distinguishing them.   [3] Aristotle, *Nicomachean Ethics*, 11.7–8.

[4] Aristotle, *Metaphysics*, 1074b30 (Lambda 9).

sorts: religious skeptics and philosophical skeptics. Although, Hegel believed, each possessed something in the way of truth, each fixed itself too one-sidedly on that truth.

Against the pietists Hegel complained that their skepticism took the form of fleeing from the knowledge of God and taking refuge in feeling.[5] Not that Hegel was utterly opposed to feeling. He put great emphasis on the subjective side of religion and associated this subjective side with the Holy Spirit.[6] He went so far as to commend the theology of his day for advancing to "the recognition of the consciousness of subjectivity as an absolute moment" in religion. In religion, he asserted, there is the danger that God will be regarded as an object lying far away from the subject. Hence the importance of feeling: in devotion and the heart this separation between God and the individual is overcome. This was the truth Hegel was willing to grant to pietism. However, by the 1820s, following some conflict with pietists, Hegel argued that they had wrongly come to oppose feeling to thought, with a resulting loss of all objective knowledge. Their overweening emphasis on subjectivity meant that "the present age [was] concerned with religion, with religiosity, or with piety, in which no regard is had for what is objective . . . We cannot know God [according to pietism] as an object, we cannot cognize him."[7] Hegel's insistence on the objective knowledge of God stems from his desire to regard the Trinity as the truth about God and, moreover, as the means by which the truth could be known. That is, it is because God is a Trinity that God is knowable and revelatory. He feared that the pietistic emphasis on feeling and subjectivity rendered the knowledge of God, properly speaking,

[5] For a general orientation to Hegel and the religious setting of his day see Laurence Dickey, "Hegel on Religion and Philosophy," in Frederick C. Beiser, ed., *The Cambridge Companion to Hegel*, Cambridge Companions to Philosophy (Cambridge: Cambridge University Press, 1993). See also Hodgson, "Hegel's Christology," 26–27 and Philip M. Merklinger, *Philosophy, Theology, and Hegel's Berlin Philosophy of Religion, 1821–1827* (Albany: State University of New York Press, 1993), ch. 5.

[6] Georg Wilhelm Friedrich Hegel, *Lectures on the Philosophy of Religion*, ed. Peter C. Hodgson, trs. R. F. Brown, et al., vol. III: *The Consummate Religion* (Berkeley: University of California Press, 1984), 140–142.

[7] Ibid., 166–167. See also *Hegel's Philosophy of Mind*, trs. William Wallace (Oxford: Clarendon Press, 1894), 305–306 (this is Hegel's *Encyclopedia of the Philosophical Sciences*, §573).

impossible. As we have seen, this was not an unfounded fear; Schleiermacher's theology was a likely object of Hegel's scorn, for it forbade just the sort of objective knowledge that Hegel regarded as the zenith of human knowledge. The point of contention between them is whether the knowledge of God is knowledge of God's activity or of God's being. Do we, as Schleiermacher would have it, lack words for describing the being of God in itself, apart from creative and saving activity, or does the being of God, in its revelatory structure, supply us with those words, as Hegel asserted? This issue, of fundamental importance to a doctrine of God, was, as we shall see, resurrected in the twentieth century in the theology of Karl Barth.

Against the Enlightenment, Hegel complained that its theology was void of truth. He was attracted to its devotion to rationality but held that it was so fixed on avoiding superstition that it ended up possessing the mere form of truth, lacking all content, including the truth contained in religion.[8] It limited, he charged, its own content and purpose to the extinction of error. Worse, it measured finitude by a being's degree of specificity (its "determinateness"). The more particular a being, the greater its finitude. As a result, it thought of the infinite God as being without determinations and predicates.[9] Such a God would be an utter abstraction, with the result that the theology of the Enlightenment was "nothing but abstract understanding masquerading under the name of reason."[10] In Hegel's judgment, although the Enlightenment had a useful function to perform by way of criticism, its theology fell far short of the mark, for like pietistic theology it had given up the search for truth and contented itself with the empty abstractions of its own understanding that it called God.

Hegel proposed to overcome the religious and philosophical types of skepticism by means of a philosophical comprehension of religion and theological doctrines. This maneuver set him against both the pietists and the Enlightenment theologians: against the

[8] G. W. F. Hegel, *Phenomenology of Spirit*, trs. A. V. Miller (Oxford: Clarendon Press, 1977), 329 (§541). [9] Ibid., 340 (§557).
[10] Georg Wilhelm Friedrich Hegel, *Lectures on the Philosophy of Religion*, ed. Peter C. Hodgson, trs. R. F. Brown, et al., vol. I: *Introduction and The Concept of Religion* (Berkeley: University of California Press, 1984), 126.

former, who held that philosophical comprehension is impossible, against the latter, who believed there is nothing true in religion that would justify the attempt at comprehension.

The theory behind the attempt at philosophical comprehension of religion was that philosophy could reconcile religion and the rationality of the Enlightenment if religion were to take refuge in conceptual thinking.[11] The problem, as Hegel saw it, was that religion (and from now on we shall confine ourselves to Christianity, which Hegel called the "consummate" religion) possesses the truth but does so in a form that does not allow that truth to be conceptually known. That inappropriate form is "representation" (*Vorstellung*). The reconciliation Hegel proposed consisted in a transition from representational thinking to conceptual thinking, a transition that involves transcending the non-essential representational form, retrieving the truth contained in the representations, and restating that truth in conceptual terms. Of all religious doctrines, none was in greater need, Hegel believed, of such conceptual comprehension than the doctrine of the Trinity, first because its content is the truth of all truths and second because its representational form made it highly susceptible to rationalistic critique and rejection. As we shall see, the philosophical deciphering of this doctrine is, Hegel believed, the key to solving every philosophical perplexity and religious mystery.

What is representational thinking? Hegel's meaning may be made clearer by taking as an example the view of Jesus that one finds among religious believers. In this religious mode of thought, Jesus is thought of in representational terms. Whereas once (i.e., when alive on Earth as a historical being) he could be sensuously perceived, now he is no longer available as an immediate object of perception. Instead he is something that is known; however, Jesus is not, for believers, an object of conceptual thought, strictly speaking, since conceptual thought deals with universal concepts and believers continue to think of Jesus as a definite human individual with particular qualities and perceptible features. As Hegel says, Jesus has been given, in the Christian faith, a universal character by being "merely dipped superficially in the element of Thought" and

---

[11] Hegel, *Lectures*, III:161–162 (Manuscript) and III:245–246 (1824 lectures).

being preserved in it as a sensuous mode. The result is that Jesus has been "merely raised into the realm of picture-thinking, for this is the synthetic combination of sensuous immediacy and its universality or Thought."[12] This example illustrates a point made in Hegel's *Encyclopedia*: representation lies between sensuous perception (in German philosophical terminology, "intuition") and thought. Sensuous perception is characterized by immediacy – the object of perception is given to the subject who needs no intermediary to perceive the object. Thought is characterized by universality; it has to do with truth, which is essentially a matter of generality. Representation stands higher than sensuous perception, for in representation the intuition has been "internalized," i.e., the object is no longer something immediately given. Instead, the object in representation is an idea (we may loosely say) about which we may think. Nevertheless, representation is not yet conceptual thought for "the intuitional contrast still continues to affect [representation's] activity, and makes its concrete products still 'syntheses.'"[13] By "synthesis" Hegel means that representation combines the figurative character of intuition with the universality of thought. Representation is genuinely a form of thought, for its object is no longer given in sensuous immediacy; however, it is not yet conceptual thought, for its objects are always thought of in a figurative or pictorial manner. Other examples of representation in religious belief include angels, demons and Satan. In each case there is some thought, some idea, that we fail to grasp conceptually and which instead is clothed with sensuous forms: bright lights, wings and haloes in the case of angels, grotesque malevolent creatures in the case of demons. What is important to note is the way in which Hegel's critique of doctrine contrasts with the rationalistic critique of the Enlightenment. Whereas a rationalistic critique would regard religious doctrines as vacuous and risible, Hegel believed that within the representations lay ensconced important truth.[14] With respect to the Trinity, Hegel was convinced that the ecclesiastical doctrine, or at least its popular exposition, was thoroughly

---

[12] Hegel, *Phenomenology*, 462–463.   [13] *Hegel's Philosophy of Mind*, 214 (*Encyclopedia*, §451).
[14] *Hegel's Philosophy of Mind*, 299 (*Encyclopedia*, §565) and *Phenomenology*, 463 (§765); Schlitt, *Hegel's Trinitarian Claim*, 202–203 asserts that Hegel showed a higher regard for representation in the lectures on the philosophy of religion than in the *Phenomenology of Spirit*.

representational – three heavenly beings with the familial relation of father and son. What was required, Hegel believed, was to raise the content of the doctrine from its representational form to a conceptual form so that its universal truth would be evident.

Hegel's daunting challenge was to overcome the limitations of representation. With respect to the Trinity, these included the following: (1) Whereas conceptual comprehension manages to hold seeming opposites in a unity, in representation the mind fails to see the unity. Thus in the doctrine of the Trinity representation takes the logical components of this doctrine and portrays them as separate beings.[15] In truth, Hegel held, the doctrine of the Trinity is about the logical dynamics of the idea of God but representation portrays the Trinity as three heavenly beings. (2) Whereas conceptual comprehension grasps the necessity of truth, i.e., it sees why God is a Trinity, representation fails to see the necessity. Its knowledge of God as Trinity is based on authority (e.g., church teaching), but not on thinking through to the truth itself.[16] (3) Whereas conceptual comprehension grasps the truth in pure concepts (which is the way appropriate to knowing the truth), representation portrays speculative truth in picture images. It portrays the Trinity by means of the natural relations between father and son and employs such natural terms as generation.[17] In general, the problem that Hegel found with representation is that it is insufficient for attaining truth. Attaining truth, he believed, depended on seeing the unity of apparent opposites. Representation, however, holds things apart: not only the persons of the Trinity as separate beings, but also God and the world. It represents God as an entity separate from the world and beyond human thought. Consequently, there is, in Hegel's judgment, a paradoxical character to the Christian faith: in faith and feeling separation from God is overcome; contrariwise, in representational thinking God is portrayed as separate and other. Hegel's goal of philosophical comprehension aimed at retrieving the truth of faith and feeling and transcending the limitations of representation.[18]

---

[15] *Hegel's Philosophy of Mind*, 299 (*Encyclopedia*, §565).   [16] Hegel, *Phenomenology*, 465 (§771).
[17] Ibid., 465–466 (§771).   [18] Ibid., 477 (§787).

THE NATURE OF CONCEPTUAL COMPREHENSION:
THE *BEGRIFF*

Having shown the weaknesses of representation, it is necessary to examine what Hegel intended to replace it with – conceptual comprehension. Hegel's advocacy of conceptual comprehension is his response to Kant's philosophy in particular and to the philosophy of the Enlightenment in general. This is because representation is a function of the understanding (*Verstand*). When we think according to the understanding, we think by means of the categories whose functions and limitations Kant had described. However, it is just that sort of thinking that is incapable of conceptually grasping the truth, for the faculty of understanding lacks the required suppleness and fluidity that would enable comprehension of the logical dynamics of the Trinity. In other words, the understanding operates statically. As a substitute for the understanding, Hegel proposed reason (*Vernunft*) as the instrument of comprehension. We can see, then, that Hegel's critique of religious doctrines was based, not on an opposition of faith to reason, but on the opposition of understanding to reason. Doctrines fall into one-sided error only when they are expounded by means of representational thinking that employs the understanding.

Not surprisingly, Hegel's critique of Kant is identical to his critique of representation: Kant's philosophy of finite understanding, instead of connecting us with reality, separates us from reality by erecting a barrier between the concepts by which we think and the things about which we think (the "things in themselves"). Thought does not get beyond the thinking subject and the object remains something external to thought.[19] The problem with the understanding is that it is an "abstracting and separating intelligence which clings tenaciously to the separations which it has made." Kant held the forms of thought (i.e., concepts) to be merely subjective and empty of content.[20] Kant could locate only one source of content for thought – sense perception. In his judgment, reason alone, without sense perception, "can spin nothing but idle

---

[19] Georg Wilhelm Friedrich Hegel, *Hegel's Science of Logic*, trs. W. H. Johnson and L. G. Struthers, 2 vols. (London: G. Allen & Unwin, Ltd., 1951), I:55.

[20] Ibid., I:58 and I:61–62.

fancies."[21] Accordingly, Kant believed that conceptual thought about God is impossible because the concepts of the understanding are merely subjective and do not really apprehend entities themselves.[22] Hence, for Kant, the doctrine of the Trinity is either a mistake (if it is thought to depict God) or an encoded way of referring to our moral relation to God. Most odious to the understanding are the contradictions in the doctrine of God and the divine attributes, contradictions that the understanding undertakes to resolve on its own. Hegel, however, believed that the idea of God (whose ecclesiastical form is the doctrine of the Trinity) "is itself the resolution of the contradictions posited by it." The idea of God, with its Trinitarian, dialectical form, *is* the setting forth of contradictions and their resolution. Reason, which achieves conceptual comprehension of this setting forth and resolution, is therefore the proper thought about God.[23]

Reason is marked by dialectical thinking, which Hegel believed to be the true method of all knowledge, including the knowledge of God. Dialectical thinking is the true method because each entity, including God, is a unity of opposites and so possesses a dialectical movement. The key to grasping Hegel's view of dialectic is the notion of negation, which is not annihilation, but "definite negation," the negation of particular content. An example is the process of life from seed to plant. The plant in its immediate (i.e., undeveloped) form is the seed. However, in order to become an actual plant the seed must be "negated," i.e., the form of the seed must set itself aside by producing something that it itself is not – the developed plant. That is the meaning of negation: the development of something different from the original and immediate state. The result of this negation is "a new concept, but a higher, richer concept than that which preceded," enriched by the negation: the actual plant is the unity of the seed and its negation.[24] Unlike reflective understanding, which treats such forms as fixed determinations and mentally holds them apart, dialectical reasoning holds them together in organic unity.[25] Reason is therefore a relating activity whereby separate forms are transcended and

[21] Ibid., 1:56.   [22] Kant, *Critique of Pure Reason*, B352–B353 ("Transcendental Illusion").
[23] Hegel, *Lectures*, III:278 (1827 lectures).   [24] Hegel, *Logic*, I:64–65.
[25] Ibid., I:58.

related. For Hegel, the contradictions of forms constitute the nature of what is self-existent. To be real is to partake of the dialectical movement of life, whereby immediacy produces negation, resulting in the unity of opposites. This movement is "the principle of all physical and spiritual life."[26]

How does dialectical thinking apply to the Trinity? Hitherto we have seen Hegel's desire (1) to criticize the form of religious representations while (2) preserving their content in an appropriate form. This twofold aim was based on the premises that (1) religion is the knowledge of truth and (2) the truth is not adequately conceived in religion. The questions are, what is the truth of the doctrine of the Trinity and what is the appropriate manner of conceiving it?

QUESTIONS OF METHOD

Before proceeding any farther, however, certain questions of method arise, partly because of the various possible ways of interpreting Hegel and partly from the perplexities of his philosophical system. One issue pertains to the structure of Hegel's philosophical system. The system (as set forth in the *Encyclopedia*) has three main parts: logic, philosophy of nature and philosophy of spirit. The first part, logic, culminates in a discussion of the absolute idea. The third part of the system consists in three parts: subjective spirit (roughly equivalent to psychology); objective spirit (law, conscience and social ethics); and absolute spirit. In turn, absolute spirit is composed of three divisions: art, revealed religion and philosophy. In a further exposition, Hegel offered lectures on the philosophy of religion which, predictably, have a threefold structure: the concept of religion, determinate religion (religions other than Christianity) and revelatory religion (Christianity), which corresponds to the "revealed religion" of absolute spirit. As can be seen, the third part of the system, philosophy of spirit, has for its climax absolute spirit. The question here is, what is the relation of Hegel's logic to the rest of his system, in particular to the philosophy of spirit? What is the relation of the absolute idea to absolute spirit? The importance of

---

[26] Ibid., I:67.

this question for understanding Hegel's doctrine of the Trinity is that he discussed the Trinity at length only in the works portraying the philosophy of spirit: *Phenomenology of Spirit, Encyclopedia,* and *Lectures on the Philosophy of Religion.* What is the core of Hegel's philosophy – logic or the philosophy of spirit? If the former, then his discussion of the Trinity could be interpreted as nothing more than a concession to the orthodox theology of his day and as an ancillary aspect of his interests. If logic is the core of Hegel's philosophy, then he is best understood as providing a doctrine of ontological categories and as having only peripheral interest in the spheres of reality in which these categories are instantiated. That is, Hegel in this view would not be considered a metaphysical thinker.[27] The answers to these questions determine how seriously we should take Hegel's talk about God, whether such talk is central to his system or is merely an attempt at sounding orthodox.[28]

Hegel's books and lectures frequently discuss God. He did not hesitate to take the theology of his day to task for the inadequacy and even heterodoxy of its views. However, what are we to make of this talk about God? Although Hegel's developed views of God occur in the books and lectures on the philosophy of spirit, there is a statement in the *Science of Logic* that has drawn the attention of expositors: Logic "shows forth God as he is in his eternal essence before the creation of Nature and of a Finite Spirit."[29] The view that I adopt is that "God" is the word used in religion for that which in philosophy is known as absolute spirit. Absolute spirit is the totality that includes logic and the finite world (nature and finite spirit). That is, God is that inclusive totality that comprises all that

---

[27] For an exposition of this view see Klaus Hartmann, "Hegel: A Non-Metaphysical View," in Alasdair MacIntyre, ed., *Hegel: A Collection of Critical Essays,* Modern Studies in Philosophy (New York: Doubleday & Co., Anchor Books, 1972), 101–124. For critical comments on this approach see Thomas E. Wartenberg, "Hegel's Idealism: The Logic of Conceptuality," in Frederick C. Beiser, ed., *The Cambridge Companion to Hegel,* Cambridge Companions to Philosophy (Cambridge: Cambridge University Press, 1993), 121–124.

[28] That religious interests were close to Hegel's concern can be seen from his letter to August Tholuck in *Hegel: The Letters,* trs. C. Butler and C. Seiler (Bloomington, IN: Indiana University Press, 1984), 250 and Lawrence S. Stepelevich, "Hegel and Roman Catholicism," *Journal of the American Academy of Religion* 60/4 (1992): 673–691.

[29] Hegel, *Logic,* I:60. For a further exposition of this interpretation, see Merklinger, *Philosophy,* 152–153 and Dale Schlitt, "The Whole Truth: Hegel's Reconceptualization of Trinity," *The Owl of Minerva* 15 (1984): 175–179.

is: the world of matter and the forms of thought – not independently of each other, but their unity. In this interpretation, logic represents, not the core of Hegel's system, but the form of dialectical thinking that is required to grasp the true form of reality. The doctrine of the Trinity, therefore, is not ancillary to Hegel's purposes, but is in fact the apex of the system, for only here is there a final reconciliation of thought (logic) and being (nature and spirit).

Does this make Hegel a metaphysical thinker? Not if metaphysics means a philosophical account of an entity that is independent of the finite world. It is clear that, in Hegel's system, God is not a being or a particular self-conscious personality. God is not actual apart from the world. Yet we cannot deny Hegel's metaphysical interests. He was concerned with concrete existence and with finding the best means of comprehending it. Therefore, we should not drive a wedge between the *Logic* and the rest of the system, as though Hegel were concerned only or mainly with the logical forms of thought in their abstract character. "God" is an essential part of the Hegelian system because "God" designates absolute spirit. While the *term* "God" may be dispensable, the system is incomplete without the *concept* of absolute spirit. In conclusion: when allowances are made for the distinction between representation and conceptual knowledge, we should take what Hegel says about God at face value. Accordingly, the doctrine of the Trinity is the culmination of the Hegelian system. Of course, this is not to claim that Hegel's doctrine is orthodox – that is another matter.

Another issue of method is the fact that most of Hegel's discussion of the Trinity is contained in lectures, not in published books. An indication is needed of how reliably these lecture notes express his convictions.[30] As a matter of fact, there is every reason to believe that the lecture notes are highly reliable. Hegel lectured on the philosophy of religion four times: 1821, 1824, 1827 and 1831. Hegel's own manuscript, used for the 1821 series of lectures, is available.[31] Student transcripts are available for the 1824 and 1827 series and for part of the 1831 series. Further, Hegel used a student transcript of the 1824 lectures in preparation for his 1827 lectures,

---

[30] For a statement as to the principles used in the recent edition of the Lectures, see Hegel, *Lectures*, I:8– 52.   [31] Ibid., I:9–12.

indicating a degree of approval for that student transcript.[32] These facts allow confidence not only in the general tendency of Hegel's Trinitarian thought but also in the subtle changes that characterize the transition from one lecture series to another.[33] As a point of method, then, I adopt the following principle: In discussing Hegel's doctrine of the Trinity, exposition will begin with the *Phenomenology* and the *Encyclopedia*, and then proceed to the lectures – first to the manuscript, then to the notes. In this way, the undisputed writings can function as a control over the use of the lecture manuscript and transcripts.

THE IDEA OF REVELATION

Hegel's doctrine of the Trinity may be approached from many directions. One convenient direction is the idea of revelation. The idea of revelation is an appropriate way of understanding Hegel's doctrine of the Trinity for two reasons. First, Hegel used it to justify his confidence in our ability to come to the knowledge of God; second, he regarded it as the special mode of being of spirit, a concept that informs his understanding of the Trinity.

As to the first point: Hegel asserted that God is revelatory because God is not envious, a view that Hegel drew from Plato and Aristotle. As a result, as we have seen, Hegel argued against those of his contemporaries who declared God to be unknowable; on the contrary, he affirmed, God is eminently knowable.[34] It is for this reason that Christianity is the revelatory and consummate religion: in it God is known for what God is.[35] But if we ask why God is revelatory, the answer is the second point mentioned above: God is spirit and therefore revelatory, intrinsically knowable and in fact truly known. It is essential to spirit that it be revelatory. But this does not mean that spirit reveals something; instead its mode of being is to reveal itself.[36] For these reasons, the Trinity is, according to Hegel, neither a mystery nor a secret in itself. It is mysterious to the reflective understanding, but only because this latter,

---

[32] Ibid., I:15–16.

[33] Jaeschke, *Reason in Religion*, 292–297 and Hodgson, "Hegel's Christology," 23–40.

[34] *Hegel's Philosophy of Mind*, 298 (*Encyclopedia*, §564).

[35] *Hegel's Philosophy of Mind*, 298–299 and Hegel, *Lectures*, III:63–64 (lecture manuscript).

[36] *Hegel's Philosophy of Mind*, 164 (*Encyclopedia*, §383).

adhering to hard and fast categories, is unable to grasp the movement that is spirit and revelation. Understanding regards the moments of this movement as contradictory to one another, so that doctrines such as the Trinity (with its dialectic of identity and difference) are inconceivable.[37]

Granted that revelation is a way of approaching Hegel's concepts of spirit and of the Trinity, what does revelation say about them? Hegel usually associates revelation with the terms "universality" and "particularity." In customary use, these terms are contraries; they exclude each other, for nothing can be both universal and particular in the same respect. Even in the history of philosophy they have been separated into different realms of being, a universal being defined as what can be predicated of many things, a particular being an individual entity. Hegel, while allowing them to be contraries, did not regard them as mutually exclusive. More exactly, he believed that through dialectical thinking it could be seen that each implies the other, that there is a logical movement from one to the other. In particular, Hegel's position was that anything universal would, like all moving things, generate something different from itself, its own other. This other of the universal is the particular. According to Hegel, this self-particularizing of the universal, this self-negation and differentiation, is revelation.[38]

This understanding of revelation will most likely strike the reader as unlikely, to say the least. Nothing in abstract concepts like universality and particularity, or even in the dialectical movement whereby universality gives rise to particularity, seems remotely connected to customary notions of revelation. However, the matter becomes more clear once we see that Hegel identified this particularizing of universality in the first place with something routinely regarded as revelation: the natural world.[39] Of course, Hegel did not think of the natural world as revealing something about God, as though from it we could gather a list of predicates to ascribe to God (e.g., intelligence, power). Instead, he held that the world is a moment in God's life, the moment of particularity. To

[37] *Hegel's Philosophy of Mind*, 304 (*Encyclopedia*, §573) and Hegel, *Lectures*, III:281–283 (1827 lectures).   [38] *Hegel's Philosophy of Mind*, 163 (*Encyclopedia*, §383).

[39] *Hegel's Philosophy of Mind*, 164 (*Encyclopedia*, §384).

say it is a revelation of God is to say that it is God's self-revelation, the result of God passing over from universality to particularity. Revelation, in this sense, is equivalent to creation: what religious language calls the act of creation is in philosophical concepts known as God's self-othering, self-negating and self-differentiation.

There is another application of "revelation" and that is to Jesus Christ. In Jesus Christ, God is revealed because in this man God has again passed out of universality and entered the sphere of particular being. The example of Jesus Christ makes clear that Hegel understood revelation to be a matter of appearance. God's transition from universality to particularity is not merely some logical transition; it is also becoming present for our sensuous awareness – appearing.[40] Revelation thus points to two modes or elements of God's being: universality, in which God is an object of thought, and particularity, in which God is an object of sensuous perception. As with the case of nature, we again have the dialectical movement of the concept (universality that particularizes itself).

But why should this movement, whether understood as creation and Jesus Christ (in religious terms) or as differentiation and negation (in philosophical terms), be identified with revelation? The answer is that Hegel employed the religious term "revelation" to denote the dialectical passage from universality to particularity and the return from sheer particularity to concrete universality, i.e. individuality. This movement, Hegel believed, is what the word "God" refers to and what the doctrine of the Trinity represents. So, when religious people misleadingly affirm that God creates something that is different from God or appears as a particular being, then implicitly God is truly known, for God is the religious name for the process of setting forth something different and then overcoming the difference. As a result, the religion that represents God as setting forth something other than God and then overcoming this difference is the religion of revelation – here God is truly known for what God is, even if the religious community employs natural and other inappropriate language to represent this truth.[41]

I have appealed to the idea of revelation as a means of getting some orientation to Hegel's doctrine of the Trinity. As we have

---

[40] Hegel, *Phenomenology*, 461 (§§761–762).   [41] Hegel, *Lectures*, III:190 (1824 lectures).

seen, revelation refers to the self-particularizing of universality, a movement that is identical with God's life. However, another step is required to see why this movement implies that God is a Trinity. To say that God's life is structured according to the dialectic of universality and particularity means that God's life develops according to what Hegel called the concept (*Begriff*). More precisely, God's life *is* the concept. According to Hegel's logic, the three moments of the concept are universality, particularity and individuality.[42] It is because of the specific nature of the concept that the Trinitarian names are applied to God.

At this point, however, it is necessary to call attention to a distinction of importance both to Hegel's philosophy and to Christian theology. The distinction is between the Trinity in its eternal being and in its historical manifestation. The former is sometimes called the ontological or immanent Trinity; the latter is usually referred to as the economic Trinity. Clarifying the relation of the ontological and economic Trinities has been the subject of considerable discussion among theologians and, as we shall see, constitutes one of the fundamental points of debate in twentieth-century Trinitarian discussion. Hegel had a distinctive contribution to make to this discussion, so that close attention to his use of terms will prove instructive. In the *Phenomenology of Spirit* and the *Encyclopedia*, Hegel did not use "Trinity," although he did refer to "Father," "Son" and "Holy Spirit." In the manuscript for the lectures on the philosophy of religion, Hegel referred to the triune God and meant by it the ontological Trinity.[43] Hegel did not use "Trinity" with reference to the economic Trinity of history, preferring to speak of God or spirit becoming actualized (another technical Hegelian term, to be discussed later). Symptomatic of this reluctance to use "Trinity" to denote the economic Trinity is the fact that he normally did not refer to Jesus as Son,[44] reserving "Son" for the entire sphere of particularity, embracing the world of nature and finite spirits.[45] In conclusion, "Trinity" meant for

---

[42] Hegel, *Logic*, II:234. See also *Hegel's Philosophy of Mind*, 299–300 (*Encyclopedia*, §§567–569).
[43] Hegel, *Lectures*, III:77–78 and III:83.   [44] Jaeschke, *Reason in Religion*, 315–316.
[45] This becomes especially clear in the 1831 series of lectures, in which he used as a structuring device the kingdoms of the Father, Son and Spirit to denote the idea of God in its universality, in the sphere of finite reality, and in the Christian community.

Hegel the ontological Trinity of eternity. However, we would receive a distorted picture if an exposition of Hegel's doctrine of the Trinity were to confine itself to those few and brief texts in which he explicitly discussed this ontological Trinity. It is characteristic of Hegel's method to be suspicious of distinctions such as that between the ontological and economic Trinities and in fact his doctrine of the Trinity cannot be understood apart from seeing how the economic Trinity of history finds its pattern in and is the actualization of the ontological Trinity of eternity.

THE ONTOLOGICAL TRINITY OF ETERNITY: THE IDEA OF GOD IN THE ELEMENT OF THOUGHT

As mentioned above, Hegel analyzed God and revelation with the logic of the concept: universality, particularity and individuality. These represent the three elements or modes of God's "being."[46] Corresponding to these three elements are states of subjective consciousness by which the human mind relates to God: thought (corresponding to universality), representation (more accurately, "sensible perception," corresponding to particularity) and subjectivity (corresponding to individuality).[47] In the element of universality, God is the eternal idea of God in and for itself, an object of thought. In the element of particularity, God appears in (more accurately, as) the world of nature and finite spirit, culminating in Jesus Christ. Here God is available to sensuous perception. Finally, in the element of individuality, God is represented as the Holy Spirit, the Christian community's reconciled union with God. In this element God is known through the subjectivity of faith, which encompasses both the feeling of oneness with God and the authentic (if not philosophically adequate) knowledge of God. These three together, the idea, finite reality, and the reconciled community, constitute absolute spirit, which is Hegel's term for what is ultimately real.

---

[46] It is necessary to use quotation marks with "being" because, as was discussed above, God is not, according to Hegel, a being. What precisely God is will be discussed later in the chapter.

[47] The clearest expositions of these states of subjective consciousness are found in the 1824 and 1827 lectures. Hegel, *Lectures*, III:187 and III:271–273.

Where does the ontological Trinity of eternity fit into this scheme? "Trinity" denotes God in the element of universality, known in thought.[48] But what *is* this Trinity? The first thing to note is that spirit in the element of universality is an abstraction; the Trinity does not denote the full actuality of spirit,[49] for spirit becomes actual only following the particularity of nature and finite spirit, and after finite spirit has experienced alienation and reconciliation. In other words, spirit becomes actual only in the element of individuality. So the Trinity is not to be thought of as an actual being, to say nothing of three actual divine beings. Rather, we may say that in the element of universality, thought's object is the idea of God, an idea that is the epitome of dialectical movement. "Trinity" therefore is the religious version of what philosophers know as the logical form of spirit, a form that is the subject matter of logic. Accordingly, "Trinity" is not "God" in the usual religious sense of the term or even in Hegel's idiosyncratic sense. It does not refer to a heavenly being; it is not actual spirit. It is, when properly understood, one logical moment of actual spirit, namely the concept (or form).

Two questions present themselves: First, why does religious thinking represent God as a Trinity? Second, why did Hegel associate spirit in the element of universality with the ecclesiastical doctrine of the Trinity?

As to the first: Why is the abstract concept of God represented as a Trinity by religious thought? Why does this thought not represent God as a solitary being?[50] The answer is that the doctrine of the Trinity is the representational way of portraying the truth, which consists in the dialectical movement of differentiation and reconciliation.[51] Of course, religious thought represents this truth in forms that are wholly inadequate to the truth, forms such as three personal divine beings. Nevertheless, the truth lies ensconced

---

[48] Hegel, *Phenomenology*, 466–467 (§772); *Hegel's Philosophy of Mind*, 299–230 (*Encyclopedia*, §567).

[49] Hegel, *Phenomenology*, 465 (§769); Hegel, *Lectures*, III:275; and Schlitt, *Hegel's Trinitarian Claim*, 12.

[50] Recall that in this chapter "religion" refers to Christianity. Although Hegel had, for his day, quite a rich view of the religions of the world and was interested in the ways in which various religions represented God as a Trinity, for purposes of simplicity only the Christian representation of God is here considered.

[51] Schlitt, *Hegel's Trinitarian Claim*, 72–73.

in these forms and this makes Christianity the religion of revelation. Further, the fact that the doctrine of the Trinity represents the *abstract* concept of God is no prejudice against its truth because even this abstract form is a form of spirit. Since spirit is the process of differentiation and reconciliation in each of its forms, even this abstract concept exhibits this dialectic. In fact, it would be most accurate to state that this concept, of which the Trinity is a religious representation, *is* the dialectical process of differentiation and reconciliation in its most abstract form. So, when orthodox Trinitarian dogmatics states that the Father eternally begets the Son and that (in Roman Catholic and Protestant theologies) the Spirit proceeds from the Father and the Son, Hegel understands these relations of origin to be pictorial ways of expressing the logical dialectics of differentiation and reconciliation. In generation the Father begets the Son (i.e., the first moment of spirit negates itself by producing its own other); yet the Son is God (spirit's other is the negation of spirit, yet it is still spirit); the Holy Spirit proceeds from the Father and the Son as the bond of love that unites them (i.e., spirit's other does not remain simply other; spirit consists in this unity amid distinction, the overcoming of negation and differentiation that does not mean the extinction of difference but instead means retaining difference in the context of reconciled unity). For these reasons, Hegel believed that the doctrine of the Trinity sets forth the movement of spirit and therefore has "a purely speculative content" and the "whole truth"[52] although expressed in representational form.

The second question is why Hegel associated the Christian doctrine of the Trinity with his understanding of the dialectics of the concept. The answer to this has two parts. First, Hegel understood philosophy to be the comprehension of reality by means of precise concepts. Hence, although his system does begin with a logic of legendary density, that logic stands in the service of comprehending the spheres of reality, i.e., nature and spirit. It was part of his method to grasp history and ideas; his first work, *The Phenomenology of Spirit*, is a testimony to that method. For this reason, the history of religion and of religious ideas must form part of his system.

---

[52] Hegel, *Lectures*, III:78–79 (manuscript).

Hegel's system could not tolerate as significant a part of human history as Christian doctrine lying uncomprehended outside his philosophy. Second, if we ask why it was the *Christian* idea of God that Hegel identified as best expressing the truth about spirit, it is difficult to resist the conclusion that his upbringing and presuppositions shaped by training in the Christian intellectual tradition inclined him to develop his philosophy in just the way he did. Certainly, we may point to significant points of similarity between his doctrine of the Trinity and that of the dominant Augustinian-Thomistic tradition in theology. Nevertheless, we should not exaggerate the affinity between Hegel and Christian theology; plenty of critics were at hand then and are present now ready to testify to the fundamentally unChristian, if not anti-Christian, character of his philosophy. In the end, we must judge that as Hegel worked out his philosophical convictions in the light of the cultural and religious situation of his day, he came to identify with the main tenets of Christian theology *as he understood them*, keeping in mind that he believed he understood them better than the theologians did.

Having set forth in a general way the main points of Hegel's speculative interpretation of the Trinity, we turn now to a more detailed examination of the specifics of the ecclesiastical doctrine.[53]

For one thing, Hegel reminded the reader that, although differentiation is found in the idea in the element of universality, such differentiation was to be distinguished from the self-particularizing of the universal as it passes over into nature and finite spirit. The differentiation within the element of universality transpires as and within the process of dialectical thought. Only in the differentiation that results in particularity does finitude come about; only here does the appearance of spirit in finite form occur.[54] The point is that the idea's differentiation in the element of thought is not productive of reality; it remains within the realm

---

[53] Since his most extensive statements on the Trinity are found in the lectures on the philosophy of religion, most of this exposition is taken from those lectures, mainly the first three series (1821, 1824 and 1827) since these are the fullest.

[54] *Hegel's Philosophy of Mind*, 300 (*Encyclopedia*, §568); Hegel, *Lectures*, III:77–78 (manuscript), III:189 (1824), III:275 and 278–280 (1827).

of the ideal and therefore can be characterized as abstract.[55] The particularity that finitude carries is not yet in consideration and the pure universality of the idea remains undisturbed in spite of the differentiation that takes place in this element.[56] It is for these reasons that "Trinity," which is spirit in the form of universality, cannot refer to a being or to anything actual. Although religious thinking attributes actuality to this Trinity and believes God to be this Trinity, in truth, according to Hegel, the real reference of "God" is actual spirit, which presupposes the particularization that constitutes finitude and the reconciliation that constitutes the Christian community.

Hegel was also concerned, in various ways, to enforce the considerable difference between conceptual comprehension and all other forms of understanding the Trinity. Apart from conceptual thought, Hegel believed only faith is an appropriate way of accepting the doctrine. For whereas faith rests content with the "happily naive forms of representation"[57] used in the doctrine, attempts at grasping the doctrine by means of the understanding were sure to go wrong. Although Hegel did not wholly approve of these "happily naive forms" and thought that notions such as love are more suited to expound the truth of the doctrine than these forms,[58] at least in faith we accept the doctrine and with it the truth. Attempts at analyzing the doctrine with the hopelessly inadequate human understanding fixate constantly on the logical conundrums and cannot advance to the truth. It was not that Hegel denied the presence of contradictions in the doctrine; as we have seen, it was the reality of those contradictions that convinced Hegel of the doctrine's truth, for truth, in his opinion, consists in the movement of negation and differentiation, in other words contradiction. What Hegel objected to was any attempt by the human understanding to "remove the contradictions and the determinations that contain the contradiction."[59] Human understanding seeks to do this by

---

[55] Hegel, *Lectures*, III:275 and III:279 (1831).   [56] Ibid., III:191 (1824).

[57] Ibid., III:79 (manuscript).   [58] Ibid., III:194 (1824).

[59] Ibid., III:79 (manuscript). In the 1824 and 1827 lectures, Hegel made the point that the doctrine of the Trinity is indeed a secret and a mystery, but only for the understanding and thinking rooted in sensation. It is neither a secret nor a mystery for conceptual comprehension and for faith; in both God is truly known. See III:192 (1824) and 280–283 (1827).

portraying God as a unitary being, thus removing the internal distinctions that constitute the Trinity. The problem with this maneuver, according to Hegel, is that this unitary God, void of all internal distinctions, is only another sort of abstraction, for it depicts God as standing over against the world as a solitary being with only an external relation to the world. In other words, this unitary vision of God is as one-sided as the idea of God in the element of thought, but suffers the additional absence of internal differentiation, so that it does not even have the shape of spirit. Again, Hegel had no objection to contradictions; however, truth demands that spirit itself (in this case, the idea in the element of universality) both set forth and overcome the contradiction. Hegel found this in the ecclesiastical doctrine of the Trinity and not in the view of God proposed by human understanding.

There were, in particular, two "awkward factors" arising from analyzing the doctrine by means of the understanding: the application of number to the Trinity and the use of the concept of personality.[60]

Concerning the use of number, "That three times one is only one appears to be the harshest and . . . the most irrational demand." The problem here, Hegel suggested, lies in a misunderstanding of the concept of number. For the understanding, the number one signifies "absolute separation and splintering."[61] That is, as is so often the case with the understanding, the number one is taken to mean exclusivity. We have already seen this with the understanding's view of God: God is one and is therefore separate and enclosed. Hegel's response was to point out his own view of number (expounded more fully in the *Science of Logic*), according to which the number one is "dialectical in itself and not something autonomous." That is, the concept of the number one, like the concept of God, cannot be rightly thought without thinking of another concept that negates it. As a backup argument, Hegel adduced the example of matter which, although numerically one, negates this oneness by its gravitational attraction of *others*. Even the concept of matter cannot be thought without passing over into its negation.[62] What we observe here is Hegel's constant attempt at

[60] Ibid., III:81 (manuscript).   [61] Ibid.
[62] Ibid., III:82. See also III:192–193 (1824) and III:284–285 (1827).

overcoming the theology of the Enlightenment, especially its incapacity to reason correctly and the resulting deficiencies in its doctrine of God.

Concerning the application of the notion of personality in the doctrine, Hegel's task was compounded by the fact that it was the ecclesiastical doctrine itself that employs this term. On the one hand, the use of "person" points to differentiation in the idea – the Trinitarian persons are not the same; they differ from one another. Hence we can see here an aspect of dialectical movement. On the other hand, as the Trinitarian persons are absolutized, as he believed they often are in representational thought, the result is three separate Gods. In this case the dialectical relations of the idea are destroyed by the separateness and absoluteness of the persons. How to conceive the three persons as one seems to be "the most stark contradiction."[63]

The resolution of this contradiction Hegel found in the concept of love, which he identified with the concept of spirit and which he defined as "intuition of oneself in another.[64] The point is that love embraces two aspects simultaneously: unity and difference. In order for love to occur, there must be a beloved who differs from the lover. Even in self-love we can recognize a distinction between the self as subject of love and the self as object of love. And yet, love is not only difference, for the lover's identity is found in union with the beloved. Hegel called this a "being-outside-ourselves." The lover would not be the lover without the beloved and the beloved would not be the beloved without the lover. So, the difference between lover and beloved includes a unity.[65] (We may note parenthetically the similarities and differences of this analysis to the Thomistic-Augustinian-Leibnizian view of the Trinity. In the latter, when love is used as the main vehicle of analysis, mention is always made of love itself as the third. Going back to Augustine, it was customary to identify the Holy Spirit with love because love is what binds lover and beloved, just as the Spirit, as the love that proceeds from Father and Son, binds them together. In Hegel's discussion of love and its Trinitarian implications, the

---

[63] Ibid., III:82 (manuscript).   [64] Ibid., III:83 and III:78 (manuscript).
[65] Ibid., III:193–194 (1824) and III:276 (1827).

role of the Spirit is muted, perhaps because dialectical thinking is inherently a matter of original unity, differentiation through negation, and overcoming of differentiation in an enriched unity. That is, whereas early Christian thought had to labor to find a place for the Holy Spirit in its conceptions, Hegel's dialectic lends itself to advancing beyond the duality of lover and beloved to their unity. Nevertheless, some interpreters have wondered whether Hegel's Trinity is really a bi-nity, i.e. composed of two moments or persons, not three.[66] Hegel's inference was that the Trinitarian persons are neither completely insubstantial nor absolute, separate personalities. Indeed, "Love [consists] in giving up one's personality, all that is one's own . . . [It is] the supreme surrender [of oneself] in the other."[67] The concept of love implies that the Trinitarian persons cannot be absolute and separate. Instead, each has its being only in the other; the Trinity exhibits the same unity-in-difference that love and other spiritual relations do.[68] The persons are real in the sense that the idea of God in the element of universality truly is self-differentiating and not a mere unit. However, they are not actual beings.

Having settled accounts with attempts at grasping the Trinity through the understanding, Hegel engaged anticipations of the Trinity in other religions. While granting that other religions possess gods in triads, Hegel was quick to point out that such triads do not constitute in these religions "the first, absolute determination, which lies at the basis of everything." Instead, they were merely parts of the beliefs of these religions, with no constitutive significance. In Hegel's judgment, "the ancients [did] not know what they possessed in these forms."[69] However, the main problem with all pre- and non-Christian triadic conceptions of God is their failure to perceive that the first principle (which corresponds to the Father in the Trinity and to the idea in the element of universality

---

[66] Jörg Splett, *Die Trinitätslehre G. W. F. Hegels*, Symposion: Philosophische Schriftenreihe, ed. Max Müller, et al., no. 20 (Freiburg: Verlag Karl Alber, 1965), 145. Responses to this charge are given by Jaeschke, *Reason in Religion*, 308 and Herbert Huber, *Idealismus und Trinität, Pantheon und Götterdämmerung: Grundlagen und Grundzüge der Lehre von Gott nach dem manuskript Hegels zur Religionsphilosophie* (Weinheim: Acta Humaniora, 1984), 100–103.

[67] Hegel, *Lectures*, III:125 (manuscript).

[68] Schlitt, "The Whole Truth," 179 and Huber, *Idealismus*, 97–98.

[69] Hegel, *Lectures*, III:80–81 (manuscript).

in Hegel's system) is no less spirit than the second and third principles. In other words, the first principle is as knowable and dialectically structured as the other principles. Hegel pointed out that many conceptions of God begin with a first principle that is inconceivable and uncommunicative. As examples he adduced speculations like Philo's and the Gnostics'. They then posit a second principle such as wisdom or reason that is the principle of revelation, comprehensibility and creation. Hegel's dispute with these conceptions is that they allowed only the second and not the first principle to be spirit. Only the second can be known; only the second is a principle of movement. This contradicted Hegel's conviction that even the first principle, the idea in the element of universality, contains movement and is therefore fully knowable. In other words, even the idea in the element of universality is spirit – it differentiates itself and then overcomes this differentiation.[70]

THE TRINITY OF HISTORY

Having explored Hegel's views of the so-called ontological Trinity of eternity, the task remains of grasping his thoughts about the Trinity of history. This is an important task, because the idea of God does not attain actuality until the Trinity has unfolded in history. As already noted, this Trinity differs from the ontological Trinity through its incorporation of finitude and the appearance of God in finitude. There is a structural similarity between the two Trinities, for both involve the movement of differentiation, negation and otherness. But the idea of God in the sphere of universality contains only implicitly what is found explicitly in the sphere of particularity.[71] The second moment, that of particularity, involves, not a differentiation that remains within the immediate unity of the idea, but instead a differentiation that brings about being that is in some sense external to and estranged from the idea in its eternal unity. Differentiation and negation must, in Hegel's view, be fully played out if spirit is to be actualized. This full playing out involves a great deal more than the merely internal differentiation of the idea in the element of universality. Consequently, the element of

---

[70] Ibid., III:83–86 (manuscript) and III:195–197 (1824).
[71] Ibid., III:86–87 (manuscript).

appearance and representation and the element of individuality and subjectivity are essential to understanding the Trinity for they are essential to the idea. The idea of God includes the finitude of particularity and its reconciliation with the universal.

However, this talk of particularity and finitude being essential to the universal and infinite sounded to religiously orthodox ears like pantheism.[72] Hegel's theology appeared pantheistic to many in his day, first, because in his system the world of nature and finite spiritual beings is a part of the divine life, and, second, because according to the Hegelian system God is not actual apart from the historical process that includes the world of nature and finite spirits. In particular, there was a chronic complaint against idealists of all sorts that they identified God the Son with the world (i.e., the element of particularity) in a pantheistic sense. Now Christian thought has always recognized a close connection between the second person of the Trinity and the world. This recognition goes back to the New Testament, in which the eternal Word (in the Fourth Gospel), the pre-existent Christ (in the Pauline letters) and the Son (in the Letter to the Hebrews) is named the agent of creation, the being through whom God creates and who in some sense is the purpose and goal of creation. Still, the closest theology ever came to identifying this pre-existent being with the world was Arian theology, in which the pre-existent Christ was identified, not with the world as such, but with a particular creature. Although Christian theology recognizes the similarity between the begetting of the Son and the creation of the world, it still draws a rather firm distinction between God and the world. Doctrines such as providence are intended to show that God is not cut off from the world; however, there is no denying that Christian theology understands the world *not* to be identical with either God or a part of God.

What Hegel was attempting to do was make the world part of God's life while still maintaining a distinction between this life in its finite manifestation and that life in its eternal form, before the world so to speak. The difficulty was that Hegel's understanding of the dialectical process means that this divine life is not actual apart from the finite world. This in turn means, as we saw previously, that

---

[72] See Jaeschke, *Reason in Religion*, 312–314 for a discussion of the issues.

in some sense the eternal form of the divine life is abstract and one-sided. When Hegel added that the dialectical movement, including the self-particularizing of the universal in the finite world, is a matter of logical necessity, then the theologically conservative among his hearers were made anxious, fearful that God's freedom was compromised in the Hegelian system.

In response to the charge of pantheism, Hegel's *Encyclopedia* contained, in the final section on philosophy, an extended explication of pantheism. First, he took the moral high road, by declaring philosophy (i.e., his own) to have a better grip on God than the "new" theology and piety and by equating the new piety with the Enlightenment rationalism that Hegel despised – both being vacuous.[73] Next he analyzed the concept of pantheism and proclaimed that it must mean the belief that finite things as such are God pure and simple. Hegel, of course, had no difficulty in showing not only that his own philosophy was not guilty of this charge but that in fact no one had ever subscribed to such an absurdity.[74] Whether such a straw-man argument convinced anyone is an open question.

The main issue is the adequacy of Hegel's conception of the Trinity and God's relation to the world. The place to begin is Hegel's understanding of the term "Son." On the one hand, in the 1831 lectures on the philosophy of religion, Hegel adopted a Trinitarian outline for the idea as represented in religious thinking: the kingdoms of the Father (universality), the Son (particularity) and the Spirit (individuality).[75] This connects "Son" clearly with the realm of finitude. On the other hand, as early as the 1821 lectures, he distinguished the eternal Son from the temporal Son and emphasized the distinction because "the false interpretation may arise . . . to the effect that the eternal Son of the Father . . . is *the same as* the physical and spiritual world."[76] So, "Son" denotes the moment of differentiation, first in the element of universality (where the unity of the idea is unbroken), then in the element of particularity and finitude (where real other-being occurs).

---

[73] *Hegel's Philosophy of Mind*, 305 (*Encyclopedia*, §573). See Hegel, *Lectures*, I:159 and III:261–262 for Hegel's opinion that philosophy had in his day superseded theology as the bearer of orthodox theology.

[74] *Hegel's Philosophy of Mind*, 306 (*Encyclopedia*, §573). The exposition of his point on the basis of religious literature in history continues on for seven or eight pages.

[75] Hegel, *Lectures*, III:362.   [76] Ibid., III:87.

But then how does "Son" in this latter sense relate to Jesus Christ? The answer to this question falls under the discussion of Hegel's Christology, a highly complex and highly controversial subject. All that can be accomplished in this chapter is a brief review of the main points.

Having interpreted the Biblical story of the Fall according to the idea of differentiation,[77] Hegel established and described the human condition of estrangement from God. It is this separation, characteristic of the second moment of particularity, that must be overcome in the third moment of individuality, represented religiously by "Holy Spirit." However, in this history of particularization and estrangement, Jesus Christ has special status. He is the culmination and furthest extent of estrangement and separation and he is also the beginning of individuality and reconciliation.

Hegel's Christology, then, begins with the moment of particularity, in which the idea of God is known by us in the form of representation, which here means sense perception. Here the idea of God appears to us in sensuous form – Jesus Christ. What exactly is it that appears in Jesus? It is the unity of divinity and humanity. As we are conscious of this unity, we grasp the truth that the divine idea is our own substantial nature – not that we are God in a crudely pantheistic sense, but that our true humanity lies in being united with God.[78] This is Hegel's ultimate answer to the charge of pantheism: it is not that the finite world as such is God; the finite world considered in its finitude is an abstraction – it lacks actuality in the same sense in which matter, according to the ancient Greek philosophers, lacks actuality apart from form. What is actual is not the world as such, either in whole or in part, but the world in its union with the idea of God. The unity of the divine and the human that is found in Jesus is implicitly or potentially true of all finite spirits, but not in a naturalistic way. It is not a unity immediately given by virtue of the fact that we are human; instead it is available only in and through Jesus and the Holy Spirit. This incipient unity in Jesus, then, is a signal moment in human history; it marks the implicit overcoming of estrangement and our entering

[77] Ibid., III:90–108 (manuscript).   [78] Ibid., III:109 (manuscript).

the realm of freedom. But it is also a significant moment in the divine life as well, for, as will be discussed later, it is the furthest extent of estrangement within God.

The next issue concerns the necessity for the idea to appear in sensuous form. This necessity lies in the fact that, since knowledge of this unity is the universal destiny of humanity, this knowledge must be available to all humanity in its immediate condition, i.e., without presupposing any philosophical sophistication on its part. In other words, the unity must *appear* to us, not as the object of intellectual cogitation, but as the object of sensuous perception. No other means (short of conceptual comprehension) of communicating this truth to humanity, whether "feelings, representation[s], or rational grounds," would carry with it the certainty that perception of the immediate presence of the unity does.[79]

Immediately, however, a question is raised about this sensuous form: Is it Hegel's contention that Jesus Christ *is* the unity of the divine and the human or that what is crucial is the *belief* that he is the unity? Certain statements in the *Phenomenology of Spirit* suggest the latter view: "That absolute Spirit has given itself *implicitly* the shape of self-consciousness [i.e., in Jesus] . . . this now appears as the *belief of the world* that Spirit is *immediately present* as a self-conscious Being . . . Thus this self-consciousness is not imagination, but is *actual* in the believer."[80] The historical importance of this issue emerged after Hegel's death, when David Friedrich Strauss, in *The Life of Jesus*, proposed that the idea is united with and actualized in, not an individual (Jesus Christ), but the whole of humanity, effectively relegating the doctrine of the incarnation to the status of myth.[81] In contrast to Strauss, Hegel's ultimate view, argued in the lectures on the philosophy of religion, is that the idea must appear in the form of a single, self-conscious individual. The reason for this necessity lies in the nature of the dialectic and its union of opposites. That is, the universal must be united with its most extreme opposite, an entity in the realm of particularity.

---

[79] Ibid., III:110–111 (manuscript).   [80] Hegel, *Phenomenology*, 458 (§758).
[81] David Friedrich Strauss, *The Life of Jesus Critically Examined*, ed. Peter C. Hodgson, trs. George Eliot, Lives of Jesus Series (Philadelphia: Fortress Press, 1972; repr., Ramsey, NJ: Sigler Press, 1994), 779–780 (§151). For an extended discussion of the related philosophical issues see Jaeschke, *Reason in Religion*, pp. 317–324. Chapter four of Jaeschke's book traces the debate about Hegel's philosophy of religion in the first decades after his death.

Further, this entity must be self-conscious (i.e., human), because self-consciousness (which, like love, implies unity and difference) corresponds to the dialectics of the idea (unity amid differentiation and negation).[82] Finally, this self-conscious individual must be unique – the unity must occur only in it; if there were several such individuals, then the divinity with which they would be united would be a generic abstraction that they all shared.[83]

Our question was, "What does "Son" refer to?" In the course of answering that question we were led to discuss Jesus. But we can now see that there is a problem in applying "Son" to Jesus. "Son" denotes the moment of differentiation and, in the sphere of finitude, estrangement. But Jesus, as the unity of divinity and humanity, represents for Hegel the overcoming of difference and estrangement. Hegel's philosophical elucidation of "Son" makes it difficult, within his system, to consider the historical Jesus to be the Son.[84] The enormity of this demerit depends on our view of religious language and the importance of maintaining continuity with the terminology of the Christian tradition. Hegel felt no compunction in this matter, since terms such as "Trinity" and "Son" arise in the sphere of representation which, as noted previously, falls short of the perfect form of truth.

There is, however, one sense in which Jesus does signify differentiation and that is his death. Death is, according to Hegel, the pinnacle of finitude and of negation. The death of Jesus is the idea of God's greatest instance of self-estrangement – the extremity of particularity – and therefore contains within it the death of God.[85] Christ's death is the negation of the immediate presence of divinity.[86] However, this death is also the beginning of reconciliation, for in it there is a unity of absolute extremes – God is here identical with the other-being that has died – and natural finitude (Jesus' immediate existence) is overcome.[87] Here the particularity of the unity dies away and passes over into a universal form – faith in the community of the Spirit.[88] Therefore, the

---

[82] Hegel, *Lectures*, III:113 (manuscript).   [83] Ibid., III:114 (manuscript).
[84] Jaeschke, *Reason in Religion*, 312–316.
[85] Hegel, *Lectures*, III:124–125 (manuscript); Hegel, *Phenomenology*, 476 (§785).
[86] Hegel, *Phenomenology*, 462 (§763).
[87] Hegel, *Lectures*, III:125–127 (manuscript).   [88] Hegel, *Phenomenology*, 475 (§784).

Biblical representations of the resurrection and ascension in fact mean the negation (or overcoming) of death, a double negation.[89] Jesus' death is the negation of the unity – the death of God, the moment of extreme particularity and estrangement; his resurrection and ascension are the negation of that negation, the beginning of reconciliation.

THE SPIRIT: THE IDEA IN THE ELEMENT OF INDIVIDUALITY

However, even though Jesus represents reconciliation, he does so for all humanity only implicitly. Actual reconciliation in a universal form was handled by Hegel under the rubric of the Spirit. Finding the culmination of reconciliation in the Holy Spirit was natural for Hegel for several reasons. First, the Holy Spirit is, of course, spirit *par excellence*, and in Hegel's philosophy spirit is the reconciliation of opposites, whether this is found in self-consciousness, love, or thought. Second, as noted previously, the theological tradition itself understood the Holy Spirit to have a unitive function within the Trinity. The Spirit is the bond of love between Father and Son. Third, it is a persuasive interpretation of the doctrine of the Spirit found in the New Testament. In the Pauline letters, life in the Spirit is contrasted with natural and carnal human life and comprises a degree of freedom unknown in the natural life. According to the Fourth Gospel, the Spirit could not be sent until Jesus ascended to heaven; moreover, the Spirit is understood there as the presence of Jesus in a universal fashion. These representations would appeal to Hegel and support his conception of the Spirit and its relation to Jesus.

Why is there a Holy Spirit? Because spirit must progress on from particularity to concrete universality (which is individuality), from the immediacy of Jesus as the sensuous presence of God to the Spirit as the presence of God for faith. In scriptural terms, this means that Jesus Christ must go away so that the Spirit may come. In Hegelian terms, it means that the moment of particularity, which is the negation (difference, otherness) of universality

---

[89] Hegel, *Lectures*, III:131 (manuscript).

(the idea in itself) is itself negated (in Jesus' death) and thereby sublated[90] into universal self-consciousness (in the faith of the community). Alternately, the universal self-consciousness that is implicit in Jesus Christ becomes explicit in the community's faith.[91] Further, the death of Jesus is not only the death of particularity, it is also the death of "the abstraction of the divine Being," i.e., of the idea of God in the element of thought. That is, in the Holy Spirit, the idea of God has attained actuality; previously it was abstract.[92]

What is the Holy Spirit? First, we must be clear about what the Holy Spirit is not. The Holy Spirit is neither a person nor a being. It is commonly represented as such by the religious consciousness, but philosophy recognizes that ascribing this sort of absoluteness to the Spirit would destroy the unity of the idea of God. In Hegel's words, "Holy Spirit" rendered conceptually is "infinite subjectivity, not represented but actual divinity, the *presence* of God, not the substantial in-itself of the Father or of the Son and of Christ, who is the truth in the shape of objectivity. The Spirit is rather what is subjectively present as the divestment into the objective intuition of love and its infinite anguish."[93] Let us examine each of these aspects in turn.

Infinite subjectivity. The death of Jesus means that the sensible presence of God comes to an end. On the one hand, this is a calamity for religious consciousness, for it arouses the painful feeling that God is dead. This feeling reflects the perceived loss of reality as the visible appearance of God is taken away. On the other hand, with the loss of its object, religious consciousness turns inward. The unity of divinity and humanity that was sensuously present in Jesus becomes subjectively and universally present in the Christian community.[94] This subjectivity is infinite because it is not the finite, one-sided subjectivity of mere feelings or sentiments. Infinity here signifies the regaining of universality. With respect to

---

[90] "Sublate" is the standard, if infelicitous, English translation of *Aufheben*. It pertains especially to the third moment of dialectical movement. It signifies two things: one, the return to the unity that characterized the first moment and, two, the preservation of the difference of the second moment. When the moment of difference is sublated, its one-sided character is overcome and it is reunited with the first moment without thereby being annulled. In this way, the third moment consists in unity amid difference.

[91] Hegel, *Phenomenology*, 473 (§781).   [92] Ibid., 476 (§785).

[93] Hegel, *Lectures*, III:140 (manuscript).   [94] Hegel, *Phenomenology*, 476 (§785).

the full actualizing of spirit, the limitation of Jesus was his individuality. Although in Jesus the universality of the knowledge of the unity of divinity and humanity was implicit, its full actualization requires that each individual know this to be true of himself or herself. Thus the Holy Spirit is the community's knowledge of its union with God, a knowledge that is not limited to a few and is not represented as having occurred only in one.[95]

Not represented but actual divinity. This phrase means that, following the death of Jesus, religious consciousness progressed from the sphere of representation and sensible apprehension of the unity to a universal knowledge of this unity. In Jesus, certainty about the unity arose from its sensuous immediacy: Jesus, the unity itself, was sensibly present. Now, however, certainty is a matter of faith. Faith is certainty of the truth. But this certainty does not rest on rational grounds or experiences or feelings or evidence. It instead derives from the actuality of spirit. In other words, in this sphere the community knows its unity with God in a way that corresponds, although without philosophical form, to the way in which philosophers know the truth in conceptual comprehension. Religiously expressed, this means that God gives the community its faith, that it rests on the witness of the Spirit.[96] It is a conviction that rests, not on external grounds, but on the community's consciousness of its unity with God in the Spirit. More precisely, this conviction *is* the community's consciousness of its unity with God in the Spirit. This consciousness is the actuality of spirit. Here what is religiously referred to as "God" first attains full actuality.

The presence of God, not the substantial in-itself of the Father or of the Son and of Christ, who is the truth in the shape of objectivity. The idea in the elements of universality and particularity, taken alone, are spirit, but only implicitly and potentially, for spirit is the unity of the two. Or, in terms used in the *Phenomenology of Spirit*, prior to the full actuality of spirit in the community of faith, spirit knows God as thought or essence (in the element of universality, represented in religion as the eternal Trinity) and as being or existence (in the realm of particularity, culminating in Jesus Christ). But taken in themselves, i.e., abstractly and apart from each other, these remain

[95] Ibid., 461–462 (§§762–763).　　[96] Hegel, *Lectures*, III:149–150 (manuscript).

one-sided. Only in the full actuality of spirit does God come to be the unity of thought and being, of essence and existence.[97] Of course, this unity does occur in Jesus, but only in an individual and sensuous form. Dialectics demands that this unity attain a universal form. So, the Holy Spirit is actual spirit, spirit having become actual through self-particularization to the point of the death of Jesus and through the overcoming of this particularity in the community of faith.

The Spirit is rather what is subjectively present as the divestment into the objective intuition of love and its infinite anguish. Love is characteristic of the community of faith because love is the concept of spirit itself and the community is the actuality of spirit.[98] But the love Hegel intended is not any sort of romantic or friendly love. It is instead the love that arises out of the infinite anguish of the cross. The cross, as noted previously, is paradoxically the moment of greatest anguish and the moment of greatest love: anguish because here an infinite loss occurs – the death of God; love because this death means the giving up of particularity and its transformation into something higher, a truth represented religiously as the resurrection and ascension of Christ. This transformation is love because it is reconciliation (the negation and overcoming of finitude).[99] In other words, "love" here functions as a code word for the third moment of Hegelian dialectics, for the unification of opposites. In the case of Jesus, this meant the surrender of his life to death; for the community, the ethical meaning of love is the giving up of everything worldly and particular and finite.[100] Specifically, it means holding worthless the values of natural humanity and finding our value only in the subjectivity of faith and the Spirit. External and worldly distinctions of power, position and gender are given up, opening the possibility for a universal justice and for freedom. Friendship and sexual love are subordinated and even sacrificed to this higher love, for they are based on particularity – the attraction of one person for another. The higher love that arises out of infinite anguish grounds a new sort of human relation, one based on an objective content – the Spirit.[101] In religious

[97] Hegel, *Phenomenology*, 461 (§761).   [98] Hegel, *Lectures*, III:140 (manuscript).
[99] Ibid., III:131–132 (manuscript).   [100] Ibid., III:137 (manuscript).
[101] Ibid., III:138–139 (manuscript).

representation, the Holy Spirit is the source of this love; in Hegel's rendition, this love, this overcoming of the particularity of natural humanity and its transformation into universality, *is* spirit in its actuality.

With this, the exposition of Hegel's doctrine of the Trinity is at an end. The only remaining task is to note his final comments on the doctrine in its relation to conceptual comprehension. We have noted that the Trinity is a religious representation of the dialectical movement of universality, particularity and individuality. I have argued that Hegel took the doctrine seriously and believed he was giving a faithful elucidation of its truth. However, Hegel also held that the credal representation of the Trinity is inadequate. The problem is not just that it uses pictorial images such as father and son; it is that the use of these images means that the reconciliation of opposites that is actual spirit is as yet, in the community of faith, incomplete. The unity of divinity and humanity that the Holy Spirit represents for religious consciousness is real and is known to be real in faith; however, religious thought still represents God as a being distinct from the world and the Trinitarian persons as distinct personal beings. Faith has grasped the truth about the unity, but has not grasped it in a form adequate to the truth. In short, the truth is known by faith but not *conceptually* comprehended.[102] This is an important point, for the dialectical method demands the reconciliation of opposites. One set of oppositions is form and content. Since the content of the unity of divinity and humanity is dialectical, the form also should be. But it is only in conceptual comprehension that a truly dialectical form is attained.[103] Only here is there a complete reconciliation between the form of truth and its content. Consequently, only here is spirit actual in the fullest sense.

CONCLUSION

This recitation of German Trinitarian thinking has disclosed three motifs – the Word (revelation), reflective selfhood and history – whose counterpoint shapes the contours of that thinking. What were the contributions of Hegel to this tradition?

---

[102] Hegel, *Phenomenology*, 463 (§765).
[103] *Hegel's Philosophy of Mind*, 303–304 (*Encyclopedia*, §573).

First, we may note that his understanding of revelation was a marked departure from that of the eighteenth century and of the reformers. Although Hegel believed himself to be rendering faithful expositions of Christian Scriptures and creeds, he did not feel himself bound by traditional exegesis or by customary modes of interpretation. His attitude was the result of his conviction that he had captured the overall thrust of the Scriptures and creeds and in fact had done so in a way superior to that of theologians. We may charitably allow that this thought arose out of a meditation on the significance of Scripture and creeds in light of his idealist convictions. But even these convictions were shaped by the larger Christian tradition, which has idealist elements of its own. So, the contribution of the central texts of Christianity to Hegel's doctrine of the Trinity was not inconsiderable. Nevertheless, we are justified in asserting that, for Hegel, the most significant facet of these texts was not their textual authority, i.e., their character of being written documents functioning as authorities for the Christian church. It is instead the fact that Hegel believed he had in these texts rediscovered, with the aid of dialectical thought, the ultimate truth. What of the Melanchthonian understanding of the Word, with its emphasis on salvation and its abhorrence of speculation? It can be safely said that such a concern did not loom large in Hegel's thought. Of course, he was just as opposed as was Melanchthon to *idle* speculation with no relation to the urgent concerns of the Christian life. However, the entire Hegelian philosophy was a protest against the division between God's eternal and inner being and God's revelation, a division of great importance to theologians like Melanchthon.

Second, history played an important role in Hegel's thinking about the Trinity. Unlike theologians such as Reimarus, history for Hegel meant more than a method for discerning the meaning of the Bible and for criticizing traditional doctrines whose putative historical foundation was tenuous or even non-existent. For Hegel, history signified not so much human history as it did divine history – the conviction that the being of God cannot be separated from the historical processes of the world, whether in the realm of nature or in the realm of spirit. As a central conviction, this notion of God's historicity functioned in two ways for Hegel. First, it provided him with a means of understanding the concept of the economic Trinity, that is, the doctrines of Christ and the Holy Spirit, as well as ancillary doctrines such as salvation and the church. Second, it provided a way of understanding the eternal Trinity. In Hegel's thought the eternal life of God was presented as a movement whose historical instantiation brought about the economic Trinity – Jesus Christ and the Holy Spirit. The economic Trinity was for him a moving image of an eternal reality, for this eternal reality possesses a movement that is structurally identical to the historical movement, even if it occurs outside time. History, then, is an important constituent of Hegel's understanding of the Trinity, for he believed that the being of God is essentially historical.

Third, selfhood was a central component of Hegel's view of the Trinity. Drawing on the tradition extending back to Augustine and Thomas and more proximately to Leibniz and Lessing, Hegel represented the doctrine of the Trinity as the exposition of God's subjectivity. Here God is a single subject, an eternal act of self-consciousness or self-reflection. The interior motions of the single divine mind are the direct referents of the doctrine of the Trinity. Accordingly, the category of reflective selfhood constitutes an aspect of Hegel's account of the Trinity that possesses fundamental importance. Further, just as the concept of history underwent significant changes in the transition from deism to idealism, so the concept of the self developed from that of Leibniz and Lessing to that of Hegel, notably in the expressly dialectical structure of selfhood.

Finally, we may ask about the place of Hegel in the history of Trinitarian thought. Although his philosophy proved something of a dead end in philosophy, as evidenced by the astounding reactions against it in the later nineteenth century, Hegelian motifs in Trinitarian thought have survived and have resurfaced in the twentieth century in unexpected ways. First, looking back, it is clear that the fact that there is any contemporary interest in the doctrine of the Trinity at all owes a great deal to Hegel. In spite of such innovative approaches to the Trinity as those of Lessing and Schleiermacher, the doctrine was on the way toward becoming a little-used religious ornament at the beginning of the nineteenth century. This is not to claim that theologians were always happy with the idea of the Trinity that resulted from Hegel's meddling; even at the end of the nineteenth century a great many theologians had simply given up on the doctrine and others were content largely to repeat the traditional doctrine like a litany that has become familiar and tedious. As a result, the twentieth century began as inauspiciously for the doctrine as had the nineteenth. Nevertheless, when it experienced a powerful resuscitation in the theology of Karl Barth, its Hegelian character was unmistakable, if altered. Further, as will appear in the final chapter, the impressively Trinitarian theology of Wolfhart Pannenberg is unthinkable apart from Hegel.

CHAPTER FIVE

Liberal theology

INTRODUCTION

After the outburst of Trinitarian thought, led by Hegel, in the first half of the nineteenth century, Protestant fascination with the doctrine of the Trinity evaporated rather abruptly in the closing decades of the century. Of course, conservative Protestants remained steadfastly loyal to it; however, the rising influence of Albrecht Ritschl and his students bode ill for the doctrine of the Trinity and it was not until Karl Barth's *Church Dogmatics* that a theological system that was sympathetic to the doctrine of the Trinity was able to supplant the influence of liberal theology. In this chapter I will look at the fate that befell the idea of the Trinity at the hands of liberal theologians such as Albrecht Ritschl (1822–1889), Wilhelm Herrmann (1846–1922), Adolf von Harnack (1851–1930) and Ernst Troeltsch (1865–1923). In particular, I will examine Ritschl's own representation of the Trinity and then analyze the reasons for the liberal theologians' lack of enthusiasm about the doctrine.

THE DOCTRINE OF THE TRINITY ACCORDING TO ALBRECHT RITSCHL

Ritschl's positive account of the Trinity is found in his *Instruction in the Christian Religion*, in volume III of *Justification and Reconciliation*, and in lectures he gave in 1881–1882.[1] His statements in *Instruction in the Christian Religion* are the simplest, so I will begin there.

[1]   Albrecht Ritschl, "Instruction in the Christian Religion," *Three Essays*, trs. Philip Hefner (Philadelphia: Fortress Press, 1972); Albrecht Ritschl, *The Christian Doctrine of Justification and Reconciliation: The Positive Development of the Doctrine*, ed. H. R. Mackintosh and A. B.

The opening words introduce us to two of Ritschl's favorite ideas: special revelation and the community of believers. According to Ritschl, the community's knowledge of God arises from special revelation. But by special revelation he meant Jesus Christ and the Holy Spirit,[2] not truths about the eternal being of God miraculously communicated in the Bible. As a result, his view of Jesus differs significantly from that which we find in Protestant scholastic theology. In the *Instruction* as well as in other works, Ritschl employed some traditional epithets with Trinitarian significance but construed them in a distinctive way. So, for example, he described Jesus as the "end of creation," meaning that Jesus was the prototype of humanity and that Jesus embodied God's own purpose, the kingdom. He called Jesus the lord of the community, meaning that, as the founder of the community whose purpose is the kingdom, Jesus was the original object of God's love and the mediator of that love to the members of the community.[3] He believed Jesus to be unique because Jesus was the first to have God's intended purpose for humanity (i.e., the kingdom) as his own purpose. Ritschl conceded a unity between Jesus and God the Father but interpreted it in terms of this unity of purpose. The deity of Jesus means, according to Ritschl, his possessing the same attributes as God does – love, grace, faithfulness and freedom over the world.[4]

These ideas, adumbrated in *Instruction*, were elaborated in *Justification and Reconciliation*. In particular, Ritschl more forthrightly discussed the pre-existence of the Son of God, a topic not mentioned in the *Instruction*. Ritschl was willing to allow that one might speak of the Son pre-existing as an object of God's eternal mind and will. This notion bears a superficial resemblance to the Augustinian and Thomistic representation of the Son's generation as being analogous to the mind's conceiving an idea. Strictly speaking, however, Ritschl was not thinking of the Son's pre-*existence*, for he meant only that God eternally knows and loves Jesus as the lord

Macaulay (New York: Charles Scribner's Sons, 1900); the 1881–1882 lectures are partially reproduced in Rolf Schäfer, *Ritschl: Grundlinien eines fast verschollenen dogmatischen Systems*, Beiträge zur historischen Theologie, no. 41 (Tübingen: J. C. B. Mohr (Paul Siebeck), 1968), 203–206.   [2] Ritschl, "Instruction," 221.   [3] Ibid., 225 and 229–230.
[4] Ibid., 231.

of the kingdom. Ritschl's point is that the Son is eternal but not an eternal *being* – only a sort of idea in God's mind, the eternal knowledge of Jesus Christ.[5] Ritschl justified this understanding of the Son because *for God*, though not for us, there is no interval between God's eternal purpose – the Son – and its historical accomplishment – Jesus Christ: "Christ exists for God eternally as that which He appears to us under the limitations of time."[6]

The Holy Spirit's deity and existence are, according to Ritschl, similar to the Son's. Ritschl did not regard the Spirit as a hypostasis, that is, as a subsistent being, but he was willing to grant a sense in which talk about the eternity of the Spirit is meaningful. As in the *Instruction*, the Spirit is in *Justification and Reconciliation* described as the knowledge that God has of God's own self. Since the historical Spirit of the community corresponds to God's eternal self-knowledge, the creeds rightly describe the Spirit, i.e., the Spirit of the community, as proceeding from God.[7] Here again, Ritschl was willing to preserve some of the traditional Trinitarian terms, although investing them with his own view of God.

Ritschl's most extensive statements about the Trinity are found in his lectures; however, even these statements are brief and in summary form, a fact that suggests his lack of interest in the matter. In the lectures he proclaimed adamantly that the Trinity must be discussed only at the end of the theological system. The reasons for his judgment were that this doctrine presupposes an understanding of the Trinitarian persons and that only this location accords with the theological principles of the Reformation. This last rationale may be surprising since John Calvin and Philip Melanchthon placed the Trinity toward the beginning of their theologies. However, Ritschl was thinking about where the doctrine *should* be placed, if Protestant theology is to be a truly Biblical theology, taking its departure from revelation in Christ, not from a slavish adherence to tradition.[8] Since Protestant theology must be a Biblical, not a philosophical, theology, it must take its point of departure from what the Bible expresses – the historical experience of salvation in Jesus. The doctrine of the Trinity, then, must follow the doctrines of the Son and the Spirit.

[5] Ritschl, *Justification and Reconciliation*, 470.   [6] Ibid., 471.   [7] Ibid., 471–472.
[8] Schäfer, *Ritschl*, 203.

Ritschl next firmly tied the doctrine of the Trinity to revelation, by which he meant Jesus Christ. He laid particular emphasis on the baptismal formula of Matthew 28:19 and especially on
its reference to the one name of Father, Son and Spirit. Since he
believed that "name" signifies God as manifest, he interpreted
the Trinity of the baptismal formula as God revealed to us. As
a result, he dismissed the common distinction between the so-
called economic and historical Trinity of revelation and the
so-called ontological and eternal Trinity of essence. Such a distinction violated his axiom that one cannot know God apart
from revelation, for it implied that God's being in itself differs
from the revelation of God to us. If, he reasoned, God is fully
manifest in Jesus Christ, then our knowledge of God revealed as
Trinity is at the same time knowledge of God as God truly and
eternally is. To imagine an eternal nature of God behind God's
revelation in time is to render revelation in Christ accidental and
trivial.[9]

Ritschl next sought to explain the relation of the three persons
to the one God, succumbing to the temptation to comment that
the traditional doctrine of the Trinity was not very clear on this
point. Briefly put, he stated that the "content" (*Inhalt*) of the three
is identical, for it is the one God who is revealed as Father
through the Son and through the Holy Spirit within the community. Yet the three are truly distinct, for the Son is the organ
of revelation and the Holy Spirit is the bearer of revelation in the
community.[10] We may observe that although he asserted the dis-
tinctness of the Trinitarian persons, his opinion about the reality
of the persons was far different from the traditional view. The
Son is not a being; rather, God eternally knows the man Jesus
whose vocation is the kingdom and who therefore is the Son.
Apart from Jesus, the Son has ideal reality as the object of God's
love and purpose but lacks the subsistent reality ascribed to the
Son by orthodox theologians.

Finally, Ritschl observed that the value of the doctrine of the
Trinity lies in its distinguishing Christianity from monotheisms
such as Judaism and Islam that emphasize law. The doctrine of the

---

[9] Ibid., 203–204.   [10] Ibid., 204–205.

Trinity preserves Christianity as a religion of freedom by making redemption central. As such, the doctrine is, in Ritschl's words, the seal on our knowledge of God.[11]

It may prove instructive to compare Ritschl's and Zinzendorf's views of the Trinity for both illustrate the ambivalence of the Lutheran tradition about the systematic relation of Christology as a principle of religious knowledge to the doctrine of the Trinity.[12] Both argued that revelation is our only source of knowledge about God and both argued that there is no revelation of God except Christ. Both laid the emphasis of their concerns on what is usually called the economic Trinity precisely because they asserted the indispensability of revelation. Both were judged heterodox by conservative theologians. In both cases, their epistemological convictions went hand in hand with their insistence on being faithful to Luther's theology and resulted in their neglecting the so-called ontological Trinity.

This comparison suggests that Ritschl's view of the Trinity is not a singular anomaly in the history of Protestant theology. It bears similarities to the views of others who understood and applied Protestant theological norms in ways that diverge from the mainstream. However, Ritschl's writings about the Trinity are notable for their brevity. His thoughts about the Trinity in these three works amount to no more than a dozen pages. Other liberal theologians wrote far less. In the remainder of the chapter I will explore the reasons for their reticence.

THE SPIRIT OF MELANCHTHON IN LATE NINETEENTH-CENTURY THEOLOGY

The appeal to Luther

One reason for the hesitancy these theologians showed toward the doctrine of the Trinity was their interpretation of Luther.[13] In brief, they believed that Luther's doctrine of salvation and the controlling importance of that doctrine for his entire theology ren-

---

[11] Ibid., 205.

[12] For references from Ritschl's writings to his appreciation for certain aspects of Zinzendorf's theology see Grover Foley, "Ritschls Urteil über Zinzendorfs Christozentrismus," *Evangelische Theologie* 20 (1960): 314–326. See especially 315–317.

[13] On the general character of Ritschl's interpretation of Luther see David W. Lotz, *Ritschl*

dered the traditional doctrine of the Trinity unnecessary and mis-leading.

We may ask whether Ritschl and his students correctly inter-preted Luther. Given the weight they placed on Luther's theology as the purest expression of Christianity since the New Testament, this question has some importance. It is not difficult to find schol-ars who dispute the Ritschlian interpretation of Luther, whether with respect to Luther's doctrine of the Trinity or to the general principles of his theology. However, the Ritschlians had a rejoin-der: while proclaiming themselves faithful expositors of Luther's theology, they also declared that they understood Luther better than he himself did. Whether or not their judgment is correct, it is good to remember that the liberal theologians regarded themselves not as innovating but instead as continuing the reforming work of Luther. This reminds us that the heritage of the Reformation was far from unambiguous. The thoughts of Luther and Melanchthon were capable of leading in several directions.

The liberal theologians' main problem was that Luther himself affirmed the doctrine of the Trinity in its traditional form. He did so because, as we have seen, he regarded the Bible in orthodox fashion as a source of all manner of religious truths.[14] In response the Ritschlians distinguished Luther's hermeneutics, which emphasized Christ and salvation as the Bible's central message and which, they held, represented Luther when he was true to his evangelical insights, from his orthodox posture toward Scripture, which they said resulted from Luther's inability to implement these insights. Their task was made all the more difficult by the fact that the subsequent Lutheran theological tradition had largely adopted the orthodox view and like Luther routinely turned to Scripture in what the Ritschlians regarded as an unsound way. So Ritschl and company not only had to pit Luther against Luther, but also Luther and themselves against the Lutheran tradition.

One of the most incisive evaluations of Luther was given by Harnack. On the one hand, he believed, Luther had brought an

---

& Luther: A Fresh Perspective on Albrecht Ritschl's Theology in the Light of His Luther Study (Nashville: Abingdon Press, 1974). For critical remarks see especially 121–139. See also Karl Hammer, "Albrecht Ritschls Lutherbild," *Theologische Zeitschrift* 26 (1970): 117–122.

[14] Adolf Harnack, *What is Christianity?*, trs. Thomas Bailey Saunders (New York: Harper & Row, Harper Torchbooks, The Cloister Library, 1957), 291–292.

end to the history of dogma by rescuing faith from the intellectualistic contamination into which it had fallen; on the other hand, Luther had consciously retained certain dogmas and thus established a problem for later generations to work out. The problem rested on the fact that, according to Harnack, these dogmas lack any firm connection to evangelical faith.[15]

Harnack expatiated on the reasons for Luther's retaining such dogmas as the Trinity. First, Luther believed them to be scriptural. Second, he failed to think out the relation of dogma to faith comprehensively and systematically.[16] Third, he did not recognize how greatly his new insights differed from the standpoint of traditional dogma. Fourth, he retained respect for the ancient councils. Finally, the dogmas afforded him a foil in his attacks on Turks, Jews and fanatics.[17] In Harnack's judgment only someone who was superhuman could have effected a theological revolution like the Reformation without retaining outmoded ideas, so that we are not surprised at the presence in Luther's theology of incommensurate ideas.[18] The result of Luther's confusion, Harnack suggested, was a contradiction within the Reformation between evangelical faith and the old system of dogma that obscured that faith.[19]

Harnack regarded his own historical investigations as the attempt to bring to completion what Luther had begun – the elimination of doctrines not required by evangelical faith as he understood it. He proposed to resolve the contradiction that Luther had bequeathed to the Lutheran tradition by affirming the part of Luther's theology he called Luther's Christianity[20] and denying the system of dogma that Luther had conservatively retained. In this way he sought to rescue Luther from his own failures and use Luther against Lutheran orthodoxy.[21]

---

[15] Adolf von Harnack, *History of Dogma*, trs. Neil Buchanan, et al. (New York: Russell & Russell, 1958), vol. VII, 226–228.   [16] Ibid., VII:227.   [17] Ibid., VII:242.
[18] Ibid., VII:229–230.
[19] Ibid., VII:243–244; Harnack, *What is Christianity?*, 291–292; Wilhelm Herrmann, *The Communion of the Christian with God: Described on the Basis of Luther's Statements*, ed. Robert T. Voelkel (Philadelphia: Fortress Press, 1971), 150.
[20] Harnack, *History of Dogma*, VII:230.
[21] For Ritschl's stance on this issue see David W. Lotz, "Albrecht Ritschl and the Unfinished Reformation," *Harvard Theological Review* 73 (1980): 349–357. A similarity between pietists and liberal theologians on this issue is suggested by Gerald Parsons, "Pietism and Liberalism: Some Unexpected Continuities," *Religion* 14 (1984): 226 and 228.

Having separated the religious wheat from the dogmatic chaff in Luther's theology, the next task for the Ritschlians was to deploy the harvested part of that theology against the enemies that confronted them.

Ritschl undertook this task on epistemological grounds, contrasting Luther's approach to the knowledge of God with what he called a scholastic approach.[22] By this he meant any attempt that seemed excessively metaphysical. As an example of such an approach he adduced the traditional arguments for God's existence. Ritschl had no quarrel with metaphysics as such, but he did object to using, in theology, a metaphysics such as Aristotle's that inquires into being as such and that ignores the distinctive marks of spiritual being. Further, the idea of God obtained from metaphysical arguments is inextricably tied to our experience of the world and cannot transcend the world. These arguments fail to yield objective knowledge of God and "give us no guarantee that anything real corresponds to the thought in our minds."[23] Against this sort of natural and speculative knowledge Ritschl presented revelation as the only means of knowing God that satisfies our religious interests.[24]

Asserting the preeminence of revelation for our knowledge of God, Ritschl and his students equated revelation with Jesus Christ and denied the validity of general revelation and natural knowledge of God.[25] Their rationale for denying metaphysics, general revelation and natural knowledge is not to be found in *a priori* epistemological theories, but instead in their conviction that faith has to do with God's activities toward us in Christ and not with abstract knowledge or historical facts scientifically obtained.[26]

---

[22] Albrecht Ritschl, "Theology and Metaphysics," *Three Essays*, trs. Philip Hefner (Philadelphia: Fortress Press, 1972), 152; Harnack, *History of Dogma*, VII:214. For a critical analysis of what may have been the liberals' one-sided interpretation of Luther, see Hammer, "Albrecht Ritschl's Lutherbild," 118–122 and Paul Wrzecionko, *Die Philosophischen Wurzeln der Theologie Albrecht Ritschls. Ein Beitrag zum Problem des Verhältnisses von Theologie und Philosophie im 19. Jahrhundert* (Berlin, A. Töpelmann, 1964). For a summary of Herrmann's views on the subject see Risto Saarinen, *Gottes Wirken auf uns: die transzendentale Deutung des Gegenwart-Christi-Motivs in der Lutherforschung* (Stuttgart: Franz Steiner Verlag Wiesbaden GMBH, 1989), 64–72.

[23] Ritschl, *Justification and Reconciliation*, 214 and 216.   [24] Ibid., 22 and 213.

[25] Ritschl, "Theology and Metaphysics," 153.

[26] Ritschl, *Justification and Reconciliation*, 212–213.

With revelation equated with and restricted to Jesus Christ, the next question was, who or what is Christ? This, of course, is the question of all questions for Christian theology. Ritschl insisted that his Christology was soundly based on the historical actuality of Jesus in its effects on the Christian community.[27] He inferred that the authentic knowledge of God, resting on revelation in Christ, consists in the judgment that Christ is God. Here he cited Luther's *Large Catechism*. He drew from the *Catechism* the lessons that to be a God is to be the source of salvation and that, consequently, we recognize Christ as God because Christ is our redeemer.[28] Christ, then, for Ritschl was not the Jesus discovered by historical science, but was instead the redeemer and revealer of God who, because he is the redeemer and revealer, is accounted by us to be divine.[29] We can see why, according to Ritschl, mere historical facts and speculative reasoning have no value for faith, insofar as faith consists in trust: they cannot possibly bring to us the redemption that only Jesus mediates.

Although the Ritschlians' epistemology was Christocentric, their theology was *theo*centric because Jesus, as the mediator, brings us into communion with *God*.[30] This stance is a most unpromising beginning for any doctrine of the Trinity, for it concentrates completely on the effect that Christ has on us as we are brought into relation with God. The doctrine of the Trinity customarily begins with the relation of one divine person (the Son) to another (the Father); the Ritschlians began with our relation to God through Jesus. It is not at all clear that a divine-human person is required to bring about that relation, especially when we consider the view of salvation that the Ritschlians affirmed.

It may be helpful to pause here and compare the Ritschlians with Karl Barth on this subject. There are some striking similarities. Both agreed that theology is based only on revelation. Both identified revelation with Jesus Christ. Both took pains to preserve the church's teaching from the permutations of historical

[27] Ibid., 2–3.
[28] Ibid., 392–396. The relevant sections of the *Large Catechism* may be found in *The Book of Concord: The Confessions of the Evangelical Lutheran Church*, trs. and ed. Theodore G. Tappert (Philadelphia: Fortress Press, 1959), pp. 365–368. See also Herrmann, *Communion*, 142–143.   [29] Ritschl, *Justification and Reconciliation*, 388–389.
[30] Harnack, *What is Christianity?*, 144.

scholarship. The main difference is that the Ritschlians regarded Christ as the person, represented to us in the New Testament, whose personal life mediates our relation to God; Barth thought of Christ as the incarnate Word of God attested by the New Testament witnesses. For Ritschl, revelation is to be found in Christ's relation to God and in his own life of lordship over the world.[31] For Barth, revelation is to be found in the person of the God-man, the assumption of the flesh by the divine. This difference, described already in the nineteenth century as the opposition of Christology "from above" (beginning with the incarnation) and "from below" (historically oriented), encapsulates the reason for the Ritschlian hesitance to develop the idea of the Trinity and for Barth's vigorous defense of the doctrine.

Revelation, then, according to the liberal theologians, pertains directly to Christ and especially to redemption in Christ. This is to say that it is soteriological in character. Ritschl noted with approval that Luther and Melanchthon agreed that our knowledge of Christ amounted to a knowledge of the saving benefits that come to us from Christ.[32] Luther, Ritschl maintained, had rebelled against a style of theology that was overly preoccupied with metaphysical considerations such as Christ's nature and the divine essence. That is why, Ritschl claimed, Luther declared the Trinitarian and Christological dogmas to be incomprehensible and worthless for faith, at least if faith means trust.[33] In the place of such theology he had substituted a form of theology that portrayed the worth of God and Christ for us in salvation.[34] Ritschl thereby denied that theology has any interest in God's being as it may be apart from revelation, even in an eternal Trinity supposedly lying behind God's revelatory acts in history. Liberal theologians could find the doctrine of the Trinity congenial if it could be related to salvation;

---

[31] Ritschl, *Justification and Reconciliation*, 237, 388–389 and 437–438.

[32] Ibid., 392–396; Ritschl, "Theology and Metaphysics," 203; Harnack, *History of Dogma*, VII:198 and 226. For Herrmann's views of the soteriological character of revelation see *Communion*, 148–150 and 173–175.

[33] Ritschl, *Justification and Reconciliation*, 395 and 398; Harnack, *History of Dogma*, VII:224–225.

[34] For a qualification of the usual view that Ritschl was interested only in the significance of Jesus for us, see Hans Vorster, "Werkzeug oder Täter? Zur Methodik der Christologie Albrecht Ritschls," *Zeitschrift für Theologie und Kirche* 62 (1965): 55–56. See also Harnack, *History of Dogma*, VII:198, 214 and 226.

however, insofar as it were represented merely as a philosophical truth about God and not a truth derived from the experience of salvation, it could have no interest for faith.

The Ritschlians' preoccupation with salvation and their use of it as a controlling idea in theology is far from uncontroversial. They demanded that theology begin with the situation of humanity in the world and that we regard God as the answer to the problems associated with the human situation. While this approach does have the advantage of preventing theology from becoming a merely scientific inquiry, even Ritschl's sympathetic expositors have faulted him for confining God to the significance God has for human concerns.[35] There is a thin line between regarding God as the correlate of human need and restricting the importance of God to God's importance for us. We should keep in mind that one of the selling points of the doctrine of the Trinity has been that this doctrine keeps us from merging God and the world in thought. It does so by compelling us to recognize that God has a life apart from God's relations to the world. One result of a radically Christ-centered theology, where Christ is understood as the historical person who carried out the will of his Father, is that the theologian is forbidden to consider God beyond the immediate scope of human salvation. If this path is pursued, then some other way must be found to safeguard the freedom of God lest we think of God as a mere instrument for human well-being.

The liberal theologians asserted that because authentic Christian doctrine is based upon revelation in Christ, it really is knowledge of God. As noted above, they held that metaphysical accounts of God are not knowledge; they are abstractions from our experience of the world and so remain bound to the world. Ritschl cited Luther to the effect that these metaphysical accounts are "without redemptive value and ruinous"[36] and the faith based on them is self-deceptive, for it represents God as a metaphysical being; such a being could never be the object of religious faith.[37] Ritschl appealed to Philipp Jacob Spener for a genuinely Lutheran

---

[35] James Richmond, *Ritschl: A Reappraisal. A Study in Systematic Theology* (London: Collins, 1978), 115; Lotz, *Ritschl & Luther*, 121; and David L. Mueller, *An Introduction to the Theology of Albrecht Ritschl* (Philadelphia: Westminster Press, 1969), 165.

[36] Ritschl, "Theology and Metaphysics," 203.

[37] Ritschl, *Justification and Reconciliation*, 213.

view of faith and religious knowledge: the truly scientific proof of Christianity's truth must be sought in the way indicated by John 7:17 ("Whoever wills to do the will of God will know that the doctrine of Christ is true").[38] Religious truth, Ritschl argued, cannot be verified by metaphysics but instead confirms itself in faith and trust.

Paradoxically, then, the way to epistemological certainty regarding God is not, according to Ritschl, through supposedly objective metaphysical truths, but instead through a subjective path: that "sphere of experience which nothing save the religious conception of God can explain." That is, the only authentic argument for God's existence is found in the dynamics of our spiritual life and in the necessary role that the idea of God plays in this life.[39] Faith, according to Ritschl, must take the form of unconditional trust and consequently must be the opposite of dispassionate, scientific knowledge based on universal concepts.[40] Here Ritschl proved himself to be a faithful adherent of modern Protestant theology, one of whose main tasks had always been to fashion a religious epistemology that would attain objective knowledge from a subjective starting point – faith. As we have seen in previous chapters, the doctrine of the Trinity's stock rose and fell as theologians affirmed or denied that any Trinity could be derived from this subjective starting point.

The Ritschlians believed not only that the Reformation's new understanding of salvation was attended by a new understanding of Christ but also that it was accompanied by a new conception of faith and doctrine. Orthodox Christology, they asserted, fascinated with the union of the divine and human in Christ, inevitably separated them and laid the accent on the divine. They believed Luther's theology, unlike orthodox theology, did justice to the human life of Christ.[41] Further, they charged, orthodox theology separated doctrine from faith. One could, they asserted, believe the orthodox doctrine without possessing saving faith; worse, this doctrine had been erected by the church into a condition for salvation. In Luther's view, however, confession of Christ's deity is not a condition of faith; it is instead a concomitant of justifying faith, for

---

[38] Ibid., 8, 24–25 and 226.   [39] Ibid., 222.   [40] Ibid., 6.
[41] Herrmann, *Communion*, 153–154.

to recognize his deity is to know that through Christ God is gracious. Recognition of God in Christ is simultaneously our justification by faith and our acknowledging Christ's deity. It is justification by faith because to know God in Christ is to know God as gracious.[42] It is acknowledging Christ's deity because "the most important element in the confession of the Deity of Christ" is the thought that "when the historical Christ takes such hold of us, we have to do with God Himself."[43]

These statements disclose the Ritschlians' implacable insistence that doctrine and saving faith go hand in hand. They feared that otherwise faith would be reduced to an intellectual assent to doctrine. The issue, according to Herrmann, is between the orthodox doctrine of Christ that is in truth religiously vacuous and whose validity rests on historical authority and the authentically Lutheran doctrine of Christ whose truth is directly experienced in redemption.[44] The Ritschlians were convinced that the ancient Trinitarian and Christological dogmas went hand in hand with an authoritarian view of faith, according to which faith consists in an act of cognitive obedience. Accordingly, they held that the relation of dogma to faith is equivalent to the relation of law to gospel – a relation of perennial interest to Lutherans. They argued for an open attitude toward church dogma, asserting Christian freedom on matters that would illegitimately bind the human conscience. This sentiment, although an application of Luther's theology that Luther himself would not recognize, nevertheless demonstrates the liberal theologians' desire to thoroughly revamp theology according to their vision of the Reformation's original insights.[45]

The lesson that Ritschl and his followers drew from their use of Luther was that theology cannot be a comprehensive system of knowledge about God in the manner of scholastic theology. It must instead restrict itself to those doctrines that directly bear upon

[42] Ibid., 163–164; Harnack, *What is Christianity?*, 270–271.

[43] Herrmann, *Communion*, 143.

[44] Ibid., 172–174. See also Harnack, *What is Christianity?*, 270–271 and Dietz Lange, "Wahrhaftigkeit als sittliche Forderung und als theologisches Prinzip bei Wilhelm Herrmann," *Zeitschrift für Theologie und Kirche* 66 (1969): 94.

[45] G. Wayne Glick, *The Reality of Christianity: A Study of Adolf von Harnack as Historian and Theologian*, Makers of Modern Theology, ed. Jaroslav Pelikan (New York: Harper & Row, 1967), 208–209; Lange, "Wahrhaftigkeit," 89 and 94.

salvation. They did not so much deny the doctrine of the Trinity for its irrationality or for its exegetical deficiencies as push it to the unimportant periphery of theological concern. As we have seen, Ritschl sought to preserve the doctrine in some form, but it could never play an important role in liberal theology. Those Ritschlians who did deny the Trinity, Harnack and Troeltsch, did not waste much time in their denials, for it had already lost all importance for theology.

The influence of Friedrich Schleiermacher

Luther convinced the liberal theologians that theology must take salvation as its point of departure. This conviction suggested the difficulty of affirming the Trinity insofar as its connection with salvation was perceived to be slight. Schleiermacher's theory of Christian doctrine reinforced this conviction.

A conservative theologian of this period could well have agreed with Luther about the soteriological basis of theology and gone on to affirm the doctrine of the Trinity on the grounds that it sustains the doctrine of the atonement and so has the soteriological basis that the Ritschlians demanded. If the liberal theologian answered that the traditional view of the atonement is not the authentically Christian one, the conservative could respond that the traditional account of the atonement as well as the doctrine of the Trinity rest on revelation in the Bible, an opinion that Luther had surely shared. What the Ritschlians required in response was a view of revelation, doctrine and the Bible that would avoid Luther's antiquated view of verbal inspiration. In short, they needed the theology of Schleiermacher, particularly his account of doctrine and the Bible.[46] Schleiermacher's account of doctrine, its origin and its relation to revelation was used by the Ritschlians to show that the church's doctrine of the Trinity cannot be regarded as a direct restatement of revelation.

Briefly stated, the orthodox representation of doctrine holds

---

[46] For an orientation to Ritschl's relation to and use of Schleiermacher see James M. Brandt, "Ritschl's Critique of Schleiermacher's Theological Ethics," *Journal of Religious Ethics* 17 (1989): 51–72, especially p. 53 on Kant and Schleiermacher, and Mueller, *An Introduction*, 33–37.

that church dogmas, enshrined in creeds, are summaries in technical language of the doctrines that are given in revelation. Western and Eastern Catholics and orthodox Protestants have all agreed on this point, disagreeing only on the question of whether post-Biblical teaching is inspired or whether only the Bible is inspired. All these affirm the dogma of the Trinity because they believe it faithfully describes God and has been revealed by God in the Bible. Protestants such as Calvin were initially nervous about requiring affirmation of the creeds that contained the dogmas. They insisted that the language of the dogmas could not be required as articles of faith, since the words themselves were human in origin. Nevertheless, even Calvin came to require affirmation of the truths that the creeds attempt to state.

Schleiermacher's innovation on this subject consisted in the view that neither church dogma nor Biblical text is a restatement of truths known to and revealed by God. He agreed with the orthodox that dogmas enshrined in confessional documents are expositions of Scripture, or at least that they are intended to be,[47] but he disagreed with their view of revelation and of revelation's relation to Scripture. The orthodox believed that dogmas have their ultimate origin in the mind of God. They are the human counterpart to God's self-knowledge.[48] Schleiermacher held that dogmas and the Bible itself have their ultimate origin in the human religious consciousness. To be sure, Schleiermacher believed this religious consciousness is a response to revelation and can be traced back to God's revelatory activity; however, he denied that this activity consists in the communication of doctrinal truths. Dogmas, Schleiermacher asserted, have a doctrinal form because in Christianity human religious consciousness had developed sufficiently for religious feelings to be communicated with great definiteness.[49] Christian teaching has come to have a doctrinal form because of certain features of human nature, not because it was communicated in that form by God.

---

[47] Friedrich Schleiermacher, *The Christian Faith*, ed. H. R. Mackintosh and J. S. Stewart (Philadelphia: Fortress Press, 1976), 112–118 (§27).

[48] See Richard A. Muller, *Post-Reformation Dogmatics*, vol. I, *Prolegomena to Theology* (Grand Rapids, MI: Baker Book House, 1987), 128–129 on the distinction between archetypal and ectypal theology.   [49] Schleiermacher, *The Christian Faith*, 76–83 (§§ 15–16).

Schleiermacher's influence may be detected at the beginning of Ritschl's *Justification and Reconciliation*:

The material of the theological doctrines of forgiveness, justification, and reconciliation is to be sought not so much directly in the words of Christ, as in the correlative representations of the original consciousness of the community. The immediate object of theological cognition is the community's faith that it stands to God in a relation essentially conditioned by the forgiveness of sins.[50]

Although Ritschl did not here cite the inspiration of Schleiermacher, his view of theology and its object is unthinkable apart from the prior work of Schleiermacher. What is affirmed by both is that theology not only arises from faith but is an exposition of faith and that it is not a restatement of revealed truths. Christian theology, according to Ritschl and Schleiermacher, can be crafted only from within the community of faith. Although Schleiermacher differed in important ways from the liberal theologians, his account of doctrine reinforced the soteriological thrust of their theology by defining faith as religious consciousness and not as assent; moreover, he gave them a means of criticizing particular doctrines while affirming the truth of the Christian religion. He accomplished this by distinguishing religion, as a relation to God, from the doctrines that express our relation to God but are, as expressions, secondary in importance to the relation itself and are not a condition of it.

Herrmann's *The Communion of the Christian with God* also leans on Schleiermacher's analysis of doctrine. As Herrmann presented it, the task of theology as traditionally conceived is to systematically connect together the ideas of the Bible or other classic witnesses to faith. For Herrmann, however, theology's task is instead to show how it is that these ideas arise out of the soul's communion with God. The traditional view assumed the priority of the doctrinal ideas and then sought to get individuals to appropriate for themselves those ideas as objects of belief; Herrmann regarded the ideas as products and expressions of faith and therefore as

---

[50] Ritschl, *Justification and Reconciliation*, 3. See also Ernst Troeltsch, *The Christian Faith*, trs. Garrett E. Paul, ed. Gertrud von le Fort, Fortress Texts in Modern Theology (Minneapolis: Fortress Press, 1991), 19, 48, and 111–112; Wilhelm Herrmann, *Systematic Theology*, trs. Nathaniel Micklem and Kenneth Saunders (London: George Allen and Unwin, 1927), 19, 30, 62 and 64.

secondary. For him the vital point is getting individuals to have the same communion with God that produced the original thoughts expressed in Scripture.[51] Herrmann drew the consequence that doctrinal uniformity among believers is not only not possible, it is not even desirable, for if doctrines are truly expressions of communion with God, then these expressions will vary as individuals vary.[52] As with Ritschl, there is an evident similarity to Schleiermacher's account of doctrine.

Finally, we may consider Ernst Troeltsch's lectures on theology. Troeltsch cited Schleiermacher expressly and approvingly for having rejected traditional Protestant dogmatics and for having thoroughly rethought the nature of theology from the ground up.[53] He commended Schleiermacher for conceiving of theology as *Glaubenslehre* (the teaching or doctrine of faith) and not as dogmatics. For Troeltsch, such a conception points to the way in which theology as "permanent laws drawn from the dogmas of an inspired Bible" differs from theology as the expression of Christian piety.[54] His adoption of Schleiermacher's view is revealed in the following: "Like Schleiermacher, we too build on the contemporary consciousness of the community. A theology of consciousness does not seek the definitive exposition of all Christianity; it only seeks to comprehend contemporary Christianity."[55]

Adopting Schleiermacher's view reinforced for the Ritschlians several ideas they had drawn from Luther. First, it supported their epistemological point that religious knowledge arises from our relation to God in redemption. It did so by asserting that religious feeling, which is the ultimate source of doctrine, has to do with the effect that God's activity has upon us. In the case of Christianity, this activity is the redemption accomplished through Jesus Christ. Doctrines are thus, in this opinion, removed from the immediacy of revelation and set forth as representations of this redemptive relation between God and self. The implication, according to Schleiermacher, is that doctrines such as the Trinity cannot be

---

[51] Herrmann, *Communion*, 40–42.   [52] Ibid., 10–12.

[53] Troeltsch, *The Christian Faith*, 14–15.

[54] Ibid., 16 and Ernst Troeltsch, "The Dogmatics of the History-of-Religions School," *Religion in History*, trs. James Luther Adams and Walter F. Bense, Fortress Texts in Modern Theology (Minneapolis: Fortress Press, 1991), 100–101.

[55] Troeltsch, *The Christian Faith*, 19. See also 48 and 111–112.

regarded as directly portraying the nature of God. Schleiermacher had provided a description of the origin of doctrines that was appealing to the liberal theologians because it correlated divine acts with the human response of faith.[56]

Second, Schleiermacher's account of doctrine reinforced their contention that Christianity is an experiential, not a cognitive, matter, that its doctrines are thoroughly religious and not at all metaphysical or theoretical. They favored Luther's view of justification but not his conservative retaining of traditional doctrines. Schleiermacher's theology added a vital wing to their intellectual edifice by separating religion from doctrine, thereby allowing them to cite Luther's groundbreaking insights into justification without having to accept Luther's own conservative retention of traditional doctrines. In other words, they believed that Schleiermacher had related religion to doctrine as Luther *should* have done. Schleiermacher's contributions allowed the Ritschlians to criticize the orthodox view of faith. The Ritschlians had objected that orthodox theologians had required assent to doctrines as a condition of faith. They did so because they thought of faith's object as cognitive truths, something to which intellectual assent might be given. They failed to see that it is the person of Jesus that is the object of faith.[57] Following Schleiermacher's analysis of doctrine, the Ritschlians argued that doctrine is an expression of faith and that it is logically subsequent to faith.

In short, in spite of many vital differences between the theologies of Schleiermacher and those of the Ritschlians, Schleiermacher's view of doctrine enabled the Ritschlians with good conscience to claim the heritage of the Reformation. His thought provided them with a way of assessing the character and worth of doctrinal statements and asserting the superiority of faith to doctrine. He also provided them with a justification for their desire to emphasize those features of Luther's thought according to which our knowledge of God is restricted to what can be said of our relation to God.

---

[56] According to Ritschl in *Justification and Reconciliation*, 22–23 and 34, both Schleiermacher and the Augsburg Confession follow the right path by expounding Christianity by means of the effects of God upon us and the "religious and moral acts which are called forth by revelation as a whole."   [57] Herrmann, *Communion*, 221–224.

HISTORY AND CRITICISM

Beside their adherence to the spirit of Melanchthon, with its practical and anti-speculative bent, liberal theologians were reluctant to embrace the doctrine of the Trinity also because of their convictions about historical criticism and its impact on the traditional doctrine.

A statement by Herrmann nicely summarizes the main point: "We theologians are ourselves cast out from the position of simple reverence for dogma because . . . we have set about investigating the sources of it. Historical study of the growth of any human ideas always tends to liberate men from subjection to those ideas."[58] Note that this claim assumes Schleiermacher's account of doctrine. Herrmann could regard the dogmas as "human ideas" because Schleiermacher had paved the way to such a view. As Herrmann went on to acknowledge, it was just this view that separated him from Luther and his contemporaries. For Luther, certain dogmas and the infallibility of Scripture were unquestioned givens; for Herrmann they had become utterly questionable.

However, although Schleiermacher had paved the way for a critical assessment of doctrines, he did not bestow on liberal theology an appreciation for the historical character of doctrine.[59] This new historical interest can be explained partly by the lingering influence on the liberal theologians of F. C. Baur and the Tübingen school of theology and partly by the progress made by the broader discipline of history – both developments occurring after Schleiermacher. As a result, the liberal theologians found Schleiermacher's theology deficient. Troeltsch, although crediting Schleiermacher with being the first to fashion a dogmatics based on a historical outlook, reproached him for failing to thoroughly carry out this task and accused him of accommodating his theology to the church's doctrinal tradition.[60] Further, developments in

---

[58] Ibid., 53.

[59] Harnack complained, in *History of Dogma* VII:234–235, that Luther also lacked historical sense. In *Christianity and History*, trs. Thomas Bailey Saunders (London: Adam & Charles Black, 1896), 24, he credited Johann Gottfried Herder with introducing the idea of history. For Herrmann's similar judgment of Schleiermacher see Robert T. Voelkel, *The Shape of the Theological Task* (Philadelphia: Westminster Press, 1968), 25.

[60] Troeltsch, "The Dogmatics of the History-of-Religions School," 91–92.

historical knowledge and methods were, in Troeltsch's estimation, so far advanced beyond what was available in Schleiermacher's day that such progress had rendered his results antiquated.[61]

Adolf von Harnack provides us with the best perspective on how the application of historical considerations inclined liberal theologians away from the doctrine of the Trinity.[62] Harnack asserted that dogmas belonged only to a certain epoch of Christian history, suggesting that their usefulness was transitory. This assertion implies not only his well-known view that "dogma in its conception and development is a work of the Greek spirit on the soil of the Gospel,"[63] but also the charge that Christianity in the period of dogma was modeling itself on the ancient schools of philosophy. Harnack identified dogmatic Christianity with an antique mode of thought, consisting in an antiquated view of history, psychology and metaphysics.[64] The result of Harnack's view was his belief that the importance of dogmatic Christianity was relative to the period in which it arose – dogma, he argued, depends on theology and theology in turn depends on the spirit of the times.[65] Dogmas can have no absolute value and are certainly not, in Harnack's estimate, simple restatements of revelation. At most they could have some value for their own era. They were, he thought, "the instrument by which the church conquered the ancient world and educated the modern nations."[66] But Harnack left the reader in no doubt that with Luther a new epoch had arisen in which dogma had begun to wither away and which was being brought to completion in Harnack's own day and work.

Harnack's view has not gone unchallenged. In our day Jaroslav Pelikan has forcefully sought to exonerate dogma. Where Harnack saw discontinuity and contradiction between gospel and dogma, Pelikan has seen a more genetic relation in which there is a continual tension between Scripture and the influence of philosophical

---

[61] Ibid., 93–94 and Ernst Troeltsch, "Half a Century of Theology: A Review," in *Ernst Troeltsch: Writings on Theology and Religion*, ed. and trs. Robert Morgan and Michael Pye (Louisville: Westminster/John Knox Press, paperback edition, 1990), 67–68.

[62] For an overview of the impact of historical criticism on doctrine see Gottfried Hornig, "Lehre und Bekenntnis im Kulturprotestantismus," *Studia Theologica* 29 (1975): 166–169 regarding Harnack and 174–178 (especially 174–176) regarding Troeltsch.

[63] Harnack, *History of Dogma*, I:17.   [64] Ibid., I:20–21.   [65] Ibid., I:9.

[66] Ibid., I:17.

modes of thought. Pelikan believes that philosophical terms have proven helpful to the church in expressing precisely what it already but inarticulately believed and taught.[67] Although we may agree with Pelikan that Harnack perhaps overstated the contradiction between New Testament teaching and later dogma, we must nevertheless refrain from wholehearted endorsement of Pelikan's understanding. On the one hand, Harnack's version of the gospel is surely oversimplistic; on the other hand, Pelikan's view seems excessively optimistic and triumphalistic, at least to the extent that the relation of New Testament to dogma is understood as one of development and expression. His view presupposes a notion of orthodoxy that is highly problematic, depending as it does on identifying orthodoxy with doctrinal *consensus*. There may yet be some truth in Harnack's notion of radical discontinuity.

More remarkable than the time-conditioned character of dogmas, according to Harnack, was their discontinuity with the gospel. In contrast to the traditional view, according to which dogmas are a repetition, in technical language, of truth revealed by God, Harnack insisted that dogma is not repetition but innovation. He specifically denied a genetic relation between the gospel and dogmas.[68] Whereas Schleiermacher criticized doctrines on the basis of their relation to religious feeling, Harnack based his criticism on their historical origin and character and lack of substantive identity with the gospel. In this way Harnack posited a historical disjunction between gospel and dogma and was then free to subject dogmas to critical judgment without danger of questioning the gospel.[69]

Historical discontinuity meant not only a gap between traditional theology and the gospel, but also a gap between traditional theology and modern theology. Ernst Troeltsch, commenting on the orthodox doctrine of the Trinity, stated: "Now that ancient cosmology has been eliminated from theology, and with the accompanying emergence of a human-historical view of Jesus, the

---

[67] Jaroslav Pelikan, *The Christian Tradition: A History of the Development of Doctrine*, vol. I, *The Emergence of the Catholic Tradition (100–600)* (Chicago: University of Chicago Press, 1971), 45–55 and 185–186.   [68] Harnack, *History of Dogma*, I:16–17.

[69] Gerald Parsons, "Pietism and Liberalism," 235–236, points out that another similarity between pietist and liberal theology lies in their respective views of Christian history and the place of orthodox doctrine within it.

Christian concept of God has grown independent of this basically Neoplatonic formula."[70] Liberal theologians such as Troeltsch capitalized on the fact that the modern historical outlook differed dramatically from the modes of thought that theologians had formerly used. On the one hand, modern historical consciousness saw previous modes of thought as relative and dependent on the intellectual conditions of their own day. On the other hand, historical consciousness itself provided a different way of approaching the object of Christian faith. Briefly put, it meant that the concepts that had previously undergirded the doctrine of God, concepts such as nature and person, were replaced by different ones such as personality. Troeltsch in particular reflected on the differences between the traditional understanding of theology and the newly emerging historical approach. Far from being a mere technique that might be merged with traditional presuppositions, the historical approach was, Troeltsch asserted, a revolution in thinking, accompanied by a new attitude toward human being.[71] In particular, the historical approach meant several things: that religious doctrines must be critically investigated as other areas of human life have come to be; that the assumption guiding the investigation of the Bible and Christianity must be the consistency of the human spirit in history; and that all historical events must be regarded as interrelated.[72] The net effect was to render all facts uncertain and to show the contingent nature of every historical phenomenon.[73]

Harnack's analysis of the doctrines of Christ and the Trinity affords an illustration of the change of thinking brought about by the historical approach. First, he noted that these doctrines combine Christian thinking about the revelation of God in Christ with the legacy of ancient philosophy.[74] Second, these doctrines are contrary to the interests of religion, for the history of their formation illustrates a pattern observed in every religion: "From the religious thought to the philosophical and theological doctrinal proposition, and from the doctrinal proposition which requires

---

[70] Troeltsch, *The Christian Faith*, 105.
[71] Troeltsch, "Historical and Dogmatic Method in Theology," in *Religion in History*, trs. James Luther Adams and Walter F. Bense, Fortress Texts in Modern Theology (Minneapolis: Fortress Press, 1991), 16.   [72] Ibid., 13–14.   [73] Ibid., 17.
[74] Harnack, *History of Dogma*, IV:128–129.

knowledge to the legal proposition which demands obedience."[75] Third, the doctrines were based on a thoroughly unhistorical view. Athanasius, he believed, erred in reducing "the entire historical account given of Christ to the belief that the Redeemer shared in the nature and unity of the Godhead itself."[76] In other words, Athanasius lacked the very historical approach that alone could rightly grasp the importance of Jesus, substituting in its place a metaphysical view resting on the concept of nature.[77] Harnack applauded the Antiochene theologians for preserving the sense of the historical Jesus that was threatened by the Alexandrian obsession with the divine nature of Christ.[78]

Liberal theologians could take up a critical attitude toward doctrines such as the Trinity because they believed that religion itself lies outside the changes of history. Christianity for them meant living as Jesus lived in lordship over the world and having the same relation to God and the world as Jesus did – a life and relation that resist historical change.[79] That is why Harnack could say that Augustine had the same "inner experience" as Paul the apostle did and why he could quote with approval Goethe's assertion that "[m]ankind is always advancing, and man always remains the same."[80] It is also why the liberal theologians could make reference to the historical Jesus, meaning by that phrase the impact that the life of Jesus has exercised over history.

In this respect, liberal theology resembled Barth's theology. Each sought to describe Jesus Christ in such a way that the changes of historical scholarship could have no effect on the importance of Jesus for theology and Christian faith. Neither allowed that history could alter the essence of Christian faith and both held that the Biblical message has a certain timeless quality.[81] Their difference, regarding our topic, lies in the meaning of revelation and Jesus Christ; beyond these admittedly weighty subjects, there is substantial agreement.

With respect to the relation between Christianity and history, Troeltsch represents a departure from the liberal fold. In "What

---

[75] Ibid., IV:137.   [76] Ibid., IV:45.

[77] See *History of Dogma*, IV:143 for Harnack's critique of the concept of nature.

[78] Ibid., IV:170–171.   [79] Ritschl, *Justification and Reconciliation*, 387–388.

[80] Harnack, *What is Christianity?*, 258 and 8.

[81] See Karl Barth's comments on Biblical interpretation in the second preface to *The Epistle to the Romans*, trs. Eswyn C. Hoskins (London: Oxford University Press, 1972), 7.

Does 'Essence of Christianity' Mean?" Troeltsch formulated an understanding of essence that allowed for both continuity and innovation within history, suggesting that it is by creative acts of individuals that the essence of something develops in history. In history, one such essence will be superseded by another as individuals appropriate the past and fashion it into an essence in combination with their personal convictions. So the essence of Christianity cannot be identified with the origin of Christianity or in fact with anything else. Instead the essence is the result of a continuous process of transformation and synthesis.[82]

In effect, Troeltsch charged the Ritschlians with being insufficiently historical. Although they were willing to subject dogma to historical criticism, they preserved Christianity itself as something above history. On this topic, then, Ritschl, Herrmann and Harnack had more in common with Barth than with Troeltsch. The Ritschlians and Barth had good reason to exclude Christianity from history, for the possibility of attaining truth and values seems to require a standpoint outside of history. Accordingly, Christian theology has customarily demanded some sort of absolute principle of knowledge – Scripture, tradition, experience, or Logos. Troeltsch's writings are a testimony to the attempt at grasping truth and values from *within* history; his demand for a thorough-going historical approach to theology and faith holds out little prospect for such an absolute standpoint as seems demanded by theology.

To summarize: the liberal theologians welcomed historical criticism as a liberation from the confining and legalistic view of dogma that had prevailed throughout the history of Christianity. Harnack in particular took the lead by showing dogmas to be relative to and conditioned by an ancient intellectual point of view so that they had historical importance but not continuing validity; by showing them to be discontinuous with the gospel, so that, far from being expositions of revelation, they were instead amalgamations of the gospel and human philosophy; and by showing that the philosophy on which they were based is discontinuous with a modern, historical way of thinking, so that individual dogmas are relics of

[82] Ernst Troeltsch, "What Does 'Essence of Christianity' Mean?" in *Ernst Troeltsch: Writings on Theology and Religion*, ed. and trs. Robert Morgan and Michael Pye (Louisville: Westminster/John Knox Press, paperback edition, 1990), 166.

ancient thinking and the concept of dogma itself is incomprehensible. For the doctrine of the Trinity, the result could at best be a benign neglect as theologians allowed it to languish unused or puzzled over its irrelevancy. Individual theologians might attempt a rehabilitation of sorts, but the effect of historical criticism was to diminish the stature of the doctrine of the Trinity from its place as a primary revealed truth about God to its role as an oddity in the system of theology.

GOD'S SELFHOOD AS PERSON

When we say that the liberal theologians made no place for the doctrine of the Trinity, we do not mean that they utterly dismissed the idea of a Trinity. Ritschl, as we have seen, interpreted the Son as God's eternal purpose, historically actualized in Jesus Christ, and the Holy Spirit as God's self-knowledge.[83] Herrmann believed that the doctrine of the Trinity summarized the knowledge of God's nature that we could infer from God's historical activity.[84] What the liberal theologians did not accept was the orthodox doctrine of three divine persons constituting the one divine being. One important reason for their stance was the idea of personality, a comprehensive idea the liberal theologians put to use for understanding God, Jesus Christ and human being.

We have seen that for liberal theologians it is the historical personality of Jesus, not his metaphysical constitution as a divine-human being, that has religious significance. The concept of personality also played a large role in the liberal understanding of human being and salvation.[85] In this section I will set forth the importance of this concept for the Ritschlian doctrine of God and its implications for the doctrine of the Trinity. Briefly put, instead of regarding God as three eternal persons they thought of God as a single personality – an understanding of God not calculated to be fruitful for the doctrine of the Trinity.

Both the traditional and liberal accounts of God used "person"

---

[83] Ritschl, *Justification and Reconciliation*, 470–472.
[84] Herrmann, *Systematic Theology*, 65.
[85] Glick, *The Reality of Christianity*, 202. He applies the term "historical axiology" to this trend in Harnack's thought (8 and 79). See also Voelkel, *The Shape of the Theological Task*, 24.

to describe God; however, the common use of the word conceals a profound disagreement about its meaning. For the Ritschlians, "person" signified a certain kind of being, namely spiritual and volitional; for the orthodox, "person" had come to mean, in Boethius' much-quoted definition, an individual substance of a rational nature.[86] For our purposes, the important part of this definition is "individual substance," with its implication that the Trinitarian persons are in some sense individually real. Although the individuality of the persons has usually been mitigated to some degree by the Augustinian-Thomistic interpretation of person as subsisting relation and by the theological concept of the circumincession of the persons, the belief that God is irreducibly three was indispensable to the traditional doctrine. The liberal theologians, at least Ritschl and Herrmann, were willing to concede a threeness in God in some sense; however, since their leading idea of God was that of personality, the emphasis in their theology inevitably fell on the oneness of God. They could have conjoined their emphases on threeness and personality only by acknowledging some sort of tritheism whereby each of the divine persons would be thought of as an individual personality.

The main question, then, is why the liberal theologians became so enamored of the notion of personality. The answer is found in their understanding of religion and of human being. Ritschlian theologians took up a conscious opposition to materialism and were fond of representing religion as the answer to an existential question posed in its starkest form by philosophical materialism. That question was about the possibility of spiritual and personal life amid the material world. The liberal theologians routinely depicted this material world as threatening human being with, we would say today, meaninglessness. The material world loomed in the liberal mind as a mechanical system into which humanity might be drawn, becoming a mere part and instrument of the cosmic machine. Most of the distinctive ideas of liberal theology –

---

[86] This definition is accepted by Thomas Aquinas in *Summa Theologica* 1.29.1. Protestant theology also largely employed this definition or one like it. See Richard A. Muller, *Dictionary of Latin and Greek Theological Terms* (Grand Rapids: Baker Book House, 1985), 226 and Robert D. Preus, *The Theology of Post-Reformation Lutheranism* (St. Louis, Concordia Publishing, 1970–1972), vol. II, 122.

freedom, value-judgments, autonomy, the kingdom of God, and personality – are best interpreted as attempts at preserving the humanness of human existence in the face of insidious matter.[87]

One of the most important passages in Ritschl's theology is the place in *Justification and Reconciliation* where he described the nature of religion. It is there that the idea of God as personality made its appearance:

> In every religion what is sought, with the help of the superhuman spiritual power reverenced by man, is a solution of the contradiction in which man finds himself, as both a part of the world of nature and a spiritual personality claiming to dominate nature . . . The idea of gods, or Divine powers, everywhere includes belief in their spiritual personality, for the support to be received from above can only be reckoned on in virtue of an affinity between God and men.[88]

This quotation establishes two points relevant for our topic. First, it argues that religion necessarily includes the belief that the saving power is a personality. Second, it asserts that the basis for this belief is the similarity between the divine and the human. The personality of God was important to the liberal theologians because it functioned as a transcendent ground and archetype of human moral personality in its struggle toward lordship over the world. The liberals thought of God as a foundation of the moral order of the universe. But for them this did not mean so much that God is the author of the moral law as that God is simultaneously the source of and the chief instance of personal being. As Ritschl put the matter: "The individual spirit is marked by every possible characteristic we think of as existing originally in God. Therefore, we may use the idea of species in order to compare spiritual beings with God, provided we make the reservation, that everything we class in the same species with God comes ever from God."[89] Ritschl was undertaking a maneuver often used in Christian theology, namely regarding God as analogous to the human person while preserving God's uniqueness as first cause. In the history of theology the maneuver

[87] Ritschl, *Justification and Reconciliation*, 17 and 199; Wilhelm Herrmann, *Die Religion im Verhältniß zum Welterkennen und zur Sittlichkeit: Eine Grundlegung der systematischen Theologie* (Halle: Max Niemeyer, 1879), 88–89 and 207; Harnack, *Christianity and History*, 46–47; Troeltsch, *The Christian Faith*, 29 and 41. [88] Ritschl, *Justification and Reconciliation*, 199.
[89] Ibid., 470.

has sometimes permitted and even encouraged a fruitful exploitation of this analogy on behalf of the idea of the Trinity. We have already noted the example of St. Thomas in this regard. At other times, however, considering God's selfhood has discouraged development of the idea of the Trinity; such was the case with the liberal theologians. Having adopted personality to designate and explain human selfhood, they applied it to God as well, arguing for a similarity between God and humans on the basis of a common possession of personality. We can see why they were not inclined to develop the doctrine of the Trinity, for their concept of selfhood, i.e., the idea of personality, does not suggest a Trinity. The Thomist idea of self does suggest a Trinity, comprising as it does the self with its intellect and will; the idea of moral personality, however, does not in itself imply a Trinity. This is not to claim that Thomas affirmed the Trinity because he deduced it from his view of the self. However, he was favorably disposed to this view of the self because he saw it as congenial to the doctrine of the Trinity. The liberal theologians, otherwise unmotivated to affirm the Trinity, were not prompted to do so because of their view of personality.

That personality is the central concept of the Ritschlian view of God can be gathered from express statements. According to Ritschl, the idea of the personality of God is the only idea that can prevent the usual scholastic idea of God from degenerating into either pantheism or deism. The idea of God as personality is, he held, "positive," i.e., not speculative, for it arose from the distinctively Christian idea of God. He also asserted its scientific character – always a plus for the liberal theologians – arguing that it alone could explain the co-existence and coordination of spirit and nature.[90] For Herrmann, the personality of God was a modern substitute for the metaphysical notion of divine substance.[91] Troeltsch enumerated the components of "prophetic-Christian personalism" as faith in the absolute value of the person, faith in the reality of an absolute standard of value, and faith in a deity who was both ground of the values and personal as we are.[92] More

[90] Ibid., 228.   [91] Herrmann, *Communion*, 177–178.

[92] Ernst Troeltsch, "On the Possibility of a Liberal Christianity," in *Religion in History*, trs. James Luther Adams and Walter F. Bense, Fortress Texts in Modern Theology (Minneapolis: Fortress Press, 1991), 345.

briefly, he defined Christianity as "the general, decisive break-through in principle to a religion of *personality*, opposed to all nat-uralistic and anti-personalistic understandings of God." Troeltsch was quick to point out that he found this form of Christianity most visible in contemporary Protestantism.[93]

It is not possible here to offer a complete assessment of this idea of personality. As indicated above, this is the idea that connects the Ritschlians' ideas of God, Christ and human being and that establishes the context in which their criticism of metaphysics and of Schleiermacher must be understood. All that can be done here is to pose some questions that indicate the direction a future inquiry could take.

First, we may ask whether personality is the best concept to use for the understanding of God. Even when personality is defined as loving will, as Ritschl specified, it still seems unduly restricted. It does not, for example, connect well with the sense of God as *mysterium tremendum* that we find in both the Bible and the history of religion. Loving will, although congruent with much of the Bible, does not account for that non-rational aspect of God that is met not only in the Old Testament but also occasionally in the New Testament.

Second, personality as the dominant category for understanding God seems to border on a theistic notion of God as a being who stands to the universe as artificer to artefact. Paul Tillich's criticism of the God of theism is appropriate here.[94] Admittedly, liberal theologians were not given to garrulous discourse about God; their opinion of theism is consequently difficult to discern. Nevertheless the emphasis on personality and the similarity that they drew between God and human beings is troubling because of the theistic connotations suggested.

Third, liberal theologians defined God's personality in connec-tion with God's own purpose, the kingdom of God. But it seems unnecessarily provincial to discuss God solely in terms of God's purpose for humanity. While there is a danger, which the Ritschlians tirelessly denounced, of going too far in the opposite

---

[93] Troeltsch, *The Christian Faith*, 63.
[94] Paul Tillich, *Systematic Theology*, 3 vols. (Chicago: University of Chicago Press, 1951–1963), I:245.

direction by describing God in purely cosmic terms and without reference to humanity, liberal theology here erred by overlooking the Biblical, or at least Old Testament, sense of the presence of God in and the purpose of God for the whole of the universe.

Finally, God's personality, according to liberal theologians, is an archetype of human personality – a perfect exemplar. While congratulating them for their sensitivity to their own cultural situation, we may nevertheless ask whether even humans are best defined by personality. Did the Ritschlians derive this understanding of human being from revelation or is their view merely an overreaction to late nineteenth-century pantheism and materialism? We may wish to judge that humanity stands in a much closer relation to the natural world than the Ritschlians were willing to allow. One does not have to be a convinced Romantic to affirm that human being is a kind of natural being and that salvation may not simply be a matter of world-transcendence.

In short, the Ritschlians attached themselves to the idea of God's personality because it performed a valuable function in their struggle against materialism. They had no need of the idea of the Trinity, for it solved none of the problems they found pressing.

CONCLUSION

With respect to the history of Trinitarian thought, the period of liberal theology is similar to certain aspects of the period of the critical Enlightenment. In both cases, theologians invoked Luther's and Melanchthon's theologies to justify their suspicion of the doctrine of the Trinity. In both cases the doctrine was not so much expressly denied as displaced from a position of importance. In both cases, this period of neglect was followed by renewed efforts to assert the Trinity as a fundamental doctrine of the Christian faith. Although it is evident today that theology will never return to liberalism in its nineteenth-century form, it would be precipitous to claim that liberal theology was a mere cul-de-sac in Christian thought. This is because the central concepts that determined this theology, including its authors' conceptions of the Word, selfhood and history, are still matters of debate today. What is revelation? How is it related to the Bible? How should God's selfhood be understood? What consequences does that understanding have on our conception of human selfhood? Finally, what is the true significance of historical criticism for our understanding of the Christian faith?

We should also note a great paradox, namely that the same three ideas – Word, reflective selfhood, and history – that formed the basis of Hegel's robust view of the Trinity were employed by the liberal theologians to a quite different effect. Of course, they assigned meanings to these ideas that differed dramatically from the meanings that Hegel assigned. Nonetheless, the paradox illustrates the point that it is these three ideas that move the history of Trinitarian thought as their meanings change over time. As the next chapter will show, these same three ideas continue to determine the contours of Trinitarian thought up to the present.

CHAPTER SIX

The twentieth century

INTRODUCTION

By the mid-nineteenth century, the main components of modern Trinitarian thought were in place; the available paths were well known and discussed. The fundamental motifs were thoroughly developed – What is the "Word"? Is it the Biblical text? Or is it Jesus Christ? Where does one stand on Melanchthon's claim that the doctrine of the Trinity is an esoteric matter disconnected from the main interests of Christian theology? How is God's selfhood to be understood – with the classical notion of Logos or with the modern notion of personality? To what does the modern understanding of historicity mainly apply – to the Biblical text or God's revelation or even to the divine being itself?

The liberal theologians at the end of the nineteenth century and the beginning of the twentieth articulated one permutation of the three fundamental motifs – Word, reflective selfhood, history – in a way that meant the eclipse of the doctrine. Their critical but also Protestant temperament prevented them from inferring the doctrine from its traditional sources.

Early in the twentieth century another variation on the Trinitarian motifs was composed, a variation that is in fact the contrapuntal inverse of the liberal theological understanding. Whereas liberal theologians stood adamantly in the Melanchthonian tradition and could not see a connection between the Word and the doctrine of the Trinity, such twentieth-century theologians as Karl Barth, Jürgen Moltmann and Wolfhart Pannenberg vehemently asserted the intimate connection between revelation and the doctrine. Whereas liberal theologians thought of God mainly as a person, twentieth-century theologians such as Paul Tillich and Rudolf Bultmann, as well as Moltmann and Pannenberg, eschewed personalistic categories. Although the category of history was no less vital in the twentieth century than in the nineteenth, the application of this category proved to be far more fruitful for developing the doctrine of the Trinity in that century than in the previous century.

The subject of this chapter is the doctrine of the Trinity in the twentieth century. Our study necessarily confines itself to theologians, for, following the collapse of idealism, philosophical interest in the doctrine grew emaciated; few philosophers expressed even slight interest. Even Hans-Georg Gadamer, whose sympathy with theology is well known, discusses the Trinity only because it illustrates an aspect of language.[1] He does not take the doctrine seriously as a subject matter in its own right, but refers to it merely to exhibit an important point in the development of hermeneutical understanding. If we ask about any philosophical dimension to twentieth-century Trinitarian thought, we find that theologians who are most concerned to rehabilitate the doctrine after the onslaught of liberal theology are beholden in one way or another to Hegel and are among the modern inheritors of his legacy.

The theologians to be discussed are Karl Barth (1886–1968), Rudolf Bultmann (1884–1976), Paul Tillich (1886–1965), Jürgen Moltmann (1926–), and Wolfhart Pannenberg (1928–). Why these and not others who might with equal justification have been considered? Karl Barth, of course, is unquestionably indispensable. There can be no doubt that, at least for Protestant theology, he nearly single-handedly rescued the doctrine of the Trinity from the oblivion it faced at the hands of liberal theology. Further, the development of the doctrine by the likes of Moltmann and Pannenberg is inexplicable apart from the spadework of Barth. Bultmann serves the purpose of reminding us that the liberal tradition did not cease in the nineteenth century but continued on. Tillich is included to represent the enduring legacy of idealism, a legacy to which Moltmann and Pannenberg also advert. Tillich shows that the idealistic tradition can be put to very different

---

[1] Hans-Georg Gadamer, *Truth and Method*, 2nd revised edition, translation revised by Joel Weinsheimer and Donald G. Marshall (New York: The Crossroad Publishing Co., 1990), 418–421.

Trinitarian uses when those idealistic impulses are mediated by existentialist philosophy and not by Barth. Moltmann and Pannenberg are chosen here to illustrate contemporary developments of the doctrine that draw on both Barthian and idealistic approaches. Whether their Trinitarian thought will prove to be enduring remains to be seen; at the present moment, they are among the leading examples of the direction in which the doctrine appears to be heading at the beginning of the twenty-first century.

Inasmuch as the fundamental motifs that determine the doctrine of the Trinity were in place by the mid-nineteenth century, this chapter proceeds thematically. Since the twentieth century's reaction to liberal theology has taken the form of theologies that emphasize revelation, this chapter will begin with a review of the various understandings of the Word and the implications for the doctrine of the Trinity. Next will be the question of God's selfhood followed by a consideration of history.

THE WORD AND THE TRINITY

Rudolf Bultmann

We begin this section with Rudolf Bultmann, for he is a bridge to the liberal theologians examined in the preceding chapter. Bultmann himself acknowledged the connection between liberal theology and the dialectical theology of the 1920s, a movement in which he participated along with Barth, Friedrich Gogarten and Eduard Thurneysen. He depicted this connection as a discussion with, not a repudiation of, the liberal theological past and saw the theology of the 1920s as arising out of conditions created by liberal theology. None of this prohibited Bultmann from disagreeing sharply with the leading tenets of the liberals, particularly with their understanding of the Word of God. Nevertheless, the fact that Barth later indicted Bultmann on exactly the charge of which Bultmann accused the liberals – dealing "not with God but with man" – suggests that Bultmann's affinity with liberal theology justifies our understanding him as a bridge between the two movements.[2]

---

[2] Rudolf Bultmann, "Liberal Theology and the Latest Theological Movement," *Faith and Understanding I*, ed. Robert W. Funk, trs. Louise Pettibone Smith (San Francisco: Harper & Row, 1969), 28–29.

Bultmann believed that one of the most profound differences between his theology and liberal theology lay in the concept of the Word of God. For Bultmann, the Word is the proclamation of two things: first that I am a sinner and second that in Christ my sin is forgiven.[3] The Word is proclamation about Christ, but *not* a teaching about Christ's divine nature. It is instead a teaching about our justification in Jesus Christ.[4] While this understanding of the Word of God serves to distinguish Bultmann from liberal theology to some extent, it also distinguishes him from Barth's theology in a way that completely determined their resulting attitudes toward the doctrine of the Trinity. Both Barth and Bultmann agreed that all authentic knowledge of God comes from the Word; however, this admission did not lead Bultmann to the doctrine of the Trinity because the Word, in his view, being the proclamation of justification, does not communicate to us information about the nature of Jesus Christ. Barth, on the contrary, because he understood the Word to be Jesus Christ himself – and not merely a proclamation about Christ – was led to embrace the doctrine of the Trinity. Since, according to Barth, it is the person of Jesus who is the Word, the doctrine of the Trinity is implied by a theology of the Word. So, while Bultmann's predilection for the theology of the Word allied him with Barth, his definition of "Word" placed him far closer to the liberal theological view of the Trinity.

Bultmann was willing to acknowledge Christ as the Word of God in a restricted sense; however, for him this signified only that Christ becomes present to us in preaching. He reasoned that just as Jesus historically was the eschatological moment when the old epoch ended and the new began, so preaching is the moment when this new beginning takes place for those who hear the Word. In fact, Bultmann held that Jesus Christ cannot be separated from preaching – preaching is a part of the saving act by which God in Christ justifies us. As a result, he could acknowledge that Christ is the Word of God only in the restricted sense that proclamation of the Word in preaching is "a continuation of the Christ event."

---

[3] Rudolf Bultmann, "On the Question of Christology," *Faith and Understanding I*, 132; "The Concept of the Word of God in the New Testament," *Faith and Understanding I*, 301.

[4] Rudolf Bultmann, "The Christology of the New Testament," *Faith and Understanding I*, 277.

Accordingly, both Christ and preaching deserve the appellation "revelation."[5] The point for Bultmann is that faith and theology deal with the Christ who is present to us in preaching as God's act of salvation, not with the historical individual who lived 2000 years ago or with the divine-human person of the creeds. Christ's being as the union of the divine and human, which was the point of departure for the early church's doctrine of the Trinity and which plays a prominent role in Barth's understanding of the Trinity, is irrelevant for Bultmann. It is no surprise, then, that there is no role for the doctrine of the Trinity in Bultmann's theology – its traditional basis (the historical Jesus as the divine-human person) was not significant for him, having been displaced by the presence of Christ in preaching.

Consistently, then, Bultmann held that the Christology of the New Testament is essentially a doctrine of justification and not a theory about the nature of Christ. In Bultmann's estimation, the possibilities for Christology are twofold: either it is proclamation and summons or it is a matter of speculative metaphysics. As with the liberal theologians, the latter was anathema to Bultmann's Protestant sensibilities. Consequently, he could understand the unity of Jesus Christ and God only as a matter of God's acting in Jesus. It could not be a matter of Jesus' unique ontology.[6] We can see that Bultmann's understanding of the incarnation differed dramatically from its customary meaning in Christian theology; this difference explains the Trinitarian lacuna in Bultmann's theology.

Not surprisingly, Bultmann was quite critical of traditional ways of looking at Jesus Christ. New Testament statements about Christ, according to him, pertain to the saving significance of Christ and to the revelation that is found exclusively in him; they do not ascribe to him a metaphysical nature. "Divinity" and "lordship," traditional buttresses of Trinitarian doctrine, in truth denote that Christ is the eschatological event; they cannot be employed so as

---

[5] Bultmann, "The Concept of the Word of God in the New Testament," 307–308; "The Christology of the New Testament," 278; Rudolf Bultmann, "The Concept of Revelation in the New Testament," *Existence and Faith: Shorter Writings of Rudolf Bultmann*, trs. Shubert M. Ogden (Cleveland: World Publishing Co., Meridian Books, 1963), 87 and 89.   [6] Bultmann, "The Christology of the New Testament," 279 and 282–283.

to yield an objective and theoretical knowledge of Christ.[7] This does not imply that for Bultmann the knowledge of God and of Christ is merely subjective and that it lacks an objective ground. He insisted, over against liberal theology, that theology has a proper object, namely God.[8] Faith is absolutely not a human attitude; to regard it as such is to lose sight of the intentionality of faith, the fact that it always has an object.[9] However, although God is the *object* of theology, theological knowledge of God is not *objective* in the scientific or theoretical sense; it is instead existential knowledge which concerns God's acting upon us. This sort of knowledge has nothing to do with God's eternal being with its metaphysical features.[10] In other words, theology is concerned only with the act of God in Jesus Christ and in the proclamation of forgiveness. Bultmann, then, was attempting to steer a course between what he understood to be the subjectivizing tendencies of liberal theology and the objectivizing nature of scientific knowledge. He wanted to establish a genuine knowledge of God, with an objectively real ground, while insisting that such knowledge is existential in character, not theoretical, and that it has to do with God's saving activity and not with the metaphysics of the divine being. We can easily detect his profound sympathies for the liberal theological agenda and for the Melanchthonian strain of theology in his strident stance against the importation of metaphysics into theology and his insistence on the thoroughly personal nature of our knowledge of God. At any rate, with his theological principles forbidding any knowledge of God's eternal being in itself, the prospects for a robust doctrine of the Trinity were slim as long as the Trinity was understood precisely as the eternal being of God

---

[7] Rudolf Bultmann, "The Christological Confession of the World Council of Churches," *Essays: Philosophical and Theological*, trs. J. C. G. Grieg, The Library of Philosophy and Theology (New York: Macmillan, 1955), 280–281, 284 and 286–287.

[8] Rudolf Bultmann, "Theology as a Science," *The New Testament and Mythology and Other Basic Writings*, ed. and trs. Shubert M. Ogden (London: SCM Press, 1984), 52.

[9] Bultmann, "On the Question of Christology," 118–120.

[10] Bultmann, "Theology as a Science," 49–50 and 54. See also Roger A. Johnson, *The Origins of Demythologizing: Philosophy and Historiography in the Theology of Rudolf Bultmann*, Studies in the History of Religions (Supplement to *Numen*), no. 28 (Leiden: E. J. Brill, 1974), 84–86 and 194–197 for an account of Bultmann's dependence on the thought of Wilhelm Herrmann for this notion of objectivizing knowledge and its incompatibility with the Christian understanding of faith and of God.

in itself. Moltmann and Pannenberg have recently tried to over-come this distinction between God's actions and God's being, seeking thereby to formulate a doctrine of the Trinity that is neither metaphysical nor theoretical.

In conclusion, there are two principal factors in Bultmann's neglect of the doctrine of the Trinity: the distinction between metaphysical and saving knowledge on the one hand and the related understanding of the Word of God and the incarnation on the other hand. Like the liberal theologians, Bultmann expressly endorsed Melanchthon's disparaging statements about the Trinity in the first edition of *Loci Communes*. In particular, Bultmann fastened on to the proposition that the knowledge of Christ consists in knowing the benefits that come to us from him, not in knowing about his natures and mode of incarnation; Bultmann thereby justified his belief in the solidly Protestant character of his views.[11] Bultmann also appealed to Martin Luther to substantiate his view of proclamation as the focus of theology.[12] With Luther and Melanchthon on his side, Bultmann felt confident in passing by the doctrine of the Trinity, for, as Melanchthon had pointed out, its connection to saving knowledge is not beyond dispute. Further, Bultmann's understanding of the Word and of the incarnation eliminated the traditional bases on which the doctrine of the Trinity had been seen as necessary. If Bultmann failed to find in the New Testament presentation of the incarnation the doctrine of the two natures of Christ, then it is understandable that he saw no need to seek other grounds for the doctrine. Given his practice of historical criticism, to be discussed in more detail later, Bultmann was not inclined to interpret the New Testament retrospectively from the perspective of later church doctrine.[13]

---

[11] See H. P. Owen, "Revelation," in Charles W. Kegley, ed., *The Theology of Rudolf Bultmann* (London: SCM Press, 1966), 25–26 for a critique of Bultmann's view of revelation and an analysis of its similarity to the liberal theological agenda.

[12] Bultmann, "On the Question of Christology," 139.

[13] See James D. Smart, *The Divided Mind of Modern Theology: Karl Barth and Rudolf Bultmann, 1908–1933* (Philadelphia: Westminster Press, 1967), 190 and 192 for commentary on the differences between Barth and Bultmann on the importance of the *person* of Christ and of the incarnation for the concept of revelation. See also James F. Kay, Christus Praesens: *A Reconsideration of Rudolf Bultmann's Christology* (Grand Rapids: William B. Eerdmans Publishing Co., 1994), 109–110 for a defense of Bultmann against Barth's charges of docetism in regard to the incarnation.

Bultmann represents the continuing influence of nineteenth-century liberal theology into the twentieth century. While he disagreed sharply with some liberal notions, at least one of his fundamental sympathies was the same as theirs – the focus on saving knowledge in Christ and the concomitant banishing of all metaphysical speculation from theology. With his distinctive understanding of the Word of God, his theology, like theirs, had no place for the doctrine of the Trinity.

Paul Tillich

Like Bultmann, Tillich was concerned with the character of our knowledge of God and with the propriety of theological language. Unlike Bultmann, he did not shy away from metaphysical reflection on God and had no qualms about discussing the being of God. As a result, Tillich did not feel Melanchthon's impediment to writing about the Trinity. Nevertheless, we must note that Tillich could never embrace the traditional doctrine of the Trinity because of a fundamental axiom of his theology: all statements about God, with one exception, are to be regarded as symbolic. The one exception is the statement that God is being itself,[14] a statement showing little promise of supporting any doctrine of the Trinity. This axiom implies that the doctrine of the Trinity is thoroughly suffused with symbols that cannot be taken literally. Armed with this axiom, Tillich was prepared to take the traditional doctrine seriously but it would always retain its symbolic content.

Even though virtually all theological language is, for Tillich, symbolic, it still has a connection with revelation; more exactly, all symbols arise out of revelation.[15] As a result, these symbols and the theological systems based on them are not merely subjective feelings or opinions; they are grounded in God and in the ways in which we relate to God in revelation. In particular, the Trinitarian symbols of Father, Son and Spirit are based on the manifestation of God as "creative power, as saving love, and as ecstatic transformation."[16] We can see from this that revelation, for Tillich, is of a highly experiential nature; like Bultmann, he rejected the view

---

[14] Paul Tillich, *Systematic Theology*, 3 vols. (Chicago: University of Chicago Press, 1951–1963), I:238.   [15] Ibid., I:110.   [16] Ibid., III:283.

that revelation consists in communicated information about God. As a result, he drew a distinction between revelation and doctrine: revelation provides the content of Trinitarian thought; theology adds a rational and logical form to that content as it formulates doctrines.[17] While both the revelatory content and the rational form are essential to theology, revelation always retains its priority in importance. This distinction between form and content allowed Tillich to subject the traditional doctrine of the Trinity to criticism. In doing so, he believed he was criticizing only the form in which the church had attempted to formulate the revelatory experiences. Criticism of the doctrine does not imply rejection of the revelatory content.

Having noted the experiential character of revelation and its distinction from doctrine, we must go on to observe that, with respect to the Trinity, revelation is of two sorts: first, there is the experience of the living God, an experience that all humans in some way have. Second, there is the experience of the new being in Jesus the Christ, which is a specifically Christian experience.[18] On this distinction rests a further refinement of great importance – the distinction between Trinitarian principles and Trinitarian symbols. Because God is the living God (symbolized as Spirit) and because life has a threefold, dialectical character, God has often been represented in the history of religion in Trinitarian ways. The universal experience of God as living results in Trinitarian representations of God. But these Trinitarian ways of representing God are not identical with the Christian doctrine of the Trinity. For one thing, the specifically Christian Trinitarian symbols (Father, Son, and Spirit) are neither found in nor deducible from the Trinitarian principles universally found in the history of religions. For another thing, whereas the universal Trinitarian principles arise out of the experience of God as Spirit, the Christian Trinitarian symbols are based more particularly on "the assertion that Jesus is the Christ." These Trinitarian principles are nothing more than a preparation for the doctrine of the Trinity; they are grounded in the life of God as Spirit and in the general features of revelatory experience.[19]

17 Ibid., III:286.   18 Ibid., II:144.   19 Ibid., I:251.

The Christian doctrine of the Trinity, employing the Trinitarian symbols (Father, Son, and Spirit), depends on a developed Christian thinking about Jesus Christ; hence it is rooted in God as Logos more than God as Spirit. Nevertheless, a developed Christology is only a necessary and not a sufficient condition of the Christian doctrine of the Trinity. What is needed in addition to Christology is a doctrine of the Spirit, for we experience the new being in Christ only through God as Spirit.[20] As we can see, the role of revelation in Tillich's theology is complex, with a dynamic relation between the symbols Logos and Spirit. Viewed in one way, his theology is thoroughly Christological, for historically the doctrine of the Trinity could not arise until the church had reflected on the significance of Jesus Christ and his relation with God; viewed in another way, the distinctively Christological aspect of his theology is a subset of a more universal understanding of God and revelation. Revelation is at the heart of Tillich's theology, but revelation is not identical with Christ.

Nevertheless, Christology is an essential condition of the Christian doctrine of the Trinity. It was Tillich's opinion that the early Trinitarian councils, Nicaea and Constantinople, were really concerned with Christology, since, he argued, their purpose was to identify Jesus Christ and the Logos. If it were not for the demands of Christology – that Christ is the divine Logos and not a creature – there would be no doctrine of the Trinity (although God would still be thought of in Trinitarian ways). Consequently, the doctrine of the Trinity presupposes the doctrine of Christ and is a support for it.[21] Accordingly, Tillich sided with Schleiermacher and against Barth on the question of the proper location of the doctrine of the Trinity in the system of theology. Schleiermacher, as already noted, argued that the doctrine of the Trinity, as the "coping-stone" of Christian theology, must come last in the system of doctrine, since it presupposes everything else, especially the doctrines of Christ and the Spirit. Barth, as we shall learn, argued that the doctrine of the Trinity, as the church's exposition of revelation, is the presupposition of all other doctrines and so should be the first doctrine. Tillich's view was that the systematic order of doctrines may differ

[20] Ibid., III:285.   [21] Ibid., II:143–144 and III:288.

from the existential order. The doctrine's "logical foundation in the structure of [divine] life" precedes "its existential foundation, the appearance of Jesus as the Christ." That is, the doctrine of Christ logically presupposes the Trinitarian structure of the divine being; however, the doctrine had to await the appearance of Christ in history. As a result, the formally stated doctrine of the Trinity must come after the discussion of Christology. Consistently, he chided Barth for turning a postlegomenon into a prolegomenon and praised Schleiermacher for correctly locating the doctrine.[22]

Ultimately, then, the doctrine of the Trinity rests, in Tillich's opinion, on two revelatory grounds – the universal experience of God as Spirit and the historical revelation of Jesus as the Christ. The former yields Trinitarian principles that are found throughout the history of religion; the latter is the basis for the specifically Christian doctrine of the Trinity. In the end, the doctrine must take its bearings from the revelation of God as Spirit; even Christology is incomplete without this revelation. Christology is the historical impulse for the formation of the doctrine; however, the content of the doctrine is already laid out in the Trinitarian principles that arise from the revelation of God as Spirit. Accordingly, we will further examine Tillich's understanding of God as Spirit later, under the heading of God's selfhood.

Karl Barth

On introducing Karl Barth into this discussion of the Trinity and the Word of God, we enter new territory. Whereas for Bultmann the Trinity was not even a consideration, for Barth it is both the first doctrine in the dogmatic system and the keel upon which every other doctrine was constructed. In contrast to Tillich, for whom Christological revelation is a supplement to the universal Trinitarian experience of God, for Barth Christological revelation is the only authentic knowledge of God. The doctrine of the Trinity is not (as it is for Tillich) the historically contingent version of a universal knowledge of God; it is instead the only possible path toward the knowledge of God.

---

[22] Ibid., I:286 and III:285.

The central importance of the Trinity to Barth's theology is evident in his understanding of the Word. To say that revelation is an essential condition of our knowledge of the Trinity is not a sufficient characterization of Barth's view. Nearly every Christian theologian would admit as much. What distinguishes Barth is his view that revelation itself is Trinitarian in form. So, whereas theologians had in the past engaged themselves in finding analogies of the Trinity in nature, Barth found the one and only analogy to the Trinity in the Word itself, which like the Trinity subsists in three forms: revelation (which means Jesus Christ), the Bible, and proclamation. Like the Trinitarian persons, the three forms are fully distinct from one another, yet each of the three is fully the Word of God and none is more so than the others. In a further analogy to the Trinity, none of the forms can be abstracted from the others: just as in the Trinity the Father is known only in and through the Son and Spirit, so revelation (i.e., Jesus Christ) is known by us only in and through the Bible and proclamation. Finally, just as the Son comes to us through the mediation of the Spirit, so the Bible becomes the Word of God for us through proclamation.[23] As Barth stated elsewhere, in the doctrine of the Trinity and in the threefold form of the Word of God, we find the "same fundamental determinations and mutual relationships."[24]

This understanding of revelation signals the overriding importance that Trinitarian thinking plays in Barth's theology. For Barth, the doctrine of the Trinity arises directly out of revelation; in turn, revelation is accurately expounded only when its Trinitarian form is exposed. In this light, Barth emerges as an inheritor of the Hegelian tradition, with its emphasis not only on revelation but also on the Trinitarian character of revelation. Both Hegel and Barth departed from the customary view that revelation provides us with information about God, to the effect that God is a Trinity. Both insisted that revelation is possible only because God is a Trinity and that God's Trinitarian being is reflected in revelation.

In seeking to understand Barth's view of the Trinity and the ways in which it represents a departure from the liberal theology

---

[23] Karl Barth, *Church Dogmatics*, vol. I, *The Doctrine of the Word of God*, first half-volume, trs. G. T. Thomson (Edinburgh: T. & T. Clark, 1963), 120–121. Hereafter referred to as *CD* I/1.   [24] Ibid., 136.

of the previous generation, it may be helpful to note Barth's agreements with Bultmann. Following this, we will have a detailed look at the points of disagreement between the two.

The following theses, drawn from Barth's view of revelation, are all points with which Bultmann agreed: First, revelation is not identical with the Bible. Revelation is instead an event with a historical character.[25] Second, revelation is a manifestation of God – an activity of God.[26] Third, it is identical with Jesus Christ – or at least Jesus Christ is the criterion by which we judge other alleged revelations.[27] Fourth, the time of revelation is important: there is an important distinction between the past of the historical Jesus and the now of revelation.[28]

However, these points of contact between Barth and Bultmann are only a prelude to a far greater chasm that emerges when these points are examined in detail. In spite of the manifest similarities between them, similarities that Bultmann was always keen to mention, there are profound differences that Barth was equally intent on making public.

The first point (that revelation is an event and so cannot be simply identified with the Bible) and the second (that revelation is the manifestation of God) can be taken together. There is no question that, by affirming these, Bultmann agreed that revelation is an act of God. In no sense did Bultmann think that revelation is merely another word for human self-understanding. Revelation is, accordingly, the manifestation of God as "the Omnipotent, Holy and Eternal One." As such, revelation is absolutely not a human act and cannot be controlled by us.[29] Yet even these assertions did not suffice in Barth's opinion. What Barth felt was necessary was a near identification of God and revelation. On the one hand, Barth wished to ensure that no wedge could be driven between God and God's revelation, as though revelation were not a full and true disclosure of the nature of God; on the other hand, Barth wanted to maintain the freedom of God so that the event of revelation would depend on God's decision. The former is necessary to guarantee that the God who encounters us in revelation is the one and only

---

[25] Ibid., 127.   [26] Ibid., 468.   [27] Ibid., 131.   [28] Ibid., 169–170.
[29] Rudolf Bultmann, "The Question of Natural Revelation," *Essays: Philosophical and Theological*, 109 and 113.

God, that there is no more real God standing behind the revealed God. The latter is necessary to avoid collapsing God into the event of historical revelation and thus robbing God of eternal and independent being. As a result, Barth ventured far beyond Bultmann by characterizing God's own being as event-like.[30] Apart from the fascinating metaphysical considerations in this portrayal of the divine being, the immediate point is Barth's concern to avoid any separation between God's being and God's act of revelation. With Bultmann, Barth wished to affirm the historically contingent and particular character of revelation.[31] Thereby both sought to distinguish revelation from any sort of universal truth to which humanity might have access through natural capacities. But Barth insisted additionally on saying something about the being of God, a subject about which Bultmann showed great reticence. Barth's motivation for considering the being of God was thoroughly Trinitarian – any distinction between God's being and God's act of revelation would, he feared, result in a version of Sabellianism, according to which revelation does not truly manifest God but instead acts as a screen behind which God is concealed. Barth feared that in a Sabellian theology humanity would not have to do with God, but only with a superficial appearance of God.[32] We see here a certain anxiety on Barth's part, traceable in Protestantism back to Luther's distinction between *Deus absconditus* and *Deus revelatus*.[33] This anxiety explains in part Barth's great antipathy to Schleiermacher, whose doctrine of the Trinity violated precisely this principle about which Barth felt so vehemently. So, the initial agreement with Bultmann as to the eventful character of revelation gives way ultimately to a profound difference as Barth wished to apply the notion of event to God's being. The significance of this move penetrates deeply into Barth's doctrine of the Trinity, for by establishing an analogy between revelation and the being of God, Barth was able to portray the eternal life of the Trinity as a sort of

---

[30] Karl Barth, *Church Dogmatics*, vol. II, *The Doctrine of God*, first half-volume, ed. G. W. Bromiley and T. F. Torrance, trs. T. H. L. Parker, et al. (Edinburgh: T. & T. Clark, 1957), 263. Hereafter referred to as *CD* II/1.

[31] See, for example, *CD* I/1, 135, 169–170, 374–375.

[32] See, for example, *CD* I/1, 349, 411 and 439.

[33] Martin Luther, *The Bondage of the Will*, trs. Henry Cole (Grand Rapids: Baker Book House, 1976), 171–174.

self-revelation of God within the eternal being of God. On this view, what transpires in revelation is a historical enactment of what occurs eternally in the Trinity. As a consequence, a language is provided by which the Trinity can be set forth in doctrine.

Barth's understanding of the third point of agreement with Bultmann (that revelation is identical with Christ) can be considered together with his understanding of the fourth (that there is an important distinction between the historical Jesus of the past and the now of revelation). As was the case with the former points, Barth agreed with these theses, but erected upon them further constructions that Bultmann could never have favored. In particular, Barth insisted that the Christ that is identical with revelation is not simply the Christ present in proclamation but is also the incarnate Word, the union of God and human nature.[34] This point cuts to the heart of the disagreement between Barth and Bultmann and it has immediate consequences for their respective doctrines of the Trinity. For Bultmann, the Word that is revelation is Jesus Christ as present in the church's proclamation of the gospel. This Christ is inseparable from the proclamation and it is difficult to avoid the conclusion that, for Bultmann, the ongoing life of Jesus Christ has become completely merged with the proclamation about him. For Barth, however, the Word that is revelation is Jesus Christ who is both historically particular and also the incarnate Logos, which exists eternally and which transcends any particular moment of revelation in the present. In fact, Barth goes so far as to claim that the incarnation of the Logos *is* revelation, for "the life of this real man was the object and theater of the acts of God."[35] Because of the incarnation – because Jesus Christ is fully divine and fully human – he represents God to us and represents us to God. In this way, he is God's revelation to us and our reconciliation with God.[36] For Bultmann, on the contrary, since the Word is virtually identical with proclamation, all the emphasis falls on the moment of preaching and sacrament and on the decision thrust on the hearer of the Word. There is in this view

---

[34] *CD* I/1, 134.
[35] Karl Barth, *Church Dogmatics*, vol. I, *The Doctrine of the Word of God*, second half-volume, ed. G. W. Bromiley and T. F. Torrance, trs. G. T. Thomson and Harold Knight (Edinburgh: T. & T. Clark, 1963), 147. Hereafter referred to as *CD* I/2.   [36] Ibid., 151 and 157.

neither need of nor opportunity for a doctrine of the Trinity. Everything that Bultmann considered vital is to be found in the confrontation of the hearer by the Word.

Bultmann, then, laid emphasis on revelation as it occurs in proclamation. Contrarily, Barth's conception of the Word, closely following Chalcedonian lines, results in a distinction between revelation in the primary sense (Jesus Christ, the incarnate Logos) and revelation as it occurs now when God chooses to employ church proclamation and the Bible to confront us. Most important for our purposes is the fact that Barth explicated the distinction between revelation then (Jesus Christ) and revelation now, as we hear the Word, in Trinitarian terms; he understood Jesus Christ to be the objective actuality of revelation and the Holy Spirit to be the subjective actuality of revelation now.[37] Whereas for Bultmann the decisive thing was the proclaimed Word and the decision it compels, for Barth it was the historical reality of Jesus Christ and the Holy Spirit as the means by which Jesus Christ actually comes to us as revealer and reconciliation.

It may be helpful here to comment on Barth's understanding of the Holy Spirit in revelation. Barth invoked the doctrine of the Spirit in order to guard God's freedom in revelation and to protect against any tendency to understand revelation in anthropological terms.[38] The concept of the Spirit guards God's freedom in revelation by reminding us that revelation occurs when and if God intends it to occur. Neither the Bible alone nor any other thing is revelation in itself; revelation does not occur until the Holy Spirit makes it possible for us to hear the Word. Similarly, the concept of the Spirit prevents an anthropological understanding of revelation by making revelation to be an act of God; neither the possibility nor the actuality of revelation is due to human capacities or actions.[39] It is this emphasis on the Spirit's role in revelation that Barth missed in Bultmann's theology and which accounts for his charge that Bultmann, like Schleiermacher, was using philosophy to assert a human potential for faith.[40] While this charge may not be fully fair to Bultmann, it may be that a philosophical analysis of human being performs a function in Bultmann's theology similar

---

[37] *CD* II/1, 1 and 203.   [38] *CD* I/1, 380 and I/2, 205.   [39] *CD* I/1, 526 and 535.
[40] Ibid., 39.

to the function of the Spirit in Barth's theology. For both, a central issue is the means by which humans come to receive revelation. Bultmann, although holding to the indispensability of the divine activity in revelation, nevertheless allowed for philosophical analysis to act as a means of freeing the Word from the ancient mythological form in which it is ensconced, thereby allowing the Word itself – and not the myth – to be heard and responded to. Barth, however, assigned to the Holy Spirit this task of making us capable of hearing the Word.[41] The Spirit is important to Barth for another reason, a reason that demonstrates with great clarity Barth's differences from Bultmann. One of the ruling ideas of Barth's theology is that God is eternally the same as what God is for us in revelation. So, just as in revelation the Spirit is the activity of God whereby God and humans stand in communion, so in eternity the Spirit effects communion between Father and Son.[42] Hence there is an analogy, or perhaps more than an analogy, between the event of revelation and the life of the eternal Trinity, a point hinted at by Barth's indication that the Word of revelation is in fact uttered by God eternally and is the means by which God has self-knowledge,[43] a statement that could imply that the eternal Word is a sort of revelation within God's eternity and that the Spirit is the state of revealedness within God's eternal being. [44]

In a further departure from Bultmann, Barth incorporated the historicity of Jesus Christ into his understanding of revelation. Jesus Christ, according to Barth, is revelation precisely in the central events of his life and in his Israelite heritage.[45] So the historical particularity of revelation that both Bultmann and Barth insisted upon is extended by Barth to the life of Jesus. This is in marked contrast to Bultmann's indifference toward the historical Jesus. Also in contrast to Bultmann's approach is Barth's use of the

---

[41] For further commentary on this point, see Smart, *Divided Mind*, 192–193.

[42] *CD* I/1, 538–539 and 549–550.   [43] Ibid., 158 and 499.

[44] See R. D. Williams, "Barth on the Triune God," in S. W. Sykes, ed., *Karl Barth: Studies of His Theological Method* (Oxford: Clarendon Press, 1979), 171–172 for a critique of this notion that the Spirit is God's revealedness, not only in historical revelation to humanity but also in the eternal life of God. The point is that if revelation is a miracle by which God is related to something radically different from God, then it is difficult to see the propriety of drawing an analogy between the Spirit's role in revelation and in the eternal Trinity.   [45] *CD* II/1, 262.

doctrine of the Trinity to answer the question, why is revelation particular and not universal? Bultmann affirmed the particularity of revelation as part of a rejection of idealism, since, in his view, revelation is not about the *idea* of reconciliation but instead about the *event* of reconciliation. The particularity of revelation is for Bultmann a complement of the concreteness of faith and its association with human decision.[46] For Barth, however, the particularity of revelation has a Trinitarian ground, for Jesus Christ is revelation; since there can be no second Son of God besides Jesus, there can consequently be only one revelation.[47] In summary, it is evident that Barth connected revelation to the Trinity in a way that completely departs from Bultmann's understanding of revelation.[48] This points us once again to Barth's Hegelian heritage and, contrariwise, to Bultmann's liberal heritage, and shows that an emphasis on the Word does not in itself result in a robust doctrine of the Trinity. Everything depends on how the Word is represented.

For his understanding of the Word Bultmann looked back to Philip Melanchthon and thus saw revelation as the gospel's call to decision and proclamation of forgiveness. The importance of Melanchthon for Bultmann's theology can scarcely be overestimated. From Melanchthon he drew the conclusion that faith is not the intellectual holding of dogmatic propositions, but rather the knowledge of Christ's benefits to us.[49] From here he further inferred that Paul's Christology was actually to be found not (as expected) in express statements about Christ's pre-existence and resurrection but instead in his doctrine of justification.[50] This appeal to Melanchthon immediately shows us that Bultmann stood in the Ritschlian interpretation of Lutheran theology, according to which Christian theology is absolutely non-speculative. By employing Melanchthon in this way, Bultmann could lay claim to an

[46] Rudolf Bultmann, "The Crisis of Belief," *Essays: Philosophical and Theological*, 6–10 and 16.
[47] *CD* I/1, 487.
[48] For a critique of Barth's conception of revelation, see Williams, "Barth on the Triune God," 153–154 and 157–158. Williams' critique focuses on the congruity of Barth's and the Bible's respective views of revelation.
[49] Rudolf Bultmann, "Grace and Freedom," *Essays: Philosophical and Theological*, 173.
[50] Bultmann, "The Christology of the New Testament," 279. See also Kay, *Christus Praesens*, 98, n. 29 for references by Bultmann to Herrmann's dictum that we know God in God's acts toward us, not in God's own being.

authentic stream in the Lutheran tradition while making use of the then-contemporary emphasis on revelation, all without having to dip into Trinitarian issues. Barth was compelled to respond and show that Bultmann's use of Melanchthon was misguided and that Melanchthon could not be rightly employed to prohibit all talk about the Trinity. Not surprisingly, Barth was of the opinion that the passage in the first edition of *Loci Communes,* in which Melanchthon seemed to abjure knowledge of the Trinity in favor of doctrines with a more directly soteriological character, had been thoroughly misunderstood by the liberal theologians. First, Barth averred, Melanchthon's statements on this point were "a transient mood but not a theological attitude." Further, those statements reflect more Melanchthon's preoccupation with soteriological doctrines such as sin and grace than his disparaging the doctrine of the Trinity. Finally, they were provoked by the treatment of the doctrine at the hands of scholastic theologians, a treatment that Barth derided as "unchurchly."[51] In short, while the reformers may, because of the peculiarities of their polemical situation, have temporarily set aside the Trinitarian and Christological doctrines "with a somewhat impatient movement," it is impossible, Barth urged, to imagine that they wished to reduce these doctrines to an account merely of the benefits of Christ for us.[52] We see here an argument as old as Protestantism itself about the nature of revelation. The one side (Bultmann, the Ritschlians, and other critics of the doctrine) and the other (Barth and other Trinitarians) both protest their faithfulness to the Word and each seeks to better the other in connecting its doctrines directly to that Word. The decisive thing is the way in which the Word is understood; that understanding is the source of each tradition's orientation to the Trinity. We can also see again the historical significance of Hegel, whose revival of the ancient Logos idea and whose exposition of the divine being as inherently self-revelatory helped to make possible the resurgence of Trinitarian thinking that Barth initiated in the twentieth century.

Having showed what the content of revelation is *not*, Barth, proceeded to state what it is: not simply the word of justification and

---

[51] *CD* I/1, 477.　　[52] Ibid., 480.

forgiveness, as Bultmann would have it, but the disclosure of
God's lordship.[53] It is this understanding of the content of revelation that distinguished Barth's view of the Trinity from Hegel's,
for lordship implies, in Barth's reckoning, God's freedom and
independence, two characteristics not conspicuous in Hegel's theology. Although, as noted, God is identical with the act of revelation, God is not simply reducible to that act. While God is fully
given to us in revelation, God always remains free – hence the
importance, in Barth's theology, of asserting that God is antecedently what God is in revelation. Although revelation exhibits
the life of the Trinity, that life retains a transcendent dimension
that is the eternal prototype of revelation.[54] Because God possesses independent life, God is free. This notion of God's freedom
is so prevalent in Barth's theology that it functions virtually as an
axiom, for Barth defined deity in terms of the freedom that is
equivalent to lordship.[55] Examples abound: whether the Bible
becomes for us the Word of God rests on God's free decision; the
criterion by which we judge the authenticity of alleged revelations
is whether they recognize and encompass God's freedom to
become God's own other; and the Holy Spirit signifies God's
freedom to become our God.[56] Every one of these points represents Barth's persistent polemic against any idealist-like attempt to
merge God with the world in any form at all. While Barth's theology of the Trinity and revelation depicts a God who radically
identifies with the world, even to the point of becoming a being in
the world, at the same time his theology seeks to preserve the utter
transcendence of God and the freedom of God to reveal or to
abstain from revealing and to create or to refrain from creating. As
cannot be mentioned too often or emphasized too strongly, the
freedom of God in revelation is associated with God's Trinitarian
being: God revealed is the Son; God veiled is the Father.[57] The
fundamental identity of Father and Son establishes the basic truth
about God as Barth saw it: that God is so free that God is free even
to become what God is not (a human being) without thereby compromising God's freedom and independence (grounded in God's

[53] Ibid., 353: "God reveals himself as lord. This is the root of the doctrine" of the Trinity.
[54] *CD* II/1, 257, 260 and *CD* I/1, 158.   [55] *CD* I/1, 352.
[56] Ibid., 178–179, 367 and 382.   [57] Ibid., 372.

fatherhood). This theological move represents Barth's response to the idealist tradition's tendency to regard the world as a moment within the divine life, thus regarding the creation of the world as analogous to or even identical with the begetting of the eternal Son. Although Hegel labored long and hard to defend himself against any hint of pantheism, theologians in later generations never were convinced that he had succeeded. Barth's Trinitarian grounding of revelation represents one more in a long series of theological refutations of the pantheistic side of idealism.

However, as we will see, Barth's polemical response to this issue inclined him to highlight the eternal life of God and to raise to the level of principle the statement that God is antecedently what God is in revelation. Moltmann and Pannenberg, although disavowing pantheism every bit as strenuously as Barth, have chosen to bring the eternal Trinity and the Trinity of revelation far closer together than they believed Barth to have done.[58] It turns out, then, that whereas Barth's theology is indirectly indebted to Hegel for certain aspects of his Trinitarian thought, Moltmann and Pannenberg have drawn upon different aspects of Hegel's thought, namely on his understanding of personhood as an intensely relational phenomenon and on his emphasis on the historicity of God's being. Although not often mentioned by these theologians, Hegel is in many ways the unacknowledged guide to their thought.

Jürgen Moltmann

Karl Barth marked a watershed in the German tradition of Trinitarian thinking. While it would be premature to announce the death of liberal theology, the writings of two of the leading theologians of our day, Jürgen Moltmann and Wolfhart Pannenberg, demonstrate that Trinitarian theology today takes its cue from Barth and not from liberal theology. It is he with whom theologians must reckon and not with the likes of Albrecht Ritschl and

---

[58] See Paul D. Molnar, "The Function of the Immanent Trinity in the Theology of Karl Barth: Implications for Today," *Scottish Journal of Theology* 42 (1989): 367–399 for a critique of Moltmann's and Pannenberg's identification of the eternal Trinity and the historical Trinity and a defense of Barth's distinguishing them. In a characteristically Barthian fashion, Molnar finds in Moltmann and Pannenberg a compromise of God's freedom.

Wilhelm Herrmann. It is Barth whom Moltmann and Pannenberg have sought to improve upon in their own Trinitarian thinking. Yet, while the influence of Barth on Moltmann and Pannenberg is patent, we can also detect an important generational shift: concerns over which Barth felt great anxiety – that God must be eternally what God is in revelation and that the chief plague on theology is the excessive subjectivism of liberal theology – are not major concerns of Moltmann or Pannenberg. In turn, their own Trinitarian thought is dominated by other concerns, such as eschatology, to which Barth gave only cursory attention. In addition, Pannenberg especially has concerned himself with rethinking the concept of revelation and has decidedly turned away from the Word-oriented theology characteristic of Barth's and Bultmann's generation. Since Moltmann and Pannenberg have only recently set forth their Trinitarian views, it is impossible to know to what extent they will supplant Barth in Trinitarian thought and to what extent they represent a divergence from or a continuation of the Barthian heritage. While it is evident that both react expressly and significantly against Barth, it is also clear that the thought of each must be regarded as a development of Barth's legacy, although a development undertaken from a more self-consciously Hegelian perspective. In this chapter we deal first with Moltmann, then with Pannenberg.

One way of discerning Moltmann's continuity with Barth's theology is to note his critique of liberal theology. This critique can be seen in his treatment of Schleiermacher, according to which Schleiermacher's main fault lay in stressing the human and subjective side of Christian experience – the way in which we experience God – and consequently in neglecting to ask how God experiences us. Schleiermacher's excessive focus on human experience precluded any profound doctrine of the Trinity, for the only sort of God that would correspond to this human experience would be a monotheistic ground of our experience. Within such a ground a Trinity of persons would be neither knowable nor significant for faith. As a result, Moltmann judges, Schleiermacher's positioning the doctrine of the Trinity at the end of his system was faithful to the basic principles of that system, but wholly inadequate when judged by the revelation attested in the

New Testament.[59] Apart from Moltmann's misunderstanding of the reason for the location of the doctrine, the point remains that Schleiermacher did think of God as being necessarily concealed inwardly and revealed outwardly in revelation. One of the merits of Barth's and Moltmann's critique of Schleiermacher is to question this distinction between God's inside and outside and to argue that the concept of revelation must bring an end to this sort of dichotomous thinking. Of course, the supposition that revelation means the total opening up and knowability of God is a Hegelian motif; Moltmann's theology at this point is unthinkable apart from its ultimate Hegelian antecedents.

Moltmann's agreement with Barth against liberal theology can also be seen in his dispute against Harnack's claims that the doctrine of the Trinity is a result of the dogmatizing of the Christian faith and that the New Testament does not support the doctrine. Against this view, Moltmann argues that there is a clear link between the doctrine and the New Testament, for the doctrine is, he believes, the most compelling interpretation of the New Testament account of God. However, he asserts, this argument can be accepted only if one first adopts a hermeneutical presupposition that differs dramatically from Harnack's – and, we will see, from Barth's. Moltmann's point here is that Harnack's distinction between the gospel and dogma is tenable only on the assumption that history is in actuality *human* history – that it is human subjects who are the principal movers of history. Such an assumption effectively limits talk about God and Christ to their significance for human morality and just as effectively deters all consideration of the Trinity.[60] Against this, Moltmann proposes a different presupposition: "The New Testament talks about God by proclaiming in narrative the relationships of the Father, the Son and the Spirit."[61] On this view, which takes the history of Jesus to be revelatory of the Trinitarian relations, the Gospels testify directly to these Trinitarian relations[62] and are in fact the primary source for our knowledge of the Trinity. The significant history is not that of human reaction to revelation but rather the history of

[59] Jürgen Moltmann, *The Trinity and the Kingdom: The Doctrine of God*, trs. Margaret Kohl (San Francisco: Harper & Row, 1981), 4.   [60] Ibid., 62.   [61] Ibid., 64.
[62] Ibid., 19.

Trinitarian relations. The doctrine of the Trinity is not something added to the Gospels, for the Gospels themselves narrate this Trinitarian history.

Moltmann's critique of liberal theology proves to cut into both liberal theologians and Barth himself. While agreeing with Barth against Harnack that the Trinity can be derived from the revelation testified to in the Bible, Moltmann criticizes Barth for inferring erroneously that revelation is about God's lordship. We note in passing the irony of Moltmann's charging Barth with not giving an adequate account of revelation, this being one of the principal indictments that Barth hurled against the liberal theology of his day. Moltmann's point is that there is an important similarity between Barth and liberal theology here, for both regarded history as the work of singular subjects, either singular human subjects (Harnack) or a single divine subject (Barth). As a result, Barth's theology is in effect just another form of monotheism that fails to do justice to the Trinity revealed in the history of Jesus.[63] Although a more detailed examination of this topic must await the discussion of God's selfhood later in this chapter, it is instructive to note once again that the decisive question is about the nature of the revelation on which the doctrine of the Trinity rests. A commitment to revelation has been a standard Protestant mark from the beginning; however, agreement on the content and implications of that revelation has proven elusive, with the result that the unity of Trinitarian thinking has been just as elusive.

At the same time, in fairness to Barth, we should take note of two matters. First, while Moltmann takes God's lordship to be a threat to human freedom[64] and redolent of nominalism, with its "language of domination,"[65] Barth himself represented God's lordship quite differently. As noted above, while it does signify God's complete and ineradicable independence, it also signals God's capacity to become what God is not, without loss of God's essential being. Although Barth's theology may well *imply* the sort of lordship that Moltmann fears, Barth's actual statements about revelation and lordship in

[63] Ibid., 63.
[64] Ibid., 64. Moltmann develops the political implications of his critique of monotheism and of his view of the Trinity in chapter 6 ("The Kingdom of Freedom") of this work, 191–222.   [65] Ibid., 56.

Church Dogmatics point to something significantly different – the equation of God's lordship and God's freedom for us. God is free to become human for us without ceasing to be the lord. Second, Moltmann's claims that Barth's theology is essentially another form of abstract monotheism and that it lacks grounds for an adequate doctrine of the Trinity, resting as it does on the concept of God's lordship, may depend on an exclusive focus on the first volume of *Church Dogmatics* in isolation from later volumes, such as the highly dialectical account of the Trinity found in the fourth volume.[66] Perhaps we can fault Barth for presenting his doctrine of the Trinity as he did. The treatment in the first volume does have the appearance of a somewhat abstract account, for nothing of what Moltmann calls the history of Jesus is presented there. Instead the doctrine of the Trinity appears, at least superficially, to be a derivation from the statement "God reveals himself as the Lord," a statement that Barth calls "analytic."[67] Not until later in the *Dogmatics* does Jesus' history come into play in a way that gives concrete substance to the doctrine of the Trinity. However, in fairness to Barth we should note that his purpose in the first volume is different from that in the fourth volume: in the first volume he was seeking to establish the Trinitarian character of revelation; in the fourth volume he discussed the redemption accomplished in Christ. Accordingly, it is clear that Barth's doctrine of the Trinity is not complete without the latter portions of the *Dogmatics*, when the concrete relation between Jesus and his Father has been set forth. This relation, it appears, is what Moltmann wishes to focus on, and perhaps it would have been preferable for Barth to have begun with the more historically concrete representation of the Trinity. As it is, Barth is susceptible to the same criticism that Moltmann aims at Schleiermacher, namely that both give us an inadequate and really monotheistic doctrine of the Trinity. The roots of this critique lie in the fact that Schleiermacher's *Christian Faith* and Barth's *Church Dogmatics* both proceed from the more abstract presentation of the doctrine of God to the more historically concrete, so that the doctrine of the Trinity is not complete until the specifically Christological portions are concluded.

---

[66] Karl Barth, *Church Dogmatics*, vol. IV, *The Doctrine of Reconciliation*, part one, ed. G. W. Bromiley and T. F. Torrance, trs. G. W. Bromiley (Edinburgh: T. & T. Clark, 1961), 157–210. Hereafter referred to as *CD* IV/1.   [67] *CD* I/1, 351.

This preliminary discussion indicates that Moltmann shares with Barth the opinion that the basis for our knowledge of the Trinity is Jesus Christ. Like Barth, Moltmann has shown no interest in the speculative-analogical approach to the Trinity although, as we will see, he has an innovative way of expounding the doctrine of the Trinity on the basis of a view of selfhood that differs markedly from Barth's. Moltmann has modified Barth's Christocentric epistemology in a significant fashion by placing the emphasis on what he has called the *history* of Jesus Christ as this is attested in the Bible.[68] Now this modification is not anti-Barthian; it could actually be regarded as a natural development of Barth's own theology. Nevertheless, there is a difference: whereas for Barth, at least in the first volume of *Church Dogmatics*, Jesus Christ is revelatory because of the incarnation (understood in Chalcedonian terms), for Moltmann Jesus Christ is revelatory because his history narrated in the Gospels discloses the Trinitarian life of God.[69]

How does Moltmann understand the assertion that Jesus Christ is a revelation of the Trinity? Principally in that "Jesus is manifested as 'the Son.'" His history is the history of "the reciprocal, changing, and hence living relationship between the Father, the Son and the Spirit." In other words, the New Testament narrates the history of Jesus in a Trinitarian way – as the ensemble of relations among the Father, Son and Spirit.[70] For example, the sending of Jesus Christ into the world by God is not represented by the New Testament as "the history of a person with a god." It is instead represented as "the history of the Son with the Father."[71] In this relation, the Son is defined in terms of that relation and in turn the Father is revealed as Father of the Son only in and through the act of sending. Further, the sending of Jesus the Son takes place in the Spirit, opening up another dimension of the Trinitarian relations.[72] This example indicates Moltmann's typical approach to the issue of revelation and the Trinity: specific events in Christ's history are revelatory of the Trinity because, as narrated by the New Testament, they depict Christ by means of Trinitarian relations.[73]

[68] Moltmann, *The Trinity and the Kingdom*, 16.   [69] Ibid., 64–65.   [70] Ibid., 64.
[71] Ibid., 74.   [72] Ibid., 72.
[73] Beside the sending of the Son, which encompasses Jesus' baptism, other significant events that reveal the Trinity include the death of Christ (Moltmann, *The Trinity and the Kingdom*, 783), the resurrection and exaltation of Christ (83–90) and the future coming of Christ (90–94).

However, an objection may be raised at this point. While these significant events in Christ's history do have a Trinitarian character, involving as they do the terms Father, Son and Spirit, do they not pertain to what is commonly called the economic Trinity, i.e., the Trinity revealed in history? How can Moltmann create a bridge between these events that reveal the historical Trinity and the eternal Trinitarian life of God? As we saw previously, Barth settled this problem with the axiom that God is antecedently in eternity what God is in revelation. This resolution stood in marked contrast to the approach of Schleiermacher, who denied that anything significant could be said about God's eternal life. As noted above, Moltmann is not completely at ease with Barth's answer to this question, for it tends, he believes, to distinguish the eternal from the economic Trinity too dramatically. In particular, Moltmann is troubled by the implication that, on the basis of God's freedom, God might not have become revelatory, so that there might not have been an incarnation and an economic Trinity. To Moltmann, this entire approach appears to make the incarnation and revelation of God rest on an arbitrary decision. It makes God's love and self-communication something extrinsic and capricious.[74] Consistent with this judgment, Moltmann must find another way of connecting the history of Jesus to the eternal Trinity if he is to avoid Schleiermacher's Sabellian resolution of this problem.

Moltmann's solution comes in a series of assertions. First, he changes the traditional Trinitarian conceptuality by distinguishing, not between eternal and economic Trinity, but between the doxological Trinity and the economic Trinity. The doxological Trinity is not distinct from the Trinity revealed in the history of Jesus; it is rather the one and only Trinity insofar as it is praised as the ground of salvation. In keeping with his overall epistemological approach, Moltmann does not claim that there is a special revelation of the doxological Trinity apart from history; instead, statements about the doxological Trinity arise from reflection on what must be true about God in order to explain the historical experience of salvation.[75] Thus there is a somewhat Kantian aspect of the doxological theology – it is not about directly experienced realities but instead about the transcendent realities that

---

[74] Moltmann, *The Trinity and the Kingdom*, 53–54.   [75] Ibid., 153.

make experience (in this case, the experience of salvation) possible. But the more prominent aspect of doxological theology is its responsive character. Here, our experience of salvation gives rise to our thanks and praise: God is "worshipped and loved for himself, not merely for salvation's sake."[76]

The second assertion by which Moltmann forms a bridge between the economic and the eternal Trinities lies in his analysis of the Biblical statement that God is love. From this Moltmann deduces that God is self-communicating.[77] Actually, this notion of self-communication is remarkably similar to Barth's notion of God's lordship; both signify the capacity to enter into another and become other without loss of self. This self-communication implies God's self-differentiating, for in the act of self-communication and to the extent that it is complete, the subject becomes the other while remaining the same. Further, such self-differentiation implies God's self-disclosure, for the act of self-communication is truly that – communication. Here God's essential goodness is revealed.[78] We should note the creative use Moltmann has made of the Hegelian heritage, with its talk of otherness and differentiation. In fact, the direct connection between communication and differentiation on the one hand and revelation on the other is a hallmark of Hegelian thought. In employing this analysis Moltmann has shown his indebtedness to both Barth and Hegel. Although couched in Biblical terms such as love, Moltmann's thought shows him to be a direct heir of the Hegelian approach to the Trinity.

By defining God as essentially love and by understanding love as self-communication, Moltmann is able to establish that the eternal, doxological Trinity corresponds to the economic Trinity revealed in the history of Jesus. The economic Trinity "is nothing other than the eternal perichoresis of Father, Son and Holy Spirit in their dispensation of salvation."[79] In other words, the eternal and economic Trinities are not to be thought of as two distinct Trinities but instead as the one Trinity in two activities, one extra-worldly,

---

[76] Ibid., 152–153.

[77] It is instructive to note that Moltmann fails to make mention of Schleiermacher on this topic, in spite of the fact that Schleiermacher likewise identified love as the essence of God and made it the cornerstone of his doctrine of God. See *The Christian Faith*, ed. H. R. Mackintosh and J. S. Stewart (Philadelphia: Fortress Press, 1976), 727–732 (§§166–167).

[78] Moltmann, *The Trinity and the Kingdom*, 57–58.   [79] Ibid., 157.

the other intra-worldly. This represents a direct rejection of the Augustinian distinction between the interior life of the Trinity which is determined by the divine essence and the external deeds of the Trinity which are matters of grace and are contingent. On this Augustinian view, the world has no ultimate significance for God, since the Trinity's eternal and purely interior life is self-sufficient and fixed apart from any relation to the world. In place of this distinction Moltmann urges us to think of the interior and eternal life of the Trinity as intimately involved with the world, an involvement characterized by the word "suffering."[80] If God is truly love, i.e., self-communicative, then the eternal life of the Trinity cannot be apathetic toward the world; the external acts of the Trinity in history cannot be merely arbitrarily chosen deeds that do not affect God; instead they must arise directly out of the essence of God. If God is truly love, then the self-giving that marks the revealed Trinity of history is characteristic also of the eternal Trinity.[81]

In summary, then, Moltmann has paid his dues to the Protestant emphasis on revelation as the only basis for asserting the doctrine of the Trinity. Like the mainstream of recent Protestant thought, he identifies the Word of revelation with Jesus Christ. However, his own emphasis falls on the *history* of Jesus, for it is in the events of Christ's life that the Trinitarian relations that are essential to God are revealed. But, in reaction to the mainstream of Trinitarian thought, this revealed Trinity is not the contingent exterior of an inward and eternal life of God; it is instead the eternal God in its self-communication within history. By identifying the economic Trinity so strongly with the eternal, Moltmann has made it plausible to erase the customary distinction between the internal and the external in God, between (to use the traditional terms) the eternal processions of the persons and their historical missions. This distinction, which Schleiermacher sought to overcome by consigning all talk of God's internal being to the realm of the metaphysical, Moltmann has sought to abolish by understanding love as the self-communicative opening up of

---

[80] Ibid., 98.
[81] Ibid., 160. We should also note Moltmann's dependence on and alteration of Karl Rahner's identification of the economic and eternal Trinities. See pp. 147–148.

the divine being to its other. The question that remains is whether, in thus defining God and in so closely connecting the economic and eternal Trinities, Moltmann has compromised God's independence from the world and, in spite of his protests, drifted over into idealistic territory in this, its most controversial tenet. This is a subject to which we will return later.

Wolfhart Pannenberg

Like the other Trinitarian thinkers discussed in this chapter, Wolfhart Pannenberg establishes and expounds the doctrine of the Trinity strictly on the basis of revelation. Like Moltmann, however, he has reacted against the theologies of the Word and, even more than Moltmann, has urged the importance of history as an essential component of this Word. So, as with the previous theologians, Pannenberg has had to face the question of the nature of revelation and the precise relation between this revelation and the doctrine of the Trinity.

Following Barth's insistence, Pannenberg is convinced that the doctrine of the Trinity should have a constitutive significance for Christian theology. Unlike Barth, Pannenberg does not regard the location of the doctrine in the system of theology to be a matter of first importance; more weighty, in his belief, is the relation of the divine unity to the Trinity and the question of which of these, the unity or the Trinity, is theologically prior.[82] On this issue Pannenberg charges that Barth's understanding of the Trinity is seriously flawed because of Barth's deriving the Trinity from the unity of God; doing so makes the unity of God prior to and better known than the Trinity. The roots of Barth's error go back, Pannenberg believes, to Augustine for whom the unity of God seems to take precedence over the Trinity and to Pseudo-Dionysius who like Barth tried to derive the Trinity from the unity.[83] The folly continued nearly unabated through the middle ages, with the shining exception of Richard of St. Victor, whose idea of deriving the Trinity from the divine love is appealing to Pannenberg,[84] and

---

[82] Wolfhart Pannenberg, *Systematic Theology*, 3 vols., trs. Geoffrey W. Bromiley (Grand Rapids: Wm. B. Eerdmanns Publishing Co., 1991–1998), I:283.

[83] Ibid., I:284–285.   [84] Ibid., I:286–287.

John of Damascus, whose system of theology *begins* with the Trinity.[85] In the mainstream, however, the Trinity was derived, not from revelation, but from the idea of God's unity.[86]

A corner in Trinitarian thought was turned by the Protestant scholastics, who insisted on revelation alone as the basis of the doctrine. Regrettably, this insistence resulted in a certain loss of structural coherence in their theology: they kept the medieval outline of theology (unity followed by Trinity) but rejected the customary derivation of the Trinity from the unity; they thus bifurcated the doctrine of God into disconnected units, one on the unity of God, another on the Trinity. In this way they opened the door to rationalistic criticism, for the disjunction between unity and Trinity made the Trinity seem ancillary to the doctrine of God and obfuscating.[87]

From that point, according to Pannenberg, two paths could be taken: one, the Hegelian path, reverted to the traditional method of deriving the Trinity from the divine unity of Spirit;[88] the other, taken by Schleiermacher's followers, sought to base the Trinity on revelation in history, namely on Jesus Christ and the Holy Spirit in the economy of salvation. Although clearly favoring this latter path over the idealist path, Pannenberg is forthcoming about its chief limitation – its inability to establish knowledge of the eternal Trinity. It could not do so because it sought to found the doctrine of the Trinity on statements within the Bible and on the Biblical data of revelation.[89] In other words, nineteenth-century followers of Schleiermacher rightly sought a basis for the doctrine in revelation alone; however, they could not span the gap between Biblical statements about historical revelation and theological statements about God's eternal and interior life. They were working with the same understanding of God's inside and outside that Schleiermacher did.

All this explains why Pannenberg is so critical of Barth and why he regards Barth's doctrine of the Trinity as a throw-back to an earlier and discredited era. In particular, Pannenberg faults him for deriving the Trinity "from the formal concept of revelation as

[85] Ibid., I:289.   [86] Ibid., I:288.   [87] Ibid., I:289–291.   [88] Ibid., I:292–293.
[89] Ibid., I:293–294.

self-revelation," a derivation that Pannenberg finds to be structurally identical to the Hegelian deduction of the Trinity from the
idea of God as absolute spirit. Although such a move uses the language of revelation, it does not, Pannenberg charges, rest upon real
revelation as attested in the Bible. It rests instead on the *idea* of
revelation. Pannenberg is a bit more generous than Moltmann in
his interpretation of Barth. He takes note of the supplemental
Trinitarian material covered in the fourth volume of Barth's *Church
Dogmatics*. About this material he notes that it, if taken alone,
"might well form the basis of a doctrine of the Trinity that derives
materially from the revelation of God." In fact, however,
Pannenberg believes that the dominating presentation of the idea
of revelation in the first volume of *Church Dogmatics* vitiates this otherwise promising line of thought.[90]

The net result of this development is, first, the need to decide on
the relative priority of the unity and the Trinity of God and,
second, the need to establish the doctrine of the Trinity on the
basis of revelation alone. This latter in turn demands a rethinking
of revelation in such a way that not only the historical but also the
eternal Trinity will be disclosed. Much of Pannenberg's writing on
the Trinity is an attempt at addressing these needs.

The problem that Pannenberg addresses is similar to that confronted by Moltmann: nineteenth-century theologians demanded
that the doctrine of the Trinity be grounded in revelation; however,
there is no express mention of the Trinity in Scripture, leaving the
doctrine on shaky ground.[91] Although the New Testament does
ascribe divinity to the Son and the Spirit, it leaves highly unclear
their relation to the Father.[92] However, this is, in Pannenberg's
view, the central issue. Every other issue – subordinationism,
Sabellianism, the unity of God, and the relation of the economic
to the eternal Trinity – can be explicated in terms of the relation
of the Son's and Spirit's divinity to the Father's. Like Moltmann,
Pannenberg holds that if we begin with the revelation attested in
the Bible, then we are led immediately to the Trinity; what needs
explaining in this view is not the doctrine of the Trinity, which is
taken immediately from revelation, but the *unity* of God, that is, the

---

[90] Ibid., I:296.   [91] Ibid., I:301.   [92] Ibid., I:302–303.

relation of the Son and Spirit to the Father. Unlike some theological approaches, neither Moltmann nor Pannenberg makes use of philosophical considerations to solve this problem of God's unity; each sees the problem of God's unity as a Trinitarian problem. It is not the unity of a being and its attributes, as in philosophy, but a unity of the three Trinitarian persons. Both Pannenberg and Moltmann hold that knowledge of God's unity must arise out of reflection on revelation. We can see, then, that Moltmann and Pannenberg have reversed a longstanding theological assumption. For centuries, natural theology could be relied on to establish the unity of God; the Trinity was the problem and the various inadequate attempts at grounding it only added to the general weakness of the doctrine resulting from the fact that it seemed ancillary to the unity of God. For Moltmann and Pannenberg, however, revelation not only yields immediate knowledge of the Trinity but also indirectly provides knowledge of the divine unity.

What, then, is the revelation that testifies to the Trinity? As noted above, it was both the accomplishment of and a barrier for nineteenth-century theology that it recognized that the Bible does not in any express way support the doctrine of the Trinity. Accordingly, Pannenberg takes the Barthian path of asserting that this revelation is not the Bible or our experience of the Bible's message, but instead Jesus Christ. However, Pannenberg is quick to announce that the focus here is not on the "person" of Jesus[93] but on his message of God's coming rule.[94] It is difficult here not to detect an anti-Barthian slur that wishes to displace emphasis from the incarnational character of Jesus Christ to what Moltmann has called the history of Jesus and to the role of Jesus in the eschatological kingdom of God. But this revelation associated with Jesus' message does not lie so much in his teaching as in his act of announcing the kingdom of God. The kingdom that he announced is God's rule, a rule that began in the history of Jesus. As the incipient moment of the kingdom, Christ's historical existence is crucial to revelation. Further, Pannenberg argues that God's own being cannot be separated from God's rule, so that the existence of God is intimately associated with the rule of God that

[93] Ibid., II:335.   [94] Ibid., I:304.

takes place in Jesus Christ. To say that Jesus is revelation signifies that he "executes" the lordship of God and inaugurates the kingdom in a way that has implications for the existence of God.[95] Finally, this revelation of God in Christ is in fact the revelation of the Trinity, for as in Moltmann's theology, the central events in the history of Jesus – his death on the cross, his resurrection, his receiving authority – disclose mutual relations among Father, Son and Spirit.[96] Therefore, the ground of the doctrine of the Trinity lies not in the words of Jesus but in the man Jesus in his relation to his Father and to the Spirit.

The question remains, how does the knowledge of the historical Trinity gathered from revelation, i.e., from the history of Jesus, yield knowledge of the eternal Trinity? The answer is twofold: on the one hand, Pannenberg does not wish simply to collapse God's existence into a historical process; as in Barth's theology the eternal Trinity remains the basis of the economic Trinity of history and revelation.[97] On the other hand, a fundamental theme in Pannenberg's theology is that "God's being and existence cannot be conceived apart from his rule."[98] This means that the existence of God was at stake in the ministry of Jesus; in some important sense, the existence of God depended on the outcome of Jesus' ministry. This is true because if God's being cannot be separated from God's rule and if Jesus both announced and inaugurated that rule,[99] then the events of Jesus' history are critical for God's being. The death of Jesus, for example, represented a potential refutation both of God's rule and of God's being. The resurrection is important precisely because it confirms both Jesus' approval by God the Father and also God's own being and rule. Accordingly, the existence and ministry of Jesus were a revelation not simply of God but of the Father as the one whose being and rule are tied to the history of Jesus.[100] In short, it is impossible for us to conceive of God the Father apart from a consideration of Jesus and his message.

All this implies that revelation is not something extraneous to God's being. This is an idea shared by Moltmann and Pannenberg:

---

[95] Ibid., I:312.   [96] Ibid., I:312–313, 314–319.   [97] Ibid., II:22.

[98] Wolfhart Pannenberg, *Theology and the Kingdom of God*, ed. Richard John Neuhaus (Philadelphia: Westminster Press, 1977), 55.

[99] Pannenberg, *Systematic Theology*, 211.   [100] Ibid., I:310.

we should not think of God as having a concealed, interior life that would be opened up to us only through a decision by God to be revealed. Although Pannenberg's axiom, that God's being is God's rule, is not a prominent aspect of Moltmann's theology, they agree in nearly making revelation something essential to God. In comparison with Barth, they severely underplay God's freedom to remain concealed. At any rate, this is the way in which Pannenberg interprets what has come to be called Rahner's Rule – that the economic Trinity *is* the eternal Trinity. Karl Rahner used this mainly to protest against the scholastic treatment of the doctrine of the Trinity whereby the eternal Trinity was expounded in a seemingly rationalistic fashion and the economic Trinity was not considered until many other doctrines had been discussed. The rule for him was a plea to connect the two more tightly in the system of theology and to maintain the soteriological focus of the doctrine. Pannenberg, however, employs the rule to assert that "revelation cannot be viewed as extraneous to [God's] deity." He is arguing for the necessity to "constantly link the trinity [*sic*] in the eternal essence of God to his historical revelation."[101]

This use of Rahner's Rule implies an alteration in the understanding of the relation of the eternal to the economic Trinity. No longer, asserts Pannenberg, should we distinguish the eternal processions of the Trinitarian persons (e.g., the eternal begetting of the Son) from the historical missions (e.g., the sending of Jesus by God and the giving of the Spirit) as though the first were essential to God and the second depended on God's will. Instead, we should think of the economic Trinity as the "actualization" of the eternal Trinity. Although recognizing the possible misunderstandings that attend this term, loaded as it is with idealistic and other connotations, Pannenberg nevertheless believes that it is most suitable because it guards the unity of the eternal and economic Trinities better than other available terms. This unity is grounded in the fact that God's revelation – God's saving acts in history – "are not external to his deity but express his presence in the world."[102] Because of this, Pannenberg holds, knowledge of the economic Trinity is in fact direct knowledge of the eternal Trinity, not merely a source

---

[101] Ibid., I:328.   [102] Ibid., II:393.

from which knowledge of the eternal Trinity may be inferentially gained. The eternal Trinity is not a being closed up within itself, possessing only accidental relations with the world. It has instead opened itself to the world in such a way that the existence of God is now at stake in the history of the world.[103] This is why God's being cannot be separated from God's rule and why the ministry of Jesus was crucial to God's rule and existence. Although the eternal Trinity remains the ontic foundation of the economic Trinity, the two are nonetheless not to be distinguished; they are one and the same God, known in just one way (i.e., revelation), and characterized by the fact that what takes place in the economy of salvation is the "self-actualization" of God's eternal Trinitarian nature.[104]

This view has implications for Christology. In traditional theological approaches, Jesus Christ is related to the eternal Son through the concept of incarnation and the incarnation is assigned to a definite moment in history. According to Pannenberg's view, however, the incarnation is not so much a punctiliar moment as something that is true of Jesus' entire history. Jesus *is* the Son because of his obedience to God and his subordination to the rule of God.[105] Since this obedience cannot in any significant sense be understood as completed, or even begun, at the birth of Christ, it would not be correct to claim that the incarnation – Jesus' sonship and divinity – is accomplished at his conception or any other distinct moment. Instead, it characterizes his entire life of obedience and subordination.[106] The obedient Jesus is the incarnation of the eternal Son because it is characteristic of the eternal Son to be obedient to the Father.[107] Here again, as in the relation of the

---

[103] See Pannenberg, *Systematic Theology*, I:222–223 and I:228–229 for his comments on his debt to and modification of the idealist conception of universal history as the revelation of God.

[104] Catherine Mowry LaCugna, *God for Us: The Trinity and Christian Life* (Harper San Francisco, a division of HarperCollins Publishers, 1993), 222–224 has recently expounded similar ideas on the basis of, but also as a correction to, certain aspects of Karl Rahner's theology of the Trinity. She has sought to abolish the distinction between economic and eternal Trinity by means of the ideas of *exitus* and *reditus*, whereby there is a single procession of persons, a single economy that eventually is manifested in history and which is then followed by a return of all things to God the Father in a sort of de-procession.   [105] Pannenberg, *Systematic Theology*, II:373.   [106] Ibid., II:385.

[107] Ibid., II:377.

eternal Trinity and the economic Trinity, we see that history and eternity are not two separated realms; the historical is instead the eternal in a particular form. Jesus Christ and the eternal Son are not distinct beings; Christ is instead the eternal Son in history. Further, the historical is an essential part of the eternal, for, once God decided to create a world, God's existence now depends on God's rule in history. This dependence was most notably evident in the obedience of Jesus who thus proved himself to be the Son.[108] This dependence of the eternal on the historical is Pannenberg's attempt at harmonizing the New Testament passages that variously associate Jesus' sonship with a pre-existent state, the virginal conception, the incarnation, the baptism and the resurrection. In Pannenberg's view, each of these ascriptions is correct because of a principle that Pannenberg calls the ontological priority of the future. Although a fuller exposition of this important concept must wait, we can note briefly that, just as God's being depends on God's rule and thus is in doubt until the end, so Jesus' sonship was in doubt until a final confirming event (the resurrection) that demonstrated that he is the eternal Son.[109] But what does it mean to say that Jesus is the eternal Son? Although the human being Jesus of Nazareth did not exist prior to his conception, it is nonetheless true that, eternally, God the Father's identity is marked by a relation to this Jesus – God the Father is eternally the Father of this man Jesus Christ.[110] Therefore, although the *man* Jesus Christ did not exist prior to his conception in Mary's uterus, the sonship of Jesus is itself eternal and it is appropriate to speak of the eternal Son which was incarnated in Jesus.

In summary, revelation is for Pannenberg as for the other leading figures of twentieth-century Trinitarian thought the sole source of knowledge about the Trinity. Unlike Barth and Bultmann, however, Pannenberg has sought to fashion a different and in his view more Biblical understanding of revelation. Drawing on the idealist philosophical notion of universal history as itself revelatory, he has identified revelation with the totality of history. Again, as with the others (with the complex exception of Tillich), Pannenberg regards the Word as identical in an important

---

[108] Ibid., II:390–391.   [109] Ibid., II:367.   [110] Ibid., II:368 and 370–371.

way with Jesus Christ; however, with Moltmann he wishes to focus on the history of Jesus – the way in which his relation with God the Father is narrated in the Gospels. Doing so, he believes, enables theology to avoid the errors into which Barth fell and to preserve God's openness to the world and to history.

GOD'S SELFHOOD AND THE TRINITY

Introduction

The second of the concepts that have determined the course of Trinitarian thinking in the German tradition is the selfhood of God. As we have seen, the speculative-analogical use of this concept represents a way of deriving the Trinity independently of historical revelation. Through much of Christian history, the speculative use of this concept in the doctrine of the Trinity co-existed with an appeal to revelation (customarily equated with the Bible) on the basis of the mostly unquestioned assumption that since the doctrine of the Trinity is given in and assured by revelation, deriving the doctrine or at least expounding it by means of speculative reflection on subjectivity was a profitable intellectual exercise. Protestants, however, spoiled this easy harmony of speculation and revelation by banishing the use of analogical thinking in the doctrine and insisting on a straightforwardly Biblical approach. However, as we have seen, a few recalcitrants, notably Leibniz and Lessing, continued to value the idea of God's selfhood as a means of proving the doctrine of the Trinity. For the most part, these obstinate devotees of speculation were philosophers and were often interested in something quite different from mere exposition of the Christian faith; their Trinitarian speculation was often part of a larger philosophical agenda. With the demise of German idealism in the nineteenth century, nearly all enthusiasm for this speculative approach evaporated.

Nevertheless, a vapor of interest has lingered. Further, as we will see, the question of God's selfhood and its relation to the Trinity has turned out in the twentieth century to be anything but settled; just as Moltmann and Pannenberg clashed with Barth on the subject of revelation, so they found themselves disagreeing vehemently with him over the issue of God's selfhood. Although no one today thinks of speculatively *deriving* the doctrine from the idea of God's selfhood as formerly, a right understanding of God's selfhood has once again become a *sine qua non* in the attempt to *expound* the doctrine.

Paul Tillich

We begin with a consideration of Paul Tillich's view of this issue. We may pass over Rudolf Bultmann because God's selfhood had nearly as little interest for Bultmann as did the doctrine of the Trinity. Tillich, however, as one of the few confessed descendants of German idealism, had an intense interest in the concept of God's selfhood and its connection to the doctrine of the Trinity.

Following in the footsteps of Hegel, Tillich regarded his doctrine of God as grounded solidly in revelation. However, the connection between revelation and doctrine is not an immediate one. First, this revelation is the disclosure not of a doctrine but rather of God's selfhood with its Trinitarian structure. The Christian doctrine of the Trinity is a distillation of that experienced revelation. Second, revelation, in his theory, gives rise to symbols, upon which theologians reflect rationally and which they employ in the formation of doctrines. The doctrine of the Trinity, then, is the rationalization of symbols that are the direct expressions of revelation. Tillich's allegiance to the idealist philosophical tradition is evident both in his emphasis on revelation and also in his insistence on taking doctrines seriously but not literally. His understanding of doctrines as symbolic expressions has direct antecedents in Hegel's notion of representational thinking in religion.

However, Tillich did differ from the idealists in one important respect. As we have seen, Hegel's philosophical account of God was based on the concept of God as subject or spirit. For Tillich, however, "spirit," although an exceedingly important term, is nonetheless a *symbol* and not a *concept*. It is indeed "the most embracing, direct, and unrestricted symbol" that we may apply to God, but it is a symbol nevertheless.[111] In other words, whereas for

---

[111] Tillich, *Systematic Theology*, I:249.

Hegel absolute spirit is the ultimate idea and unsurpassable reality, it is not so for Tillich. There is a term more fundamental for describing God, Tillich believed, and that is "life." On the one hand it is true that, like all terms (except "being itself") "life" is a symbol;[112] on the other, there is a noticeable tendency within Tillich's theology to subordinate "spirit" to "life." This tendency places Tillich definitely outside the Hegelian line of philosophical development and in the line that includes Schelling and Nietzsche, a line that rejected Hegel's understanding of God as spirit as excessively rationalistic and that wished to substitute in its place the concept of "life," with its more a-rational connotations. Not surprisingly, Tillich expressed admiration for idealism to the extent that it was "basically a philosophy of life"; his enthusiasm was more restrained to the extent that he found it unappreciative of the "divine mystery."[113] Accordingly, we must judge that the tradition, extending back at least as far as Augustine and reaching its height in idealism, in which the doctrine of the Trinity is derived or at least expounded by means of an analogical and speculative understanding of God's selfhood, appears in Tillich's theology to have been extraordinarily modified if not terminated, having turned from selfhood to life as its principal theme.

The task at hand is to observe how Tillich sought to derive or expound the doctrine from the idea of life. In spite of its emphasis on spirit, idealism was, Tillich held, basically a philosophy of life because its method was dialectical. Life itself, he declared, is dialectical and "dialectic determines all life-processes."[114] The dialectical character of life means that all life is governed by movements of separation and return; the divine life is no exception.[115] As a result, there are two points to observe about thinking about God: First, it is rational and is neither a violation of logic nor paradoxical; second, it does not consist in reflecting on an external object. As to the first point, dialectical thinking is not paradoxical. As Tillich professed, there is really only one paradox in the Christian faith, namely Jesus Christ, the appearance of the new being under the conditions of existence. Paradox expresses that which is true,

---

[112] Ibid., II:90: "Life itself is dialectical. If applied symbolically to the divine life . . ." and III:283: "The symbolic application of the concept of life to the divine ground of being."
[113] Ibid., III:284.   [114] Ibid., II:90.   [115] Ibid., III:284.

although seemingly impossible according to finite reason.[116] This does not describe Trinitarian thinking, for as Tillich noted, the Trinitarian principles are nearly universal in religious experience. Further, dialectical thinking does not violate logic. It merely follows the logic of life, with its moments of affirmation and negation. Least of all does the doctrine of the Trinity violate mathematics by suggesting that one equals three.[117] As to the second point, dialectical thinking is not the sort of thinking that remains external to its object. It does not confront the object as something that is utterly opposed to and different from the other. It does not simply reflect in thought a reality standing over against it, but instead compels itself to enter into the structure of the object. It thereby participates in the object's nature.[118]

What, then, can be said about the divine life on the basis of dialectical thinking? Principally, it signifies that being itself includes non-being and otherness and that the divine life is a movement from this otherness back to identity in an eternal motion.[119] As noted previously, this idea of God's otherness, of God's capacity to become other, has been a pervasive feature of Trinitarian theology in the twentieth century, being employed notably by Barth. The difference between Tillich's understanding of this otherness and Barth's is that Tillich saw this otherness as lying eternally and essentially within the divine being; Barth regarded otherness as something that God can freely assume or not assume. In other words, this is an issue on which Tillich retained his idealistic leanings and on which Barth decisively renounced that idealism. For Tillich the divine life is an eternal cauldron of negation and affirmation, of separation and return, of difference and identity. The doctrine of the Trinity, although an important symbol, is merely a way of expressing this life. For Barth, the divine life is indeed movement, but one that is foundationally Trinitarian. The difference can be seen in Tillich's understanding of the significance of number. For Tillich, the number three is nearly irrelevant to the idea of God; theology calls for qualitative, not quantitative thinking. The idea of the Trinity is an attempt at expressing the dynamics of the divine life and although the

---

[116] Ibid., I:57.   [117] Ibid., I:56.   [118] Ibid., II:90.   [119] Ibid., III:284.

number three is useful in depicting the process of life, it has no "specific significance."[120] For example, early Christian thought veered toward a duality, with the Father on one side and an amalgamated Logos-Spirit on the other. Further, the tendency in the Roman Catholic Church to elevate Mary testifies to the possibility of the divine's being symbolized as a quaternity.[121] While Barth spent no time defending the number three, nevertheless it is clear that for him the doctrine of the Trinity is not a symbol or expression of anything – it is itself the truth about God set forth in human terms. The doctrine is not reducible to any more basic concept of God from which the threeness of the Trinity could be derived.

The divine life, as a living process, is characterized by tensions. These opposing principles Tillich called depth and form, which are associated respectively with power and meaning. Symbolic terms from the history of religion and philosophy that portray these principles are, first, the abyss, which is drawn from the language of mysticism and which symbolizes the principle of depth and power, and, second, the symbol of the Logos, which is drawn from philosophy and which symbolizes the principle of form and meaning. With respect to the Christian doctrine of the Trinity, another set of symbols is employed for the first principle: "Father" symbolizes the first principle, the abyss, and represents it as holy love and as creator and preserver.[122] "Logos" designates the divine life in its openness and clarity – its possibility of being revealed. Whereas the abysmal aspect of God suggests the infinity and darkness of the divine life, the Logos aspect represents the definite and illuminated side of the divine, God's capacity for self-objectification.[123] The third moment in the divine life is symbolized by spirit, which is drawn from religion. Like Hegel, Tillich regarded spirit as the all-encompassing term for the divine because it represents the perfect unity of the first two principles.[124] Spirit encompasses the first two moments because it is their "actualization." God as spirit contains the first two moments and unites them.[125]

In Tillich's philosophical exposition of the doctrine of the Trinity, he borrowed from Hegel and F. W. J. Schelling. From Hegel

---

[120] Ibid., I:228.   [121] Ibid., III:292.   [122] Ibid., I:286–287.   [123] Ibid., I:250–251.
[124] Ibid., I:156.   [125] Ibid.

he derived the understanding of the Holy Spirit as the unity of the first two persons. While the notion of the Holy Spirit as the bond of love that unites Father and Son has a long history in Trinitarian thought, Hegel gave it a distinctive twist by understanding the Spirit dialectically as the concrete universal that encompasses the previous and relatively abstract moments. That is, in Hegel's philosophy, it is the third moment that incorporates the partiality, finitude and abstractness of the first two moments. The third moment is the truth for it is the totality. However, this was not at all Schelling's understanding of the Spirit. In place of Hegel's all-encompassing spirit, the unity of all things, Schelling proposed a plurality of divine persons. One could say that whereas in Hegel's system the process of dialectics means a progressive resolution of difference into a final and enriched unity, for Schelling the process of God's history results in greater numerical diversity as God becomes a Trinity of persons. Tillich on this point opted for the Hegelian understanding of spirit and interpreted the doctrine of the Trinity accordingly. That is why he could state that "God *is* Spirit,"[126] while never making a corresponding affirmation regarding God as abyss or Logos; these merely denote principles within God's life. However, in his understanding of the first principle, corresponding to the Father, Tillich relied more heavily on Schelling than on Hegel. This is seen principally in the view of this principle as the dark and infinite abyss that requires the second principle, the Logos, in order to become "distinguishable, definite, finite."[127] Whereas in Hegel's system the first principle is characterized by universality and immediacy, in Schelling's and Tillich's systems it is marked by darkness and power. This preference for Schelling over Hegel can also be seen in Tillich's repeated emphasis on God as the living God.

We can see, then, that Tillich represents the tradition of German idealism in Trinitarian thought. Although acknowledging the indispensability of revelation for the doctrine of the Trinity and even for the Trinitarian principles, Tillich also, like the idealists, attempted a philosophical reconstruction of the doctrine. In doing so, he followed the idealist, and especially the Hegelian, path

---

[126] Ibid., I:249.   [127] Ibid., I:251.

of interpreting the Trinity in terms of God's subjectivity as spirit. Although reserving "life" as a more basic symbol for God than "spirit" and thus marking a significant alteration in the idealist tradition, Tillich was the latest and perhaps the last member of a speculative tradition extending, with all sorts of permutations, from Augustine through the middle ages and Melanchthon to Leibniz, Lessing and the idealists.

Karl Barth

Not surprisingly, Karl Barth stood opposed to the entire Tillichian enterprise of giving a philosophical rendition of the doctrine of the Trinity. Nevertheless, it cannot be said that Barth disagreed with Tillich on every point, for Barth's exposition of the Trinity utilizes the same Augustinian-Thomistic and even idealistic analysis of the divine selfhood in which Tillich's was rooted. Although the notion of deducing the doctrine of the Trinity from an understanding of God's selfhood was abhorrent to Barth, he did find it useful to expound the doctrine in terms drawn partially from such an understanding. In turn, Barth's theology has become the object of an excoriating criticism leveled by Moltmann and Pannenberg, who have charged him with a thoroughly unBiblical view of the Trinity resting on a Hegelian view of God's selfhood. However, as we have noted, any representation of Barth's view of the Trinity must be supplemented by a look at his remarks in the later volumes of *Church Dogmatics*, where he depicted God's selfhood in terms far different from those found in the first volume.

We begin with Barth's definition of revelation: *Dei loquentis persona*, the person of God speaking.[128] We observe immediately that *persona* is in the singular. This fact is of no little importance and Barth was never slow to draw out its monotheistic implications. We observe further that revelation is conceived as an act of speaking. Although we should not press this language too far, the personalistic aspect of speaking should not be overlooked. Revelation is, in this view, an address by a single subject to hearers. Immediately we are connected with the Logos tradition and its

[128]   *CD* I/1:349.

association of the Trinity with the eternal speech of God in the Logos. Although Barth is far from the idealistic desire to deduce the Trinity from the concept of selfhood his understanding of revelation suggests that he shares with the idealists an appreciation for the idea of the Logos.

Our awareness of God's selfhood in revelation is enhanced when the *Church Dogmatics* notes that revelation is a "language . . . 'God's Word' means 'God speaks.'"[129] We further learn that, as a language, a speaking, revelation implies God's possession of reason and spirituality. Revelation is a communication between persons, a divine person and a human person. In fact, Barth went out of his way to emphasize that revelation, conceived as a language, is "a rational and not an irrational event,"[130] thereby underscoring the personalistic character of revelation. Barth here distinguished himself from such analysts of revelation as Rudolf Otto and Tillich who were emphasizing the non-rational character of revelation, thus distancing themselves from a personalistic view of God. Consequently, we are not surprised to hear Barth, on the basis of his understanding of revelation, ascribe personality to God and to connect personality with selfhood: "Personalness means being the subject not only in the logical sense, but also in the ethical sense." In fact, Barth warned, so little is ascribing personality to God a case of anthropomorphism, that we must regard God as the supreme person, "a free subject," and ourselves as personal in only a derivative and diminished sense.[131] As a final bit of evidence for the importance of the selfhood of God in Barth's theology, we may notice that Barth employs Martin Buber's I–Thou language to explicate further his view of revelation.[132] Here, God is expressly designated by the singular "I." The point of all this is that Barth's concept of revelation inclined him to emphasize the singularity of God's personhood, an emphasis not calculated to ensure an easy assimilation to the doctrine of the Trinity. As can be seen from the history of Christianity, stress laid on monotheism often tends to prevent the doctrine of the Trinity from rising into prominence.[133] Whether this is true of Barth's theology is an

[129] Ibid., 150.   [130] Ibid., 152–153.   [131] Ibid., 157.   [132] Ibid., 352–353.
[133] Sam Powell, "The Doctrine of the Trinity in Nineteenth Century American Wesleyanism 1850–1900," *Wesleyan Theological Journal* 18, no. 2 (1983): 33–46.

open question, but it is striking that he so heavily weights the oneness of God in the critical and opening section on revelation in the *Church Dogmatics*.

Barth's appreciation of the concept of God's selfhood is most explicitly evident in his statement that God should be thought of as "a Person, i.e. as an I existing in and for Itself with a thought and will proper to it."[134] The similarity between the way in which God is represented here and the Thomistic representation of God is patent and its significance for the doctrine of the Trinity is great. As we have noted previously, Thomas Aquinas' exposition of the Trinity is based on understanding God as a divine self with two internal motions, intellect and will. In this view, the Father is the divine self as such. The second person is the interior word resulting from the movement of intellect. The third person is associated with the movement of will or love. Likewise, Barth's portrayal of God is of a single self with two faculties, thought and will. Although the *Church Dogmatics* does not explicate the Holy Spirit as the movement of will or love in the Thomistic manner,[135] it does depict the procession of the Spirit in terms of love, much in the spirit of Augustine.[136] Further, Barth, like the Augustinian-Thomistic tradition, in places connected the second person of the Trinity with God's act of self-understanding. Using the axiom that God is antecedently in eternity what God is in revelation, Barth asserted that the Word of God is both the means by which God "gives himself to our knowledge" and the means by which God has self-knowledge. Further, Barth expressly identified the speaking of the eternal Word with God's thinking.[137] All this suggests that the eternal Word performs the same function – revelation – in eternity that it performs in history, so that the eternal speaking of the Word is in some sense a revelation within God's eternal life – a revelation of God to God. Of course, Barth nowhere states this; it is a deduction from his theology. We must remain cautious in light of statements in which Barth warned against making too much of the concept of Word and was critical of the Augustinian-Thomistic tradition for doing so.[138] Nevertheless, there is reason, in spite of Barth's critique of the Catholic doctrine of analogy, to locate Barth within the tradition of Trinitarian thought that uses an analysis of reflective selfhood to expound the doctrine of the Trinity.

The emphasis on the singularity of God's selfhood appears also in Barth's strictures against the word "person" when discussing the three Trinitarian persons. Barth exhibited on this issue a remarkable anxiety that modern personalistic connotations would be carried over and applied to each of the three persons. Hence his repeated and ardent insistence that personality and personal characteristics pertain to the singular essence of God, not individually to the three persons.[139] As a result, the doctrine of the Trinity does not in any way imply the existence of three personalities or personal beings. There is one divine I, which has repeated itself in a threefold way.[140] God's unity is neither a generic unity nor a collective unity.[141] As a result, Barth proposed that the doctrine of the Trinity, far from endangering monotheism, is in fact the Christian form of monotheism,[142] so firmly is it anchored in the unity of God.

What is amazing about Barth's tirade on this point is that it is a vital part of the twentieth century's most sustained and successful attempt to resuscitate the doctrine of the Trinity from a vague monotheism. When we recall that one of Barth's constant opponents in the *Church Dogmatics* is liberal theology, which, as noted previously, was obsessed with God's personality and had absolutely no toleration for any sort of Trinity, then Barth's continual emphasis on the uni-personality of God seems explicable only on the supposition that Barth was attempting to reintroduce the doctrine of the Trinity into theological consideration with the least possible offense. In brief, a certain uncharacteristic timidity may be evident here in Barth's thought.

In addition to being anxious over possible misunderstandings of "person," Barth was convinced that this concept was to blame for the bane of modern theology – Sabellianism. As he saw it,

[138] Ibid., 500–501.
[139] Ibid., 403. See also, for example, I/1, 537 where he was particularly exercised about denying an individual personality to the Holy Spirit.   [140] Ibid., 403.
[141] Ibid., 402.   [142] Ibid., 407.

nineteenth-century theologians, recognizing that personality had come in the modern era to be associated with self-consciousness and individuality, drew the correct conclusion that tritheism loomed with such use and fled instead in the direction of Sabellianism. In this way, they were able to preserve the one personality of God, but at the cost of making the Trinitarian persons mere epiphenomena.[143] This illustrated, for Barth, the fact that the concept of "person" suffers from a lack of clarity. The modern connotation of self-consciousness only exacerbates this lack of clarity.[144] Barth's solution to this problem was to substitute the phrase "mode of being" for "person" when discussing the Trinitarian persons. He believed "mode of being" states "more simply and more clearly" what "person" denotes.[145] It is clear that Barth was attempting to reserve the personal characteristics of God to the one essence of God who exists in the three modes of Father, Son and Spirit. He strenuously resisted any possibility of ascribing these personal characteristics to the Trinitarian persons individually. As we will see, it is at this point that Moltmann and Pannenberg are sharply critical of Barth's theology, for they believe that revelation points directly to and emphasizes the plurality of persons. Ironically, they fault Barth for the same tendency, Sabellianism (i.e., failing to concede full reality to the Trinitarian persons), for which he criticized nineteenth-century theology. We may observe here the latest stage in an ongoing debate over the nature of God's selfhood and its implications for the doctrine of the Trinity.

Barth was well aware of his proximity to the traditional Augustinian-Thomistic-idealistic path of Trinitarian thought.[146] He took note of criticisms to the effect that, in regarding the statement "God reveals himself as Lord" as analytic and from which the doctrine could be derived, he had offered a speculative proof of the doctrine in the manner of Leibniz and Lessing. Although conceding his use of rational formulations, Barth denied the charge of rationalistic speculation, arguing that he took the doctrine of the Trinity from the revelation attested in Scripture, not from general truths attained outside Scripture.[147] Barth's anxiety is

---

[143] Ibid., 411.   [144] Ibid., 408 and 410.   [145] Ibid., 412.   [146] Ibid., 397–398.
[147] Ibid., 340 and 389.

patent; he was struggling to ensure that his exposition of the doctrine should arise out of revelation and not from an analysis of the concept of selfhood. His defense against the charge of speculation rested on the distinction between purposely deriving "the Trinity from the scheme of human self-consciousness" on the one hand and on the other hand deriving it from Scripture. It also rested on avoiding the former and accomplishing the latter. However, he did acknowledge that in his reversion to the Augustinian view of the Trinity he had employed "a scheme which has admittedly no small resemblance to the scheme of human self-consciousness."[148] However, Barth was confident that he had used the Augustinian analysis only for the purpose of expounding the doctrine, not to derive it speculatively. As we will see, Moltmann and Pannenberg have found Barth's self-defense on this point wanting. It is their belief that Barth did not at all free himself from the tradition that grounded the Trinity in reflective selfhood. As far as they are concerned, it matters little whether the doctrine is being *derived* from such reflection or merely being *explicated* by it, for the result is the same – a neglect of the plurality of persons and an undue emphasis on monotheism.

Yet as noted previously, there is another side to Barth's understanding of God's selfhood and its importance for the Trinity. In the fourth volume of *Church Dogmatics*, Barth presented the doctrine of the Trinity in strongly dialogical terms and in a way that emphasized God's passing over into otherness. Already in the first volume of *Church Dogmatics* Barth had discussed revelation as God's taking, in the incarnation, the form of God's other. This form-taking is depicted as God's "self-unveiling." Thereby God becomes "His own double." Here there comes to be a distinction in God's being; God comes to be in a different mode of being. Further, this second mode of being is so different from the first mode that it is the form of that which God is not. It is proper to God, Barth asserted, to be free enough even to become what God is not, without thereby ceasing to be God. God's becoming other amounts to being God "a second time."[149] In the fourth volume, the content of this otherness is spelled out expressly in Christological terms. Jesus, as the exemplar

[148] Ibid., 398.   [149] Ibid., 363.

of human obedience and humility, "stands in the greatest possible contradiction to the being of God," whose essence is Lordship.[150] But it is not only Jesus' humility that distinguishes him from God; it is also Jesus' solidarity with sinful humanity. Barth's Christology is founded on the conviction that, in the incarnation, the Word assumed human nature in its sinful condition. As a sinner, Jesus "negates God" and is, even as the elect one, "the man negated by God" and judged and rejected by God, finally suffering the "onslaught of nothingness."[151] The crucial point here is that this Jesus, who is negated and rejected by God, is in fact God existing in a second form. God here is both accuser and accused, judge and sinner.[152] Because Jesus Christ is God in the form of an other, the subordination that is evident between Jesus and God does not imply any diminishing of God, for in becoming other God remains God. The incarnation was not a transformation of God, not a ceasing to be God.[153] Further, this dialectical relation between Jesus the Son and God the Father implies no contradiction or conflict in God.[154] It is not even a matter of paradox, antinomy, division or inconsistency; all these terms are inadequate to understanding the relation of Jesus the Son to God the Father, for they all assume that it is somehow improper for God to take on the form of God's other.[155] For Barth, the incarnation and the cross must be conceived as God's freedom in love. Without compromising the divine impassibility and transcendence, God's freedom in love enables God to become God's own opposite. God's omnipotence is such that God "can assume the form of weakness and impotence" while remaining omnipotent and thereby "triumphing in this form" of weakness.[156] Jesus Christ, then, even Jesus the sinner, is not God divested of all divine attributes, but instead is truly God whose lordship and glory are concealed.[157]

---

[150] *CD* IV/1, 163–164.   [151] Ibid., 173.

[152] Ibid., 172. See John Thompson, "On the Trinity," in John Thompson, ed., *Theology Beyond Christendom: Essays on the Centenary of the Birth of Karl Barth May 10, 1886*, Princeton Theological Monograph Series, no. 6 (Allison Park, PA: Pickwick Publications, 1986), 19 for further exposition of the crucifixion as the history between the Father and the Son. Thompson's exposition forces us to the conclusion that Barth's understanding of the Trinity given in this section of the *Church Dogmatics* is the proximate background of Moltmann's and Pannenberg's accounts of the Trinity. While in their criticism of Barth they focus on volume I of the *Church Dogmatics*, their positive formulations of the doctrine are unthinkable apart from volume IV.   [153] *CD* IV/1, 178–179 and 185.

[154] Ibid., 184.   [155] Ibid., 186.   [156] Ibid., 187.   [157] Ibid., 188 and 192–193.

The point of this extended discussion of Barth's Christology is to demonstrate the sharply dialectical character of the relation between Jesus Christ and God the Father. "Dialectical" here is used precisely in the sense in which the idealists used it, namely to denote something that exists in a dual form, whose other form is not only different but in fact the opposite, and which nonetheless, in the midst of this extraordinary otherness, remains the same – the sort of being whose identity consists in (or at least, in Barth's case, allows of) difference.

The next step in grasping Barth's account is to realize that this dialectical relation between Father and Son pertains not only to the historical man Jesus and his relation to God the Father, but also to the eternal relations of the Trinity. In particular, the humility and obedience of Jesus toward the Father are grounded in the eternal being of God. The logic of this position is inescapable, given the Barthian axiom that God is antecedently in eternity what God is in revelation: if Jesus is God in the form of otherness, but still truly God, then the obedience of Jesus is no merely human deed; it is rather God's own deed, so that "obedience cannot be something alien to God."[158] As a result, we must acknowledge, Barth affirmed, an element of subordination within the eternal Trinity – an obedience within God's eternal being, involving a superior and a subordinate.[159] Recognizing that this is something difficult and elusive, even offensive, and smacks of the heresy of subordination-ism,[160] Barth nevertheless drew the conclusion that otherness is an element in God's eternal being. God did not first come to have an other, an opposite, with the historical appearance of Jesus Christ, or with the creation of humanity or of the world as a whole. Otherness occurs within the divine life as "an original and essential determination of [God's] being and life."[161] Yet, as with the historical case of Jesus and the Father, this otherness, although extreme, does not threaten the unity of God's eternal being, for God's unity is not characterized by "singleness and solitariness," but is instead "a unity which is open and free and active . . . a unity in more than one mode of being."[162] As a consequence, the sub-ordination found within God's being does not imply any inferiority

[158] Ibid., 193.   [159] Ibid., 195.   [160] Ibid., 195 and 200–201.   [161] Ibid., 201.
[162] Ibid., 202.

or lack within God. Instead, Barth counseled us to meditate on the notion of *homoousia* and see that what is subordinate in God is not lacking in "dignity and significance."[163] Father and Son remain of the "same substance" in spite of their relation of superiority and subordination. To restate the main point, God can be subordinate and obedient without ceasing to be truly God. Although this representation conflicts with the customary understanding of God and God's lordship, it follows, Barth believed, from the revelation of Jesus Christ attested in the Bible. Finally, we observe a particularly suggestive notion that arises from this dialectical account of the Trinity: God is located *between* the first two modes of being (the Father and the Son). Although God may be said to be in each mode, God is not in each mode in its particularity or its isolation, but instead in its relatedness to the other mode. Accordingly, God may be said to subsist in the history that transpires between the Father and the Son, for God "exists in their difference, not in their identity." "His being as God is His being in His own history."[164] Over against this dynamic history of God Barth opposed an abstract monotheism that would conceive of God as standing outside all relations. The true God, however, is the living God, the God with a history.[165]

It is evident, then, that in addition to the view of God's selfhood found in the first volume of *Church Dogmatics* there is another view in the fourth volume. According to the former, God is a single personality, an individual subject of action. According to the latter, God exists as the in-between of the Father and the Son; here God enters into and becomes that which is radically opposite God. Here otherness and difference are eternal aspects of the divine being, yet without disrupting God's identity. Whereas the view of God's selfhood given in the first volume has its closest parallels with the Augustinian-Thomistic tradition, the view of the fourth volume has its greatest affinities with philosophical idealism, especially in the weight it gives to otherness and difference and the way in which these are significant for God's identity. Although nowhere in the fourth volume did Barth suggest any sort of bi-personality in God, he did emphasize plurality in God. Mention of God's plurality is

---

[163] Ibid.   [164] Ibid., 205.   [165] Ibid., 203.

not absent in the first volume, but it does not receive the degree of importance that it does in the fourth volume, which has a more dialectical character.

The reader may have noticed that in Barth's highly dialectical account of the Trinity, there has been a discernable lacuna – the Holy Spirit. In good Augustinian fashion, Barth attempted to ground the unity of Father and Son in the Holy Spirit, who, Barth offered, is "the One who affirms the one and equal Godhead through and by and in the two modes of being."[166] The problem is that there does not seem to be any need of positing a third mode of divine being in order to account for the unity. Barth had already explained that God's freedom implies the freedom to become God's other without loss of lordship, without ceasing to be God. It is not clear how the notion of a third mode of being adds to this feature of God's freedom or clarifies its importance. Further, no doctrine of the Spirit seems to be required by Barth's suggestion that the subordination inherent in God does not imply inferiority because, even in the mode of subordination, God remains God. If anything, this understanding of freedom and subordination means that the doctrine of the Spirit is not required by Barth's principles and that it is a sort of addendum juxtaposed for the sake of ortho-dox considerations. Confirming this judgment is the fact that Barth's dialectical exposition of the Trinity in the fourth volume of the *Church Dogmatics* is in fact a two-membered dialog between Father and Son, in which the Spirit has no real significance.[167] In fairness to Barth, it should be noted that the dialectical/dialogical account of the Trinity occurs in the volume on reconciliation. Had Barth lived, the projected volume on redemption might well have given a more adequate doctrine of the Spirit.

As can be seen from this brief exposition, Barth's doctrine of the Trinity and of God's selfhood is complex. On the one hand,

[166] Ibid., 202.
[167] For general purpose critiques of Barth's deficiencies regarding the doctrine of the Spirit, see Thomas A. Smail, "The Doctrine of the Holy Spirit," in John Thompson, ed., *Theology Beyond Christendom: Essays on the Centenary of the Birth of Karl Barth May 10, 1886*, Princeton Theological Monograph Series, no. 6 (Allison Park, PA: Pickwick Publications, 1986), 104–106 and Robert W. Jenson, "You Wonder Where the Spirit Went," *Pro Ecclesia* 2 (1993): 301–302. For a much more sympathetic portrayal of Barth's doctrine of the Spirit see Philip J. Rosato, S. J., *The Spirit as Lord: The Pneumatology of Karl Barth* (Edinburgh: T. & T. Clark, 1981).

he associated himself expressly with the mainstream tradition of Trinitarian thinking; on the other, he distanced himself from the speculative aspects of the tradition. On the one hand he emphasized the monotheistic nature of the Trinity; on the other, he fashioned a sort of bipolar view of God, whereby God subsists in the relation between Father and Son. On the one hand, Barth repeatedly affirmed the orthodox tradition of theology; on the other hand, he employed such striking and non-traditional concepts as God's otherness and subordination. As noted previously, when Moltmann and Pannenberg are critical of Barth, they allude to the presentation of the Trinity in the first volume of *Church Dogmatics*, with its strongly monotheistic flavor. But there can be no denying the resemblance between their own views and that presented in the fourth volume, with the result that they appear less a reaction to Barth than a development of the Barthian tradition.

Jürgen Moltmann

Moltmann is critical of traditional understandings of "person" because they fail, he believes, to take account of God's suffering and also of God's historicity. In other words, they are too bound to traditional metaphysical conceptions of God. Meditation on God's suffering will, he holds, lead us to a grasp of the historical nature of God and of the process of differentiation that occurs within God.[168] In turn, an understanding of God's historicity will lead us to an accurate knowledge of the unity and Trinity of God. In particular, knowledge of this historicity will result in a revival of the social doctrine of the Trinity in which the emphasis falls on the plurality of persons and in which the unity of God is no longer axiomatic, but becomes an issue that must be thought through again.[169] Moltmann, then, proposes a thorough reassessment of God's selfhood and personality.

Moltmann charges traditional Trinitarian thought with giving primacy to an abstract monotheism. His judgment rests on the observation that in traditional systems of theology God is

---

[168] Moltmann, *The Trinity and the Kingdom*, 26 and 30.   [169] Ibid., 19.

commonly regarded as a substance; in these systems the unity of the divine substance is established before the Trinity.[170] As a consequence, there is a tendency to view God's unity as the thing that we know first and best about God; the Trinity is known only secondarily and much less well. Moltmann is also critical of idealism, for in his view it likewise emphasizes and begins with the unity of the divine substance. Accordingly, idealism tends to reduce the Trinitarian persons to the status of modes of being, so that God as an individual self is the principal thing and the Trinity is again shunted off to the irrelevant sidelines.[171] So, Moltmann is dissatisfied with virtually all Trinitarian thought in the Roman Catholic and Protestant traditions because of its monotheistic inclinations. It all conflicts with his understanding of the centrality of the Trinitarian persons and their relations, a concern that he believes is overridden by the tradition's emphasis on the oneness of God. In place of the emphasis on God as self and as substance, Moltmann proposes categories that give weight to the social and the relational aspects of God, a proposal he believes is part of a larger trend in intellectual history.[172]

While Moltmann is critical of traditional theology and idealism in general, his most sustained criticism is reserved for Barth. Moltmann charges Barth with falling into Sabellianism because of Barth's use of "mode of being" as a surrogate for "person." Moltmann sees this as symptomatic of Barth's affinity with idealistic philosophy. He finds further evidence of this affinity in the fact that Barth uses the "reflection structure" of selfhood typical of idealists, "to secure God's subjectivity, sovereignty, selfhood and personality." Although commending Barth for beginning dogmatics with the revelation of Jesus Christ, Moltmann nevertheless believes that Barth's understanding of revelation fell under the influence of reflective logic, with its idealistic emphasis on self-distinction and self-recollection.[173] Further, Barth's understanding of revelation and the concomitant conception of God's subjectivity leave no room for the selfhood of the Holy Spirit, which consequently gets reduced to being the common bond of love between Father and Son – a sort of energy of God. The Son's selfhood is likewise

[170] Ibid., 17.   [171] Ibid., 18.   [172] Ibid., 19.   [173] Ibid., 139 and 142.

threatened because the Son, in Barth's presentation, is simply God's other, that in which God contemplates God's own being, and is not a personal being.[174]

Moltmann is also critical of Barth's conception of freedom. As we have seen, freedom is a central category of Barth's theology of revelation and the Trinity. Moltmann accuses Barth of having a nominalistic view of freedom, whereby God's freedom means God's capacity to do or refrain from doing anything that God chooses.[175] Against Barth, Moltmann proposes that freedom is a matter of friendship ("mutual and common participation in life") in which there is reciprocity and equality.[176] Although recognizing Barth's attempts at ameliorating the nominalistic aspects of freedom by linking freedom to love, Moltmann is still bothered by the fact that, according to Barth, God might have chosen not to love – that love results from the exercise of God's choice.[177] This seems to introduce an arbitrary element into God's love, whereas Moltmann understands it to be an aspect of God's nature to be outgoing and to enter into community with humanity, because God is essentially a community of persons – Father, Son and Spirit.

Moltmann also criticizes what Barth regarded as the basis of the doctrine, namely the statement that revelation is the revelation of God's lordship. Although Barth understood God's lordship to signify God's capacity to become other without ceasing to be God, Moltmann draws the conclusion that Barth's conception of lordship implies a strict monotheism "since God's lordship can only be fulfilled by a single subject."[178] As such, Barth's version of God differs little from that of liberal Protestantism, for which humanity's absolute dependence on God (implied by God's lordship) was the central category. Our absolute dependence on God (liberal theology's emphasis) and God's lordship over us (Barth's emphasis) are, in Moltmann's opinion, not significantly different.[179] In both cases, there is nothing about the God–human relation that demands or even suggests a Trinity of persons. On this point Moltmann may not be entirely fair to Barth. As was shown in the previous section, Barth understood God's lordship and freedom in such a way that relationality, otherness and difference are found in

---

[174] Ibid., 142–143.   [175] Ibid., 52–53.   [176] Ibid., 56.   [177] Ibid., 55.
[178] Ibid., 63.   [179] Ibid., 64.

the eternal being of God. To be sure, Barth was rather obdurate on the need to preserve God's independence from the world and ceaselessly repeated the injunction that God does not need the world in any way. While this sort of talk is currently unfashionable in theology, where the emphasis is much more on God's relationality than on God's independence, it is important to keep in mind Barth's intentions, which were to ensure that God is not conceived as a picturesque way of denoting human nature or some aspect of the world. While by contemporary standards Barth may have overplayed God's freedom and capacity *not* to engage in certain activities (creation and revelation, for two), it is an open question whether Moltmann, in reacting to Barth, has managed to avoid merging God with the world in just the way that Barth feared idealists had done.

Moltmann's final criticism of Barth pertains to the consequences of his view of freedom and lordship. According to Moltmann, both the liberal view and Barth's view imperil human freedom; neither can adequately ground such freedom.[180] In fact, such a view produces just the opposite ("dependency, helplessness and servitude") by projecting an image of God as an "almighty ruler of the universe" who requires "abject servitude" and presupposes a universal dependency.[181] What Moltmann is searching for is an account of the Trinity that is both congruous with and creative of human freedom and liberation.[182]

The place to begin, according to Moltmann, for an accurate knowledge of the Trinity is the suffering of God, for we can understand God's suffering only in Trinitarian terms.[183] God's suffering is found in the cross, which is accordingly "at the centre of the Trinity."[184] This is because divine suffering has direct and principal reference to the suffering of Jesus the Son for us and the suffering of the Father who gave up the Son.[185] This Trinitarian understanding of suffering leads us directly to the concept of God's love, which, as noted above, Moltmann takes to mean self-communication.[186] Because God *is* love, this self-communication (which implies also self-differentiation) is not an arbitrary act of God. Moltmann fears that Barth's emphasis on God's freedom will

[180] Ibid. [181] Ibid., 192. [182] Ibid., 218. [183] Ibid., 4 and 25.
[184] Ibid., 83. [185] Ibid., 24. [186] Ibid., 57.

thrust God's love into a secondary position, whereas Moltmann wants to make love the principal consideration in the doctrine of God.[187] Only thus can sense be made of Trinitarian divine suffering.

Established on divine love, God's Trinitarian selfhood is thoroughly relational, a point that, Moltmann believes, has been slowly dawning on theological consciousness over the centuries. Augustine began the relational understanding of "person" but then confused matters by his modalistic tendencies.[188] Richard of St. Victor improved on Augustine's formulation by defining "person" in terms of being in relation to another, thus balancing the concepts of relation and existence in a way that Moltmann approves.[189] At length, Hegel advanced the discussion further by asserting that persons find themselves only in and through others, by "expressing and expending" themselves in others.[190] As we have seen, Moltmann is not completely satisfied with Hegel's understanding of the Trinity, but he does regard his own work as building on this historical discussion about "person," a discussion whose high point is Hegel.[191]

The relationality that is essential to the God who is love pertains not only to the Trinitarian persons but also to God's relation to the world. Because Moltmann rejects the notion that God's inner being is self-sufficient and secure and that God is a pure, monadic being in itself that requires nothing else, he is compelled to acknowledge that God's relation to the world is, like the divine love from which it flows, not arbitrary. For example, the act of creation is no arbitrary deed; rather, it emerges from the love that God *is*. Moltmann goes so far as to state that not to create a world such as this one would contradict God's love. In fact, the act of creation is "part of the eternal love affair between the Father and the Son."[192] So, God's decision to create is not to be understood in terms of God's choice and will, but rather in terms of the "inner pleasure of [God's] eternal love."[193] There is, he argues, no basis for

---

[187] Ibid., 52–54.   [188] Ibid., 172.   [189] Ibid., 173.   [190] Ibid., 174.

[191] See Regina Radlbeck, *Der Personbegriff in der Trinitätslehre der Gegenwart – untersucht am Beispiel der Entwürfe Jürgen Moltmanns und Walter Kaspers*, Eichstätter Studien, neue Folge, vol. XXVII (Regensburg: Verlag Friedrich Pustet, 1989) for an extended and penetrating critical analysis of Moltmann's concept of "person."

[192] Moltmann, *The Trinity and the Kingdom*, 59.   [193] Ibid., 58 and also 112.

arguing, in the Augustinian fashion, for a distinction between the internal acts of the Trinity which would be essential and the external acts which would arise from choice. Such a distinction rests, he believes, on the mistaken notion that God's eternal being is one thing and God's acts toward the created world are another. Instead, Moltmann proposes that the inward and the outward are "intertwined," that there is a correspondence between the two.[194] As a result, events in the world have an impact on God; in particular, the cross determines God's eternal Trinitarian life. The crucifixion of Christ has a "retroactive" effect on God, so that God is eternally defined in terms of the suffering of the cross.[195] Moltmann is quick to remind us that none of this discussion about love and suffering implies the idealistic tenet that God needs the world or that God is somehow identical with the world.[196] Instead, he wishes to regard the God–world relation as occurring *within* God and as a consequence of the eternal love between Father and Son.[197]

The doctrine of the Trinity implied by this concept of divine love is a social and pluralistic one.[198] Accordingly, revelation, which is the history of Jesus Christ, implies the Trinity directly, leaving the unity of God an open question.[199] Moltmann does hold that God's unity is not that of a monad or a number; it rather assumes a plurality of persons and preserves that plurality and the separate character of the persons.[200] Consequently, "person" is not to be understood individualistically, but instead socially; personhood is a uniting activity as well as a distinguishing activity. Here Moltmann reaches back to the Trinitarian concept of *perichoresis*, the mutual interpenetration of the Trinitarian persons, in order to argue along

[194] Ibid., 98.   [195] Ibid., 160–161.   [196] Ibid., 107.   [197] Ibid., 110–111.

[198] See Henry Jansen, "Moltmann's View of God's (Im)mutability: The God of the Philosophers and the God of the Bible," *Neue Zeitschrift für systematische Theologie und Religionsphilosophie* 36 (1994): 284–301 for a critical analysis of the relation in Moltmann's thought between the concept of love and the social analogy of the Trinity.

[199] Jürgen Moltmann, "The Inviting Unity of the Triune God," *History and the Triune God: Contributions to Trinitarian Theology*, trs. John Bowden (New York: The Crossroad Publishing Co., 1992), 82. See John O'Donnell, "The Trinity as Divine Community: A Critical Reflection Upon Recent Theological Developments," *Gregorianum* 69 (1988): 21 for a critique of Moltmann's account of God's unity, to the effect that this unity is a unity of intention and not of nature and that the divine unity does not come about, according to Moltmann, until the eschatological union of God with creation.

[200] Moltmann, *The Trinity and the Kingdom*, 95.

Hegelian lines that the persons are not subsistent entities in themselves, but thoroughly relational – they are what they are only in their relations with the others. His point is that "person" is not rightly understood if grasped in terms of an individual's self-consciousness. The unity of the Trinity corresponds to and is the archetype of "a human fellowship of people without privileges and without subordinances."[201]

It is Moltmann's belief that this understanding of person, with the concomitant concept of love, is the only way to avoid the perils of subordinationism,[202] tritheism and modalism.[203] It escapes subordinationism because the divine community of persons, grounded in love and self-communication, is without hierarchy; it escapes tritheism by stressing the radical relationality of the persons, the fact that they subsist only in their relations with one another and that none is an independent entity; and it escapes modalism by granting distinctiveness and a certain separateness to the Trinitarian persons.

In spite of this striving for balance, Moltmann definitely emphasizes the plurality of the Trinitarian persons. Each is a subject of activity, not a mode of being of the one divine subject. Each possesses will and understanding.[204] For example, the Spirit is the unique subject of such activities as glorifying and unifying the Father and the Son.[205] The distinct activities of the persons are discerned in the various arenas of salvation history, such as in the Father's sending the Son or in eschatology. In each sphere, the persons have unique activities and roles and relate to one another distinctly.

In summary, Moltmann's theology represents a decisive break with Barth's with respect to the way in which God's selfhood is conceived. Or perhaps it would be more accurate to state that Moltmann's understanding of the Trinitarian persons takes up the direction indicated in the fourth volume of *Church Dogmatics* and uses that conceptuality to bludgeon Barth's account of God in the first volume. The essential issues are whether God is best understood as a single self or as three and whether God is a

---

[201] Ibid., 150 and 157.   [202] Ibid., 175–176.
[203] Moltmann, "The Inviting Unity of the Triune God," 86.   [204] Ibid., 84–85.
[205] Moltmann, *The Trinity and the Kingdom*, 126.

Trinity because God's selfhood is self-reflective or because the three subjects that constitute God inhere in one another perichoretically.

Wolfhart Pannenberg

As is the case with Moltmann, Pannenberg is highly critical of Barth's theology on several points, not least of which is the nature of God's selfhood. Pannenberg charges Barth with fashioning a doctrine of the Trinity that is substantially Hegelian and specula-tive, one derived not from a proper exegesis of Scripture but from the logic of revelation. That is, Pannenberg charges Barth with developing the doctrine of the Trinity out of the premise that God is the subject, predicate and object of revelation. What is Hegelian about this procedure is that it rests on an analysis of selfhood similar to what we find in Hegel's philosophy. Nor can Barth's repeated appeal to revelation deter Pannenberg from this judg-ment, for he notes that even Hegel associated God's self-objectivization with revelation.[206] In short, Pannenberg charges Barth with devising a doctrine of the Trinity that is based on some-thing other than the relation of Jesus to the Father, a point that is of crucial importance to Moltmann as well.

To underline the similarity with Hegel, Pannenberg asserts that, like Hegel, Barth "deduced the Trinity out of God's being subject," a deduction grounded strictly in the logical structure of selfhood. This procedure makes God's selfhood logically prior to and more important than the Trinity, which consequently appears to be merely a by-product of that selfhood.[207] Barth's error corre-sponds to the mistake of traditional theology, which placed the doctrine of the Trinity after the doctrine of God's unity and thereby abetted the impression that the Trinity is secondary to a prior conception of God. In Pannenberg's judgment, Barth's refer-ence to revelation in Christ "remains external to the structure of his argument," since the argument does not begin with Christ but with the nature of God's selfhood. Revelation thus merely

---

[206] Wolfhart Pannenberg, "Die Subjektivität Gottes und die Trinitätslehre: Ein Beitrag zur Beziehung zwischen Karl Barth und der Philosophie Hegels," *Kerygma und Dogma* 23 (1977): 30–31.   [207] Ibid., 39.

confirms what Barth had already deduced logically.[208] However, we may question the fairness of Pannenberg's indictment. Although Barth does stand in the tradition of Trinitarian thinking that has employed a specific understanding of God's selfhood, it is highly doubtful whether Barth has really derived the doctrine of the Trinity from his understanding of selfhood in a Hegelian deduction. In the *Church Dogmatics*, long before Barth came to the doctrine of the Trinity as such, he had asserted that "revelation in fact does not differ from the Person of Jesus Christ," and went on to explicate this revelation by reference to the incarnation and the reconciliation accomplished in Jesus.[209] It would seem that Christology was firmly in Barth's thinking from the beginning of the *Church Dogmatics*. Pannenberg does have a point when he notes the somewhat abstract nature of the doctrine of the Trinity in the early parts of the *Church Dogmatics*; however, it was argued above that this early account must be supplemented by the later account in the fourth volume. Pannenberg allows as much and professes that the account given in volume four could well satisfy his demand for a doctrine based strictly on revelation. However, his final judgment is that, in the "total context of Barth's theology," the concept "mode of being" is ultimately determinative,[210] a move that precludes an adequate doctrine of the Trinity. All things considered, Pannenberg chides Barth for failing to accomplish what he set out to do – rethink theology from the ground up on the basis of revelation. Pannenberg proposes to succeed where Barth failed.

Although critical of Barth for following the Hegelian path, Pannenberg finds some redeeming merit in Hegel's thought. In particular, he favors Hegel's depiction of the divine unity in terms of love. Since love presupposes a plurality of subjects, this maneuver acknowledges the Trinitarian persons as original and regards selfhood as a property of the persons individually, not of the unity. Accordingly, Pannenberg wishes to distinguish "person" from "subjectivity." He understands Hegel to have taught that the subject is certain of itself and exists with itself. Personality, contrariwise, "does not already have the form of the I from itself." Personality is something that must be won from a "life-content"

---

[208] Ibid.   [209] *CD* I/1, 134.   [210] Pannenberg, *Systematic Theology*, I:296.

that grounds the individual being of the I. In subjectivity, the other is merely a means by which the self comes to know itself; the other is the *self's* other. Personality, however, is attained through something that transcends the I and is the ground of the I. The application of this distinction to Jesus Christ is that Jesus was a person only by virtue of "his divine sending through the Father."[211] The superiority of "person" to "subject" lies in the fact that the divine persons attain personhood only through their interrelations. Unlike the structure of subjectivity, which does not require plurality, personhood both implies plurality and prevents the plurality from degenerating into solitary individuality.

This understanding of person and its superiority to the concept of subjectivity means that for Pannenberg, as for Moltmann, the plurality of the persons is a direct implication of revelation and that it is the unity of God that is problematic. This is Pannenberg's response to the question of the relation between the unity of God and the Trinity. Which comes first in the system of doctrine? Is the Trinity an unnecessary addition to the unity? Does the unity need supplementing by the Trinity?[212] Pannenberg proposes to break cleanly from traditional answers to these questions, answers that privileged the unity of God at the expense of the plurality of persons.

Pannenberg finds in the history of theology two main approaches to understanding the relation between the unity and the Trinity. On the one hand, there is the way of Anselm and Barth, which is to derive the Trinity from the unity. The reasons for Pannenberg's dissatisfaction with this approach are now clear. On the other hand, there is the way of Richard of St. Victor, who wished to derive the Trinity from the idea of God's self-love. Pannenberg finds this to be a promising approach, for it implies a plurality of persons and the personal encounter that Pannenberg, relying on Hegel, believes lies at the essence of personhood.[213] What is necessary, Pannenberg believes, is that the persons are constituted by their mutual love; accordingly, we should not view them as expressions of God's love, for this view presupposes a single divine subject that loves and that is logically prior to the Trinitarian

---

[211] Pannenberg, "Subjektivität," 37–38. [212] Pannenberg, *Systematic Theology*, I:283.
[213] Ibid., I:286.

persons. But we must also not view the persons as individually existent subjects of love, for then love does not constitute the persons but in fact presupposes them.[214] In this case the danger of tritheism looms. In short, Pannenberg is faced with the centuries-old dilemma of Trinitarian theology – avoiding an undue emphasis on both the unity and the plurality of God. Pannenberg's opinion is that there are grievous faults with previous Trinitarian thinking, for it has almost always erred in the direction of emphasizing the unity of God. Pannenberg has set himself the task of formulating a way of conceiving the persons that will do justice to their plurality without compromising the unity of God. Indebted to Richard of St. Victor and Hegel, he attempts to do so by representing "person" as a reality constituted by love and by rethinking the divine unity.

It is customary in theology to account for the divine unity by means of the category of substance. In this view, God is an entity and an utterly simple one, to use the scholastic term. Accordingly, the trick was always to accommodate the doctrine of the Trinity to this view of unity. For Pannenberg, however, this traditional approach has the whole matter exactly backward. Like Moltmann, Pannenberg begins with the plurality of persons that he finds attested in the Bible. The question of God's unity receives from him both a historical and an eschatological solution. Historically, we should not begin with preconceived ideas of how the persons are united. This we must learn from their interactions in the event of revelation in history.[215] But revelation in history is not yet sufficient to prove God's unity, for the Father has given the kingdom, and hence the Father's own deity, over to Jesus the Son; consequently, the unity of the Father and the Son is in the balance until the eschatological consummation of the kingdom. Although that eschatological event will confirm the eternal unity of Father and Son, at present the issue is very much undecided.[216] The divine existence in the economy of history, then, is crucial for the unity of God.

Like Moltmann, Pannenberg holds that the persons are separate centers of action.[217] For example, the Son has a proper and

[214] Ibid., I:297.   [215] Ibid., I:299.   [216] Ibid., I:327.   [217] Ibid., I:319.

unique role in the act of creation.[218] Now this suggestion is out of step with the mainstream of Trinitarian thought, according to which the external acts of the Trinity toward the world are not differentiated among the Trinitarian persons, but are instead unified acts of the one God. Yet Pannenberg does not intend to suggest any sort of tritheism; although arguing that distinction and plurality are the conditions of the Trinitarian relations, he contends that the life of the Trinity consists in mutual relations.[219] Pannenberg and Moltmann are proposing that a person is not a subsistent entity that first exists and then enters into relations; a person is instead something constituted by its relations. So, for all his insistence on the plurality of Trinitarian persons, Pannenberg is equally insistent that these persons are not independently existing beings; instead they exist only in their mutual relations. Now the Augustinian-Thomistic tradition had embraced this understanding of personhood all along, but Pannenberg faults that tradition for vitiating this insight by subordinating the Trinity to the unity of God and for regarding the acts of the Trinity toward the world as acts of the unitary divine nature, not of distinct persons. Pannenberg and Moltmann wish to begin with the fact that in the history of Jesus each divine person has unique acts and stands in unique relations to the other persons; in this way they wish to counteract the traditional approach of beginning with the divine unity and only considerably later addressing the Trinitarian persons and the history of salvation. Pannenberg and Moltmann insist that these acts of God in salvation history are not acts of the one God as such but rather are acts of this or that Trinitarian person. Further, they insist that it is the ensemble of relations ensuing from these acts that constitutes the life and unity of the Trinity.

Pannenberg also complains about the way in which the persons come to be distinguished from one another in traditional theology. Customarily, theologians have argued that, since all acts of God outward in history are acts of the one God and not of this or that person, the only way we have of distinguishing the persons is by reference to the relations that they have to each other in eternity.

---

[218] Ibid., II:29–30. [219] Ibid., II:28–29.

In this view, what distinguishes the Son from the Father is the sole fact that the Son is begotten and the Father is the one who begets. In every other respect, the Son is identical with the Father. Likewise, what distinguishes Son from Spirit is that the Son is begotten whereas the Spirit is "spirated," or breathed. In other words, the persons are identical to one another in essence and differ only insofar as each has a distinctive role in the eternal procession of one person from another. Pannenberg is of the opinion that this mode of distinguishing the persons is far too narrow because the relations that not only distinguish but also constitute the persons are greater in variety than those enumerated in traditional theology.[220] For example, whereas in the Augustinian-Thomistic tradition the Spirit is clearly subordinate to the Son because the Spirit proceeds from the Son (together with the Father), Pannenberg argues that the Son also depends on the Spirit, for at his baptism the Son *receives* the Spirit.[221] Of course, in order to make this argument, Pannenberg must have recourse to the historical acts of God in history. Of course, the theologians of the Trinitarian tradition never denied that the relations of the persons in history are more complex than their relations in eternity. However, in traditional Trinitarian thought, the historical relations of the persons are irrelevant to their eternal identity; for Pannenberg, the historical relations are in fact determinative of the eternal character of the persons. God is not, for Pannenberg, one thing in eternity and another in history. The Trinitarian persons are what they are because of their mutual relations in salvation history.

In a further departure from tradition, Pannenberg proposes that the relations not only distinguish the persons but also constitute them in their deity.[222] In the Augustinian-Thomistic view, each person is divine by virtue of participating in the one divine being. The relations simply distinguish one person from another. In Pannenberg's view, Jesus is the Son precisely because he proved himself obedient to the Father.[223] His subordination to the Father not only identifies him as the Son, but also constitutes him as the Son. But by claiming that Jesus is the Son because of his obedience,

[220] Ibid., I:320.   [221] Ibid., I:317.   [222] Ibid., I:323.   [223] Ibid., II:373 and 375.

has Pannenberg fallen into the heresy of adoptionism? He certainly would, if he were to profess that the historical man Jesus *became* the Son by this obedience. In fact, however, the relation of Son to Father is, for Pannenberg, eternally a relation characterized by obedience and submission; Jesus is *the* Son because his life was one of complete submission to the Father.[224] Submission is what eternally determines the personhood and deity of the Son; therefore, Jesus, the exemplar of obedience, is the incarnation of the Son. Further, because of the retroactive effect of the future on the past, we cannot point to a single moment when Jesus became the Son; God's verdict in the resurrection brought it about that Jesus was in fact the Son all along, even, in a sense, in eternity.

This mention of the retroactive power of the future raises once again the point that God's unity depends ultimately on the course of history – it is an eschatological unity. In history, Father, Son and Spirit are separate subjects of action; their unity will be proved only at the end of history, although that end will show that their unity was real from the beginning. This consideration leads us to our next topic, history.

HISTORY: THE HISTORICITY OF BIBLE AND TRADITION

Rudolf Bultmann

Of the five theologians discussed in this chapter, Bultmann's thoughts on the historicity of the doctrine are easiest to summarize, for he simply rejects the doctrine in its fundamental claims. Basic to his views on this point is the distinction between New Testament statements that designate the saving significance of Jesus Christ and those that purport to portray his metaphysical nature.[225] As the exposition of the liberal theologians demonstrated in the previous chapter, any time a theologian begins with this sort of distinction, we may expect the doctrine of the Trinity to come in for some extended criticism for its tenuous connection with the doctrines of salvation. It is Bultmann's opinion that the New Testament speaks overwhelmingly of the soteriological

---

[224] Ibid., II:377.　　[225] Bultmann, "Christological Confession," 274–275.

significance of Jesus Christ, even when declaiming on Christ's divinity.[226] New Testament mention of Christ's pre-existence is, Bultmann averred, expressly mythological. Not surprisingly, he suggested the utter dispensability of the images contained in the myths.[227] Dogmas such as the Christological and Trinitarian are consequently plainly inadequate, for they employed Greek philosophical thought to expound the New Testament faith in Jesus and this Greek thought is inherently infected, Bultmann believed, with an objectivizing tendency, whereby the divine is represented as a thing or an object within the universe of beings. Of course, objectivization is not the fault only of orthodox theology; Arians and liberals can err as well. Nonetheless, the orthodox doctrines of the Trinity and of Christ are false because they fail to understand New Testament statements regarding Christ as statements about the "event of God's acting"[228] and instead interpret them using metaphysical categories such as nature.

In summary, on this issue Bultmann represents a continuation of the attitude characteristic of such liberal theologians as Albrecht Ritschl and Wilhelm Herrmann. This attitude could be discerned as soon as Bultmann revealed the central importance that Melanchthon's dictum, "To know Christ is to know his benefits," has for his theology. With this as a leading axiom, all the focus of theology will fall on the acts of God toward us in Jesus Christ; consideration of God as such will be consigned to speculative or mythological, objectivizing thought. Since the doctrine of the Trinity has customarily been represented as a theory of God's internal life apart from the world and prior to all outward activity, it could be regarded either as irrelevant philosophical prying into the divine being or as a sinful attempt at locating God among the universe of things in order to gain some control and avoid the urgency of proclamation.

Paul Tillich

Like Bultmann, Tillich drew a distinction between revelation and the doctrine of the Trinity. Accordingly, the doctrine is not itself

---

[226] Ibid., 280–281.   [227] Bultmann, "The Christology of the New Testament," 280.
[228] Bultmann, "Christological Confession," 286–287.

revelation or something revealed and is therefore subject to free and far-reaching criticism. However, he also held that the doctrine is firmly rooted in revelation and is a rational explication of revelation. In order to reconcile these views he had recourse to the idealist distinction between form and content: although in form no religious doctrine could ever claim to be identical with the truth, with respect to content doctrines such as the Trinity are (within the constraints of their symbolic character) reliable indicators of truth.[229]

Although the doctrine itself is reliable, a bad use of it may occur if it is separated from its "experiential roots," which are the experience of God as living and the experience of the New Being in Jesus the Christ.[230] If this happens, the Trinitarian symbols become empty, devoid of revelatory content. In consequence, the doctrine comes to be regarded as itself a revealed mystery, to be believed on the basis of ecclesiastical authority and to be used to close off inquiry.[231] As a result, Tillich considered Unitarianism to be an understandable reaction to authoritarian theology, in spite of its avowed anti-Trinitarian stance and in spite of its inability to recognize the religious motives of the Trinitarian symbols.[232] A perhaps equally regrettable result of the disjunction between the doctrine and its experiential roots is found in the Protestant churches' near exclusive focus on the element of Logos within the divine life, with the result that Protestantism has become, Tillich believed, a mere tool for moral education.[233]

Since the principal thing, then, is not the doctrine as such but its roots in revelation, Tillich held that "one should approach the trinitarian dogma of the early church with neither a positive nor a negative prejudice, but with a question" about the actual effects of the doctrine – how well it expresses the divine life.[234] In fact, however, Tillich approached the doctrine with a very firm view of its liabilities. The perennial problem of the doctrine lies, he asserted, in preserving the unity of the divine amid the diversity of manifestations. Although this is a general problem in the history of religions and gives rise to polytheism, it takes, in Christianity,

---

[229] Tillich, *Systematic Theology*, III:286.   [230] Ibid., II:144.   [231] Ibid., III:291.
[232] Ibid.   [233] Ibid.   [234] Ibid., III:287.

particular forms, reflection on which made Tillich a bit pessimistic about the future of the doctrine. One form of the problem is how to understand the ultimacy of Jesus Christ. New Testament mention of the pre-existence of Christ, when taken literally, turns the Logos into a finite being within the universe of space and time. Even identifying the Logos with Jesus Christ carries its own problems, for the Logos is God's capacity for manifestation as such; it cannot be simply equated with the historical person Jesus Christ, for then God's freedom to be manifest in other ways and in other places is compromised.[235] Another form that this problem takes in Christianity arises from prayer: If prayers are directed to one of the persons in a distinctive way, then it is difficult to see how a practical tritheism is avoided.[236] A final problem arises within the Roman Catholic tradition, where Mary is venerated in such a way as to elevate her to the level of divinity. This compels us, Tillich suggested, to see that the Trinity is not about the number three; the role of Mary as a means by which the divine is manifested plainly forces us to accommodate the doctrine to this new fact and, if necessary, jettison the number three.[237]

Tillich, accordingly, urged a radical revision of the doctrine accompanied by a new understanding (presumably his understanding) of the divine life.[238] Although simply discarding the doctrine was unacceptable to Tillich, he could not bring himself to accept it in its ecclesiastical form. His solution to this dilemma was to seek out the original intention of the doctrine – its function of symbolically expressing the revelation of the divine life.[239] We can here see the form–content distinction previously mentioned at work. The content of the doctrine is the vital matter and that which must be recovered; the doctrinal form, which is the product of human rationality and symbolic expression, may be amended or cast away if the historical form of the doctrine impedes its principal function. Although Tillich, in the *Systematic Theology*, no more than adumbrated the direction such revision might take, he did single out for special consideration the need for

---

[235] Ibid., III:290.   [236] Ibid., III:289.   [237] Ibid., III:292–293.
[238] Ibid., III:292.   [239] Ibid., III:294.

Protestant theology to re-incorporate "the female element in the symbolic expression" of revelation, a need arising out of Protestantism's neglect of Mary in reaction to Roman Catholic theology.[240]

Just as Bultmann represents the heritage of liberal theology, with its sharp disjunction between God as revealed and the inner, unrevealed life of God, so Tillich represents the continuation of the idealist tradition, especially in its distinction between form and content in Christian doctrines and in its desire to allow full rein to historical criticism on the premise that the substantive core of the doctrine, being a matter of revelatory truth, will remain untouched. However, as we have seen and will see further, Tillich was not the only theologian touched by idealist thought. Barth, Moltmann and Pannenberg all owe a great debt to the idealist notion of God's own historicity, a point not of great interest to either Bultmann or Tillich.

Karl Barth, Jürgen Moltmann and Wolfhart Pannenberg

Initially, Barth's perspective on this issue is similar to Tillich's: although the doctrine of the Trinity has its ground in revelation, the doctrine cannot be read directly off Scripture – the Bible does not explicitly state the doctrine.[241] The doctrine is an interpretation of revelation, not something itself revealed.[242] To this extent, Barth shared the critical perspective of Bultmann and Tillich. However, it is no exaggeration to state that Barth was far more confident in the ecclesiastical doctrine than either Bultmann or Tillich. This is because of his opinion that knowledge of the Trinity is implicit in revelation and that consequently such knowledge is already part of the Biblical witness to revelation. The doctrine, then, is "a necessary and relevant analysis of revelation," and

---

[240] Ibid., III:293. See III:294 for Tillich's elaboration of this revision with respect to the symbols of ground of being, Logos, and Spirit.

[241] *CD* I/1, 437. For a general review of Barth's understanding of the Trinity and revelation and their connection to the doctrine of the Trinity, see Robert Theis, "Die Lehre von der Dreieinigkeit Gottes bei Karl Barth," *Freiburger Zeitschrift für Philosophie und Theologie* 24 (1977): 251–290.   [242] *CD* I/1, 353–354.

Barth regarded the development of the Trinitarian doctrine as continuous with the scriptural witness to revelation.[243] Further, Barth's confidence in the doctrine rests on yet deeper grounds, for the act of revelation is itself God's own self-interpretation. The church, when it formulated the doctrine, and the theologian, when explicating the doctrine, are not merely interpreting revelation; they are in fact interpreting a revelation that is itself already an interpretation, a self-revelation.[244] Revelation is not simply a declaration by God of some important information that humanity needs; it is instead identical with the union of the divine and the human in Jesus Christ. It is God's becoming other. This is the import of Barth's continued polemic against a modalistic understanding of the Trinity, to the effect that such an interpretation separates God from revelation. On the contrary, Barth insisted, God is not different from revelation, although in God's freedom God is not simply identical with revelation.

Understanding the doctrine of the Trinity in this Barthian sense as a necessary analysis and interpretation of the revelation attested in the Bible has proved so persuasive that writers such as Moltmann and Pannenberg no longer seem to feel the need to defend the ecclesiastical doctrine. This may be the most significant result of Barth's theology of the Trinity – the fact that theologians such as Moltmann and Pannenberg no longer agonize, as former generations did, over the doctrine and its scriptural warrants, but instead proceed directly from what they take to be the revelation attested in the Bible, confident that this revelation can be understood only in a Trinitarian way. It is no longer a question for them that the Bible points to a Trinitarian God; the only significant questions for them deal with matters discussed here: the character of this revelation, the nature of God's selfhood and personality, and God's historicity and its implications for the doctrine of the Trinity.

Now, to be sure, Pannenberg's theological project has involved him in the quest to get behind the ancient creeds and even the New Testament titles accorded to Christ, in order to locate their foundation in the history of Jesus. Following this critical procedure, he

---

[243] Ibid., 355–356.   [244] Ibid., 358.

retraces the development of New Testament Christology and the creeds, showing the "inner necessity" and "logic" of this development.[245] This method is based on Pannenberg's repeatedly stated desire to formulate an approach to Christology "from below," i.e., from history, in contrast to what he understood to be Barth's "from above" approach. In part, Pannenberg favors this approach because he believes that it matches the way in which the early church came to its Christology, namely from the resurrection and its retroactive effects on the authority of Jesus.[246] In part, he favors it because he believes it is the only way to do justice to the humanity of Jesus and to our own historical conditionedness.[247] Further, and here Pannenberg is at his most critical, such a method allows us to separate the "essential content" of the doctrine from "secondary features or distortion" that have accrued over the years.[248] However, even at his most critical, Pannenberg still affirms the fundamental validity of the doctrine. The procedure he uses is, he insists, only adopted for methodological purposes – to make clear the "revelatory historical basis" of the doctrine that was always presupposed but not explicated; Christology itself is grounded ontically in the eternal Son.[249]

Barth, then, and theologians he has inspired, brought to an end the history of criticism launched by Hermann Samuel Reimarus in the eighteenth century. That criticism had attacked the doctrine of the Trinity as a misconstrual of the Bible. Barth rendered this view obsolete by a renewed understanding of revelation and by showing that revelation both presupposes the Trinity and in turn implies the doctrine of the Trinity. Moltmann and Pannenberg have simply followed suit and modified Barth in the ways indicated previously in this chapter. What is important to note is that this renewed understanding of revelation was made possible by idealist philosophy, with its keen appreciation for the appearance of God in history. It is to the twentieth-century appropriation of this idea that we turn in the final section.

[245] Pannenberg, *Systematic Theology*, II:282.
[246] Wolfhart Pannenberg, *Jesus – God and Man*, trs. Lewis L. Wilkins and Duane A. Priebe (Philadelphia: Westminster Press, 1968), 132.   [247] Ibid., 34–35.
[248] Pannenberg, *Systematic Theology*, II:289. See *Jesus – God and Man*, 285–301 for a sustained critique of Chalcedonian Christology.
[249] Pannenberg, *Systematic Theology*, II:288–289.

HISTORY: THE HISTORICITY OF GOD

Karl Barth

In describing the twentieth-century view of God's historicity, we may pass over Bultmann and Tillich. Bultmann's theology was so preoccupied with the revelatory event of proclamation as to render his doctrine of God nearly invisible. It is more difficult to account for Tillich's lack if interest in this topic, given his idealistic proclivities. It must suffice to note that he did not share Hegel's fascination with the entrance of God into history and the implications of this entrance for the doctrine of God. Consequently, we find little mention in Tillich of the death of God and of the historical actualization of God in history, topics of great importance to Hegel. In short, Tillich seems to have passed silently over the philosophies of history that undergirded idealism. Although he retained a great many idealistic concerns and motifs, the absence of this historical dimension means that the God that Tillich portrays is a peculiarly static reality, in spite of the inclusion of otherness and non-being and the resulting ontological tensions.

Ironically, then, it is Barth who took up the idealistic theme of God's historicity, although in a much tempered form. The first thing to note is that, according to Barth, revelation has a historical character. It is an event[250] and that event is Jesus Christ.[251] As such, revelation is historically particular – it has a "once-for-all" character.[252] Not only is God's act of revelation particular and contingent but humanity's hearing of revelation is likewise particular and contingent. Revelation is not the grasping of universal truths through rational reflection, but rather the address of God to particular people in a particular here and now.[253] This is why Barth so vehemently opposed the mythological interpretation of the Bible: it was not that he took every narrative in the Bible as a literal description

---

[250] *CD* I/1, 127.

[251] Ibid., 131. Throughout this exposition it should be kept in mind that revelation can be separated from the other forms of the Word of God, the Word as written and as preached. A fuller exposition that would take account of these forms would extend the analysis of revelation to the Holy Spirit, the "subjective reality of revelation," i.e., the way in which revelation is given to us today.   [252] *CD* I/1, 135.

[253] Ibid., 169–170.

of fact but that myth deals with the a-historical and with the general. Revelation, contrariwise, is given to people occupying "a definite historical position."[254] The historical character of revelation means that it is "a concrete relation to concrete men." It is not about abstract propositions given to human beings in general about universal and metaphysical truths, but about a unique and unrepeatable event.[255] The contingency and historicity of revelation, the fact that it is not a matter of metaphysical propositions and abstract truths, means that revelation is a sort of brute fact that cannot be judged in the light of something higher.[256] Because revelation is not a matter of rational truths, it cannot be treated as an instance of a more general truth. Consequently, we cannot study and analyze it; it can only be received.

The fact that revelation possesses a historical character does not mean that it is simply a part of the nexus of humanly historical events. For one thing, revelation is not something ascertainable by the methods of historical inquiry – it is not something that could be observed and scientifically described by a neutral observer.[257] For another thing, revelation is a divine act and therefore a free one.[258] Nothing humans do can make the Bible or a sermon become the Word of God; only the Spirit can. So, revelation is historical yet it is not simply like other historical events that can be studied by historians and explained with customary methods.

Finally, revelation is historical because it makes history. Because revelation is the act of God, it has a power and it brings about changes.[259] What sort of changes? Mainly, it creates a church, a people of God, because revelation is a relation between God and particular people. In revelation humans have "acquired a future and along with that a present." Here God becomes "the object of human contemplation, human experience, human thought, human speech."[260] In revelation, then, God is historically effective.

But it is not only revelation that has a historical character. As we noted previously, the ruling axiom of Barth's understanding of the Trinity is that God is antecedently in eternity what God is in revelation. Accordingly, there is something like history within God's own

---

[254] Ibid., 373 and 376.   [255] Ibid., 374–375.   [256] Ibid., 378–379.
[257] Ibid., 373.   [258] Ibid., 178–179.   [259] Ibid., 163 and 173.
[260] Ibid., 342 and 362.

eternal life – even God's life has an event- or act-like character.[261] Further, just as in revelation God creates fellowship with us, so God is in eternity a perfect fellowship as the Spirit unites Father and Son.[262] In short, God's character and deeds in revelation are a mirror of God's Trinitarian life in eternity. God's historical dealings with humanity in revelation are a sort of re-enactment of God's own character.

Nevertheless, Barth held back from affirming anything like historical development in God and completely disavowed such idealist notions as God's dependence on the world and God's self-actualization in the world. The whole point of Barth's doctrine of the Trinity is to argue that God has an eternal life within the Trinity that negates any need on God's part for any other reality such as the world. There is already otherness and fellowship within the divine being; consequently God stands in no need of the world. So we can see the tight connection in Barth's theology between the doctrine of the Trinity and the idea of God's freedom. God is free and independent of the world because God is a Trinity.[263] Further, Barth specifically and expressly declined the suggestion that there is in God a process of actualization from non-being to being.[264] So while Barth held that there is a historical character to God's being and act, he denied that it involved any sort of development in God or dependence of God on the world. Moltmann and Pannenberg, as we will see, are not so reticent to affirm real development in God, although they never go so far as to sacrifice completely the independence of God. That vestige of Barthian theology remains a potent obstacle to any idealist tendencies in their theologies.

Jürgen Moltmann

Moltmann insists that theology must begin with the history of salvation, which is the history of Jesus and his relation to God the Father. The doctrine of the Trinity arises from this history. But it does more than arise from this history – it *is* this history. Although

---

[261] *CD* II/1, 263.
[262] Ibid., 274–275. See *CD* I/1, 538–539 for a discussion of the way in which the Spirit's role in history is prefigured by the Spirit's act in the eternal Trinity.
[263] *CD* I/1, 158.   [264] *CD* II/1, 306.

Barth and of course everyone else in the history of Trinitarian thought would agree with the thesis that the economic Trinity is no other than the eternal Trinity in its openness to the world, Moltmann is of the opinion that a more vigorous understanding of the identity of the eternal and economic Trinities is required if we are to understand the Trinity rightly.

To this end, Moltmann proposes a revision in our thinking about history.[265] The first thing needed is to get beyond the modern emphasis on subjectivity – the experience of the self – and to regard theology as the doctrine of the Trinitarian history of God with the world.[266] In particular, this means beginning theology with the suffering of Jesus on the cross, a suffering that is also God's suffering.[267] It is in this history, this suffering, that the Trinitarian relations can be perceived, for here the distinction of persons is set in relief as each person plays a unique role. It is thus that the history of Jesus reveals the Trinity.[268]

Beginning with the plurality demonstrated in the history of Jesus' suffering, theology's goal is a knowledge of God's unity; however, the result of beginning with history is that this unity will turn out to be neither the unity of substance nor that of a self-identical subject. Instead, focus on the history of Jesus will determine how we must understand the unity of the triune God.[269] The supposition is that the unity of God that we finally arrive at will be marked by the dynamism that characterizes God's historical relation with the world.

The resulting view of history departs from that of liberal theology, which portrayed history as the realm of human action and of morality and not primarily as the place of God's activity. Hence it is not surprising that liberal theologians regarded the doctrine of the Trinity as speculative, for their historical point of departure furnished them with a most unpromising premise for any consideration of Trinitarian relations.[270] Liberal theologians were inclined to understand God principally as the founder and

---

[265] See Laurence W. Wood, "From Barth's Trinitarian Christology to Moltmann's Trinitarian Pneumatology: A Methodist Perspective," *The Asbury Theological Journal* 48 (1993): 66–69 for an exposition of the larger parameters of Moltmann's reflections on history, God and eschatology. Wood especially highlights the Hegelian background of Moltmann's view of history. [266] Moltmann, *The Trinity and the Kingdom*, 5.
[267] Ibid., 21–22. [268] Ibid., 65. [269] Ibid., 19. [270] Ibid., 61–62.

sustainer of the moral world order and as the model of personality, not as a being intimately involved with the historical course of the world. This disagreement between Moltmann and liberal theology demonstrates that modern historical consciousness has taken various forms; this fact is of supreme importance for the doctrine of the Trinity. It is no exaggeration to state that the doctrine has experienced a resurgence today precisely because of an altered view of the way in which God acts in history, a view that seems to require a Trinitarian understanding of both God and history. Ultimately, Moltmann's view of history reflects idealist tendencies; liberal theology firmly rejected the idealist philosophy of history.

The history that is theology's point of departure, then, is for Moltmann the "history to which the Bible testifies." This history, however, is not the action of a singular subject; it assumes a plurality of divine subjects, for the history of Jesus, recounted in the New Testament, is at the same time the history of Jesus the Son with his Father and likewise the history of the Father with Jesus the Son. Further, the New Testament's narration of the Son's history is, at pivotal points, conjoined with a narration of the Spirit's activities, so that Jesus the Son is inconceivable apart from the Spirit. As a result, the history of Jesus is "the history of the reciprocal, changing, and hence living relationship between the Father, the Son and the Spirit." In other words, the New Testament's account of the history of Jesus is from the beginning a Trinitarian history.[271]

The Trinitarian history of God with the world compels us, Moltmann believes, to rethink the distinction between the economic and eternal Trinities. This distinction rests on an untenable disjunction between freedom and necessity in God. God is commonly represented in such a way that the eternal procession of the Son and Spirit in the Trinity is due to God's nature; consequently it is in some sense a matter of necessity. Contrarily, God's dealings with the world result from God's free decision. Such events as the creation and the incarnation are free in the sense that God might have chosen not to bring them about. God's being remains the same whether God creates a world or not. The error here, according to Moltmann, lies in defining liberty as God's capacity to do

---

[271] Ibid., 63–64.

whatever God chooses to do. In Moltmann's opinion, this view has the deleterious effect of driving a wedge between the economic and eternal Trinities and between God's freedom and God's nature. As a result, the events that transpire in history and in the economy of salvation are thought to have no essential effect on the eternal Trinity, which in turn is regarded as a life that is independent and in some measure detached from the world. This error can be corrected only by defining God's freedom as self-communicative love. Such a redefinition removes the arbitrary aspect from God's freedom, so that God's creation of and love for the world result not so much from God's free choice as from God's nature, which is love.[272] If this definition is accepted, then it must also be acknowledged that God's relation to the world – the economic Trinity – has an effect on the divine being, for if God is essentially self-communicative love, then the relation between God and the world is a two-way street, with each having an effect on the other.[273] In this way, it becomes natural to assert that God's love toward the world is the same love that characterizes the eternal relations within the Trinity;[274] as a result, the chasm between the economic Trinity and the eternal Trinity that looms in traditional Trinitarian thought is bridged. But this identity of the economic Trinity with the eternal Trinity means that any authentic doctrine of the Trinity must acknowledge the reality of suffering within the eternal Trinity. The crucifixion of Christ means both salvation for the world and also suffering within the divine being. In an important sense, then, God is affected by events in the world; the eternal Trinity is not a passionless, immutable being for which suffering is foreign. Eternally, the cross determines who and what God is.[275]

But if the eternal God suffers, does this make God dependent on the world?[276] It is one thing to affirm that God suffers with the world and is thereby substantially affected. It is another thing to state with Hegel that God depends upon the world – that God

---

[272] Ibid., 54.   [273] Ibid., 151.   [274] Ibid., 157.   [275] Ibid., 160–161.

[276] For an extended analysis and critique of Moltmann on this point, see John J. O'Donnell, "The Doctrine of the Trinity in Recent German Theology," *The Heythrop Journal* 23 (1982): 153–167 and "The Trinity as Divine Community" (cited above). Among other points of criticism, O'Donnell finds Moltmann's theology in danger of succumbing to a Hegelian understanding of God whereby God requires the world for self-actualization.

would not be God without the world. Moltmann seems expressly to deny this sort of radical dependence of God on the world. Although wishing to dissolve the distinction between economic and immanent Trinity, he seeks to preserve the relative independence of God from the world by introducing a new distinction, namely the distinction between the economic Trinity and the doxological Trinity. The doxological Trinity is not a different Trinity from the economic; it is instead the one Trinitarian God considered as an object of praise and worship. Although with respect to our knowledge of God we must begin with salvation history and the economic Trinity, in the order of being the eternal doxological Trinity is the transcendental condition of the economic Trinity.[277] By means of this distinction Moltmann seeks to avoid dissolving the Trinity into history or merging it with the world; the notion of the doxological Trinity reminds us that God is not only our fellow-sufferer and source of our salvation, but also the eternal God who inspires our praise. In the end, although Moltmann is heavily indebted to the idealist heritage and particularly to Hegel for his doctrine of God,[278] he stops short of the idealist tenet that the finite world is a necessary aspect of the divine being and that God depends upon the world. Although he is willing to speak of the world existing in God and of God's history being in "a continual relationship of reciprocity,"[279] there can be no question about Moltmann's commitment to the independent existence of God, just as the eternal Son is the presupposition of the historical Son, Jesus Christ.[280]

In summary, Moltmann proposes that, because God is self-communicative love, it is natural for God to create a world and to enter into an intimate relation with that world. But this is possible only because the love that God essentially is implies an eternal self-giving within the Trinity. God's entrance into the historical realm

---

[277] Moltmann, *The Trinity and the Kingdom*, 153.
[278] Henry Jansen, "Moltmann's View of God's (Im)mutability," 299 finds Moltmann's understanding of God as love "certainly borrowed from Hegel" and notes the Hegelian contribution to Moltmann's view of personhood. On this latter point see also Regina Radlbeck, *Der Personbegriff*, 76.   [279] Moltmann, *The Trinity and the Kingdom*, 110.
[280] Ibid., 107. See also Jürgen Moltmann, "I Believe in Jesus Christ, the Only Son of God," *History and the Triune God: Contributions to Trinitarian Theology*, trs. John Bowden (New York: The Crossroad Publishing Co., 1992), 38–39.

is prefigured and made possible by the eternal relations among the Trinitarian persons, who, because they are utterly relational, are therefore also thoroughly historical.[281] Ultimately, the involvement of God in human and salvation history rests on the eternal historicity of the divine persons, whose life is an everlasting and dynamic fellowship.

Wolfhart Pannenberg

Pannenberg's theology shares with Moltmann's many of the ideas associated with God's historicity. Like Moltmann, Pannenberg insists that the point of departure for the doctrine of the Trinity is the Trinitarian history narrated in the Gospels, in which the relations of the Trinitarian persons are revealed.[282] In particular, theology must begin with Jesus' relation to the Father in his preaching of the message of the kingdom.[283] By his absolute submission to the Father, Jesus is united with the Father so essentially that "God in eternity is Father only in relation to him." Jesus' ministry revealed God as the Father of Jesus the Son. As a result, Jesus shares the deity and rule of God the Father and the Father is eternally identified as the Father of Jesus.[284] Accordingly, as we have seen, the deity of God depends on history. For example, God's deity is at stake in the cross of Jesus, for God's rule hangs in the balance during the crucifixion; God's rule and deity were utterly questionable while Jesus was hanging on the cross. The decision about God's rule and deity is not made until Jesus is resurrected, an event that, at least provisionally, vindicates Jesus' claims and confirms God's rule and deity. The fact that God's deity hangs in the balance allows us, Pannenberg believes, to speak in some sense of the Father's suffering.[285] In a departure from Moltmann, this idea of God's deity depending on the result of the cross is about as far as Pannenberg is prepared to go in discussing the suffering of God the Father. He is actually far more interested in the resurrection than in the suffering of the cross, for it is the resurrection that demonstrates that Jesus was in fact the Son and that the Father

---

[281] Moltmann, *The Trinity and the Kingdom*, 174.
[282] Pannenberg, *Systematic Theology*, I:298–299.   [283] Ibid., I:304.
[284] Ibid., I:310.   [285] Ibid., I:314.

indeed rules. Further, the Spirit is also active in the resurrection: by raising Jesus from the dead and glorifying the risen Christ, the Spirit is distinguished from the Father and Son and emerges as a distinct Trinitarian person.[286] Overall, then, Pannenberg, like Moltmann, begins with revelation in history and proceeds from there to a knowledge of the eternal Trinity and the unity of God.

In a further important similarity to Moltmann, Pannenberg holds that God's eternal being has a distinctly historical character, for Pannenberg too wishes to overcome the distinction between the economic and eternal Trinities. This traditional distinction is unfortunate, in his judgment, for three reasons. First, it tends to separate the eternal Trinity from history and from the economy of salvation.[287] Second, it lacks substantive Biblical warrant.[288] Third, this distinction is customarily associated with the view that the persons are distinguished solely by their eternal relations of origin. According to this view, the Son differs from the Father only in the fact that the Son is begotten whereas the Father begets. For Pannenberg, however, this account is far too simplistic; the persons are, he holds, distinguished from one another by the numerous relations that arise in the history of salvation – sending and obeying, raising and glorifying, and so on.[289] In an important sense, the identities of the persons are determined by their acts in history and by the ways in which their relations emerge in history. Thus history has a determinative effect on the eternal Trinity.

As with Moltmann, this last assertion raises the question of the extent to which God's being is dependent on the course of history. Like Moltmann, Pannenberg solemnly affirms the independent being of God and wishes in no sense to be understood as falling into any sort of pantheistic identifying of God and the world. However, Pannenberg's fuller answer to this question is a bit more complex than Moltmann's, for it incorporates Pannenberg's idiosyncratic understanding of time, eternity and eschatology. Although Pannenberg denies that God *becomes* in history, he does affirm that history is the arena in which the decision about God's being occurs. Hence, there is a great similarity between God's

---

[286] Ibid., I:314–315.   [287] Ibid., I:332–333.   [288] Ibid., I:305.
[289] Ibid., I320–321.

being and rule on the one hand and the sonship of Jesus on the other. In both cases there is a historical moment that is decisive because of its retroactive effect.[290]

Perhaps the easiest route into Pannenberg's conception of God's historicity is an examination of his understanding of the resurrection of Jesus. Pannenberg's view steers a course between two options: first, that the resurrection made of Jesus something that he was not previously, namely, the Son of God;[291] second, that the resurrection merely confirmed what was always true of Jesus, so that he would still be the Son of God even had the resurrection not occurred.[292] Pannenberg insists that while the resurrection did in fact confirm Jesus' pre-Easter claims about himself, it also decided that these claims were true. Prior to the resurrection, Jesus' claims and message were anything but settled; the resurrection was that act of God that decisively confirmed those claims and legitimated Jesus' person and message.[293] Pannenberg is of the opinion that his understanding of these matters is not unique and that he is merely calling attention to a phenomenon that we are all aware of – the fact that the essence of something often depends on future events, just as the significance of a sentence in a book becomes fully clear only at the end of the book. The limitation of this analogy is that the sentence in its literal form is static, whereas the essences of beings such as Jesus are really in the process of becoming. So, the resurrection not only confirms our beliefs about the essence of Jesus' identity and message but actually brings that essence to a completion. Therefore, it is not true that the resurrection merely makes known what is true anyway, because Jesus would not be the Son of God without the resurrection. That is, regardless of his claims and deeds and the previous course of his life, the absence of a resurrection would have been a historical decision that Jesus was not the Son of God.[294]

Having seen the notion of retroactive power employed with respect to the resurrection of Jesus, we are now in a position to grasp its significance for the historicity of God's being and

---

[290] Ibid., I:331.   [291] Pannenberg, *Jesus – God and Man*, 135.
[292] Pannenberg, *Systematic Theology*, II:345–346.
[293] Pannenberg, *Jesus – God and Man*, 135 and *Systematic Theology*, II:365–366.
[294] Pannenberg, *Jesus – God and Man*, 136.

universal rule. The resurrection of Jesus is an anticipation of the day when God will exercise universal rule over the world. That eschatological day has the same confirming and actualizing function for God's deity and rule that the resurrection possesses for Jesus' claims and message. On the one hand, it is not the case that only at the end of history will God begin to be divine and to rule, just as Jesus did not begin to be the Son of God in the resurrection. God is ruling even now, in the midst of history, and does not become divine as a result of the historical process. On the other hand, it is not the case that God is divine and rules in the absence of this eschatological day in which God's rule is decisively demonstrated, just as Jesus would not have been the Son of God without the resurrection as the decisive act of God that authenticated his claims and message. As an alternative to these views Pannenberg proposes that at the present, with the future open to new possibilities, the deity and ultimate rule of God are questionable just as, in the midst of his ministry, the claims of Jesus were questionable. Not until the eschatological day will God's rule, and consequently God's deity, be fully confirmed; however, that day will not only convince humanity of God's rule and deity but also make it evident that God was in fact divine and ruling all along. Although in faith we affirm that God is in fact ruling, this rule will not be true apart from the eschatological moment that confirms this rule.

But how is it that the eternal God can be thus given over to history in such a way that God's deity is at stake? To answer this question we need to grasp Pannenberg's understanding of eternity. Pannenberg is quite taken with Plotinus' theory of eternity because it defines eternity in terms of totality. Whereas life in time is fragmented and sequential, eternity is the totality of life simultaneously present.[295] Following this lead, Boethius and Barth represented eternity in such a way that it is not opposed to time, but includes a positive relation to time.[296] In short, eternity is not the absence of time but rather embraces the totality of time.[297] Because eternity signifies the totality of time, eternity appears, from the perspective

---

[295] Pannenberg, *Systematic Theology*, I:403.   [296] Ibid., I:404–405.
[297] Ibid., I:408. In expounding this idea of eternity, Pannenberg has recourse to a Hegelian analysis, whereby eternity is a "paradigmatic illustration" of the true infinite, which is not simply opposed to the finite but also includes the finite within it.

of beings in time, to be "a fulness that is sought in the future." As a result, Pannenberg avers, the future came to have a vital role in the understanding of time, for it is only in the future that the totality of time would be completed.[298]

There is, then, a profound difference between God's eternity and our time. Because our time is incomplete, we have a future; however, God's eternity is the completion and totality of time itself. Accordingly, God, unlike us, has no future that lies outside of the divine being.[299] Nevertheless, at the eschatological day, when God's rule is evident, time and eternity will touch, for time will then have the sort of completeness that characterizes God's eternity.[300] We may therefore state that on the one hand, God's rule and being are never really in question *from God's perspective in eternity*. In God's eternity there is completion; all human history lies in the immediacy of God's presence and nothing remains to be decided. However, by creating a world with a temporal character, God has made the divine being and rule something questionable *from the perspective of those who are in time*. In time, it is not yet evident and in fact not completely true that God exists and that God rules. Only the eschatological day will decide these matters in a completely convincing way.

However, we should not let this difference between God's eternity and our time drive a wedge between the essential Trinity of God and God's acts in history. Pannenberg argues that the positive relation between eternity and time, whereby eternity is not the absence of time but rather the totality of time as simultaneously present, requires that God be, not an "undifferentiated identity," but an "intrinsically differentiated unity." In other words, God must be a Trinity if eternity is to be truly infinite (the totality of time) and not the mere opposite of time.[301] This is not to suggest that the doctrine of the Trinity implies the temporality of God. However, because God is a Trinity, the divine life consists in a plurality in totality – a plurality of persons in the totality of God's life – just as eternity consists in a plurality of temporal moments in a comprehensive totality. Because God's life is Trinitarian, God is able to incorporate the plurality of historically bound creatures

[298] Pannenberg, *Systematic Theology*, I:408.   [299] Ibid., I:410.   [300] Ibid., I:409.
[301] Ibid., I:405.

into the totality that is the divine eternity.[302] Consequently, although God is not temporal, there is a Trinitarian basis in God for the historical economy of salvation, an economy that aims at unifying the whole of history into one total reality. In Pannenberg's words, "The creation and the historical march of cosmic time are embraced by the economy of God."[303]

CONCLUSION

This brief review of five theologians has sought to show that the main concepts that establish the parameters of Trinitarian thinking in German thought were set in place by the end of the idealist period in nineteenth-century philosophy and that subsequent development in the doctrine of the Trinity largely represents the playing out of the possible combinations and permutations of these concepts. This is not to claim that nothing original has occurred in late nineteenth- and twentieth-century theology. An examination of Paul Tillich's theology suffices to demonstrate that numerous and important concepts, methods and data both in philosophy and theology have arisen since the demise of idealism. It is also not to claim that Trinitarian thought has lately been a mere replaying of idealist philosophy. Apart from the obvious case of someone like Bultmann, who continues a completely different tradition and seems to have been largely unaffected by idealism, we could point with ease to the many respects in which Barth, Moltmann, Pannenberg and even Tillich depart from central Hegelian notions.

However, it is fair to claim that Trinitarian thought would not have enjoyed its twentieth-century revival without Hegel's prior setting of the stage. Although Friedrich Schleiermacher's provocative proposal for rethinking the doctrine of the Trinity might have stimulated a renewed enthusiasm for Trinitarian thinking, as a matter of fact the tradition influenced by him attended exclusively to his critical remarks about the doctrine and ignored the potentially profitable constructive program of his theology. The fact that the fulcrum of Moltmann's doctrine of the Trinity is God's

[302] Ibid., 1:407.   [303] Ibid., 1:409.

self-communicative love is a testimony to the potential impact of Schleiermacher's theology on the development of Trinitarian theology, for it was Schleiermacher who made the divine love the cornerstone of the doctrine of God and there are remarkable similarities between his and Moltmann's views of this love. Nevertheless, in actual fact it was Hegel who gave the impetus to Trinitarian thought and enabled its resurgence after the devastating criticisms it received in the period of the Enlightenment and liberal theology. Even though idealism as a movement is dead, as evidenced by the lack of a Tillichian school of theology, it set in motion powerful ideas that, in altered and sometimes disguised forms, issued finally in the renewal of Trinitarian thinking that has been the subject of this chapter.

Postscript to twentieth-century Trinitarian thought

If I have been successful in this book, then I have shown that modern Trinitarian thinking, at least in the German Protestant tradition, is regulated by the interplay of three leading ideas, Word, reflective selfhood, and history. These ideas, in their various permutations and relations, constitute that tradition and determine the possible forms that Trinitarian thought may take. If I have been successful, then I and the reader have come to understand this tradition and have done so by grasping its intellectual components and their historical connectedness.

Of course, this tradition is not static; I have sought to document important changes in the ways in which these ideas were conceived from the beginning of this tradition to the present. It is also not limited to these three ideas. Originally, the tradition was determined by two ideas – Word and reflective selfhood. Only in the eighteenth century did the idea of history join these two. Nothing prevents yet a fourth idea from entering the tradition and altering future Trinitarian thought. There is nothing magical about the number three. Accordingly, if the tradition is not static, then the process of understanding it is also not static, but instead is as dynamic and open-ended as the tradition itself. Nonetheless, understanding of this or any other tradition from its beginning to the present is possible once its components are discerned and their historical movement is described.

What can we draw from this history about the future course of Trinitarian thought? The tradition of Trinitarian thought discussed in this book has developed in such a way that the following issues have become a matter of urgency. Regrettably, this concluding discussion can be no more than an enumeration of problems and brief indication of desirable directions. But if Trinitarian thought and with it Christian theology is to advance beyond the present, then the following issues must be addressed and resolved.

First, with regard to the concept of the Word. Barth's, Moltmann's and Pannenberg's ratification of Luther's Christocentric understanding of revelation should be regarded as the point of departure for future reflection on this subject. However, with the recent rise of interest in the historical reconstruction of Jesus' life, theologians can hardly avoid a repetition of the Jesus of history/Christ of faith debate that preoccupied theologians a few decades ago. Whatever the outcome of the next round of this debate, the theologian will be obligated to claim that the life, death and resurrection of this particular person, Jesus, is the Trinitarian life of God acted out on the stage of history. Jesus is not the Word of God because he speaks about God, but because his life, death and resurrection are a declaration of God. He is the life of God in a particular, historical form. Likewise, Jesus is not God because he had a divine self-consciousness, but instead because his life both reveals the life of God and in fact is the life of God. Acceptance of these theses, of course, would necessitate an overhaul in the way in which we think of God. God would be not so much a being about whom one could form a more or less correct concept as the sort of being that can appear to us in a wholly unexpected way, as in Jesus Christ. Further, we would have to think of the life of God as something in which we can participate when, through the Spirit, we enter into the fellowship between the Son and the Father. Consequently, the being of God would have to be thought of as a being in which we can participate, not as a monadic and exclusionary being.

Along with Luther's Christocentric understanding of revelation, Melanchthon's initial perplexity about the religiously practical value of the doctrine must also be the subject of continual labor. Fortunately, the work of Barth and the follow-up work of Moltmann and Pannenberg should convince anyone with an interest in theology that the doctrine of the Trinity is not a theory about the eternal being of God but is instead first and foremost an account of God's being for us and among us. The main task for theology on this point is to follow the lead of these theologians and consistently present theological doctrines in a thoroughly Trinitarian form. But this can be done only if it is a matter of perpetual remembrance that the doctrine of the Trinity is about Jesus Christ, God the Father and the Holy Spirit. It is about the way in which God comes to us. It is about the way in which the Christian life is lived out by participation in the being of God. To be sure, there is still work to be done in reflecting on God's eternity, but the results of such reflection must arise out of authentic Trinitarian thought.

As to historicity. Even conservative evangelical theology today accepts the historical character of the Bible and of course Protestants never had much difficulty historicizing the creeds. The challenge today is to fashion a satisfactory understanding of the Trinitarian creeds that will account for their enduring character while also preventing them from becoming dead letters of authority. Such an account would explain the creeds in their dual function of setting boundaries for the Christian faith and representing the Trinity conceptually in a culturally conditioned form. As boundary-setting documents, they would be the church's collective judgment on the theological options (such as tritheism and unqualified unitarianism) that stand definitely outside the circle of Christianity. As such, they would be interpreted as covert negations, stating what the Christian faith excludes. As conceptual representations of the Trinity in culturally conditioned forms, the creeds would have an exemplary value as classical attempts at using the language and concepts of the day to expound the Christian faith in a coherent and imaginative way. Although later generations may wish to substitute different language and concepts, the creeds would always stand as classics in the sense described. As boundary-setting documents, the creeds would in this view have a virtually permanent authority; as culturally conditioned conceptual schemes, they would have permanent authority only for those who come to believe that there is no better human way of expounding the truth. For others they would have a merely exemplary value.

The other issue in the question of historicity is God's own historical character. The central question here concerns God's relation to the world, especially as the world is understood by contemporary science. The history of theology is strewn with the remains of responses to this question that have been found wanting, the notable ones being deism, pantheism, idealism and traditional theism. What is needed is a way of representing God that neither conflates God with the universe nor makes talk of God's action in the world nonsense. It must take account of the autonomy of natural laws that need no divine interference and also the seemingly contingent, even random character of natural phenomena, transpiring without evident purpose.

Finally, the idea of God's own historicity raises the question of God's selfhood, for any view of God's relation to the world must discuss activity, being and intentionality as these are predicated of God. What is needed on this subject is a view of God that avoids the limitations of the traditional concept of personality and subjectivity. "Personality" as an attribute of God is not easily compatible with a Trinitarian view of God. "Subjectivity" has philosophical problems of its own, at least if it is understood to denote a self-subsistent being with only accidental relations. The doctrine of God of the future will have to fashion a way of speaking of God and God's activity and presence in the world that does not depend on understanding God as a heavenly analog to human beings. The doctrine of the future will understand God's action in a Trinitarian way, not in a mono-personalistic way.

The doctrine of the Trinity, frequently misunderstood, often misused, points the way forward in the doctrine of God.

Bibliography of works consulted

Althaus, Paul. *The Theology of Martin Luther.* Translated by Robert C. Schultz. Philadelphia: Fortress Press, 1966.

Barth, Karl. *Church Dogmatics.* Translated by G. T. Thomson, et al. 4 volumes in 13. Edinburgh: T. & T. Clark, 1936–1969.

The Epistle to the Romans. Translated by Eswyn C. Hoskins. London: Oxford University Press, 1972.

Beisser, Friedrich. *Schleiermachers Lehre von Gott dargestellt nach seinen Reden und seiner Glaubenslehre.* Forschungen zur systematischen und ökumenischen Theologie, Band 22. Göttingen: Vandenhoeck & Ruprecht, 1970.

Bengel, Johann Albrecht. "Abriß der so genannten Brüdergemeine." *Nikolaus Ludwig von Zinzendorf: Materialen und Dokumente.* Edited by Erich Beyreuther, et al. 2nd series: *Nikolaus Ludwig Graf von Zinzendorf: Leben und Werke in Quellen und Darstellungen,* edited by Erich Beyreuther and Gerhard Meyer. Vol. X. Hildesheim: Georg Olms Verlag, 1972.

Beyreuther, Erich. "Christozentrismus und Trinitätsauffassung." *Studien zur Theologie Zinzendorfs: Gesammelte Aufsätze.* [Neukirchen-Vluyn:] Neukirchener Verlag, 1962.

Brandt, James M. "Ritschl's Critique of Schleiermacher's Theological Ethics." *Journal of Religious Ethics* 17 (1989): 51–72.

Bultmann, Rudolf. *Essays, Philosophical and Theological.* Translated by J. C. G. Greig. The Library of Philosophy and Theology. New York: Macmillan, 1955.

Existence and Faith: Shorter Writings of Rudolf Bultmann. Translated by Shubert M. Ogden. Cleveland: World Publishing Co., Meridian Books, 1963.

Faith and Understanding I. Edited by Robert W. Funk. Translated by Louise Pettibone Smith. San Francisco: Harper & Row, 1969.

The New Testament and Mythology and Other Basic Writings. Edited and translated by Shubert M. Ogden. London: SCM Press, 1984.

Burbridge, John. "The Syllogisms of Revealed Religion, or the Reasonableness of Christianity." *The Owl of Minerva* 18 (1986): 29–42.

Dán, Róbert. "'Judaizare' – the Career of a Term." In Róbert Dán and Antal Pirnát, eds., *Antitrinitarianism in the Second Half of the 16th Century.* Studia Humanitatis, edited by T. Klaniczay, no. 5. Leiden: E. J. Brill, 1982.

Dickey, Laurence. "Hegel on Religion and Philosophy." In Frederick C. Beiser, ed., *The Cambridge Companion to Hegel.* Cambridge Companions to Philosophy. Cambridge: Cambridge University Press, 1993.

Ebeling, Gerhard. "Schleiermacher's Doctrine of the Divine Attributes." Translated by James W. Leitch. In Robert W. Funk, ed., *Schleiermacher as Contemporary.* Journal for Theology and the Church, no. 7. New York: Herder and Herder, 1970.

Fackenheim, Emil. *The Religious Dimension in Hegel's Thought.* Bloomington, IN: Indiana University Press, 1967.

Fagerberg, Holsten. *Die Theologie der lutherischen Bekenntnisschriften von 1529 bis 1537.* Göttingen: Vandenhoeck & Ruprecht, 1965.

Foley, Grover. "Ritschls Urteil über Zinzendorfs Christozentrismus." *Evangelische Theologie* 20 (1960): 314–326.

Fraenkel, Peter. *Testimonia Patrum: The Function of the Patristic Argument in the Theology of Philip Melanchthon.* Travaux D'humanisme et Renaissance, no. 46. Geneva: Librairie E. Droz, 1961.

Gadamer, Hans-Georg. *Truth and Method.* 2nd revised edition. Translation revised by Joel Weinsheimer and Donald G. Marshall. New York: The Crossroad Publishing Co., 1990.

Glick, G. Wayne. *The Reality of Christianity: A Study of Adolf von Harnack as Historian and Theologian.* Makers of Modern Theology, edited by Jaroslav Pelikan. New York: Harper & Row, 1967.

Grossmann, Walter. "Edelmann und das 'öffentliche Schweigen' des Reimarus und Lessing." *Zeitschrift für Kirchengeschichte* 84 (1973): 358–368.

Hammer, Karl. "Albrecht Ritschls Lutherbild." *Theologische Zeitschrift* 26 (1970): 109–122.

Harnack, Adolf. *Christianity and History.* Translated by Thomas Bailey Saunders. London: Adam & Charles Black, 1896.

    History of Dogma. Translated by Neil Buchanan, et al. New York: Russell & Russell, 1958.

    "Immanuel Kant." *Aus der Werkstatt des Vollendeten: Als Abschluß seiner Reden und Aufsätze.* Edited by Axel v. Harnack. 5 vols. Giessen: Verlag von Alfred Töpelmann, 1930. V:172–183.

    What is Christianity? Translated by Thomas Bailey Saunders. New York: Harper & Row, Harper Torchbooks, The Cloister Library, 1957.

Hartmann, Klaus. "Hegel: A Non-Metaphysical View." In Alasdair MacIntyre, ed., *Hegel: A Collection of Critical Essays.* Modern Studies in Philosophy. New York: Doubleday & Co., Anchor Books, 1972.

Hefner, Philip J. *Faith and the Vitalities of History: A Theological Study Based on the Work of Albrecht Ritschl*. Makers of Modern Theology. New York: Harper & Row, 1966.

Hegel, G. W. F. *Hegel: The Letters*. Translated by C. Butler and C. Seiler. Bloomington, IN: Indiana University Press, 1984.

Hegel's Philosophy of Mind. Translated by William Wallace. Oxford: Clarendon Press, 1894.

Hegel's Science of Logic. Translated by W. H. Johnson and L. G. Struthers. 2 vols. London: G. Allen & Unwin, Ltd., 1951.

Lectures on the Philosophy of Religion. Edited by Peter C. Hodgson. Translated by R. F. Brown, et al. 3 volumes. Volume I: *Introduction and The Concept of Religion*. Volume II: *Determinate Religion*. Volume III: *The Consummate Religion*. Berkeley: University of California Press, 1984.

Phenomenology of Spirit. Translated by A. V. Miller. Oxford: Clarendon Press, 1977.

Herrmann, Wilhelm. *The Communion of the Christian with God: Described on the Basis of Luther's Statements*. Edited by Robert T. Voelkel. Philadelphia: Fortress Press, 1971.

Die Religion im Verhältniß zum Welterkennen und zur Sittlichkeit: Eine Grundlegung der systematischen Theologie. Halle: Max Niemeyer, 1879.

"Religion und Sittlichkeit." *Gesammelte Aufsätze*, edited by F. W. Schmidt. Tübingen: Verlag von J. C. B. Mohr (Paul Siebeck), 1923.

Systematic Theology. Translated by Nathaniel Micklem and Kenneth Saunders. London: George Allen and Unwin, 1927.

"Unsere Kantfeier." *Gesammelte Aufsätze*, edited by F. W. Schmidt. Tübingen: Verlag von J. C. B. Mohr (Paul Siebeck), 1923.

Hill, William J. *The Three-Personed God: The Trinity as a Mystery of Salvation*. Washington: The Catholic University Press of America, 1982.

Hinrichs, Carl. *Preußentum und Pietismus: Der Pietismus in Brandenburg-Preußen als religiös-soziale Reformbewegung*. Göttingen: Vandenhoeck & Ruprecht, 1971.

Hodgson, Peter C. "Hegel's Christology: Shifting Nuances in the Berlin Lectures." *Journal of the American Academy of Religion* 53 (1985): 23–40.

Hornig, Gottfried. *Die Anfänge der historisch-kritischen Theologie: Johann Salomo Semlers Schriftverständnis und seine Stellung zu Luther*. Forschungen zur systematischen Theologie und Religionsphilosophie, vol. VIII. Göttingen: Vandenhoeck & Ruprecht, 1961.

"Die Freiheit der christlichen Privatreligion: Semlers Begründung des religiösen Individualismus in der protestantischen Aufklärungs-theologie." *Neue Zeitschrift für systematische Theologie* 21 (1979): 198–211.

"Lehre und Bekenntnis im Kulturprotestantismus." *Studia Theologica* 29 (1975): 157–180.

"Die Perfektibilitätsgedanke bei J. S. Semler." *Zeitschrift für Theologie und Kirche* 72 (1975): 381–397.

Huber, Herbert. "Das Absolute ist der Geist." *Die Flucht in den Begriff: Materialen zu Hegels Religionsphilosophie.* Herausgegeben von Friedrich Wilhelm Graf und Falk Wagner. Deutsche Idealismus: Philosophie und Wirkungsgeschichte in Quellen und Studien. Band VI. Stuttgart, Ernst Klett, 1981.

Idealismus und Trinität, Pantheon und Götterdämmerung: Grundlagen und Grundzüge der Lehre von Gott nach dem Manuskript Hegels zur Religionsphilosophie. Weinheim: Acta Humaniora, 1984.

Jaeschke, Walter. "Philosophical Theology and Philosophy of Religion." In David Kolb, ed., *New Perspectives on Hegel's Philosophy of Religion.* Albany: State University of New York Press, 1992.

Reason in Religion: The Foundations of Hegel's Philosophy of Religion. Translated by J. Michael Stewart and Peter C. Hodgson. Berkeley: University of California Press, 1990.

"Speculative and Anthropological Criticism of Religion: A Theological Orientation to Hegel and Feuerbach." *Journal of the American Academy of Religion* 48 (1980): 345–364.

Jansen, Henry. "Moltmann's View of God's (Im)mutability: The God of the Philosophers and the God of the Bible." *Neue Zeitschrift für systematische Theologie und Religionsphilosophie* 36 (1994): 284–301.

Jansen, Reiner. *Studien zu Luthers Trinitätslehre.* Basler und Berner Studien zur historischen und systematischen Theologie, edited by Max Geigner and Andreas Lindt. Vol. XXVI. Bern: Herbert Lang/Frankfurt am Main: Peter Lang, 1976.

Jensen, Kristian. "Protestant Rivalry – Metaphysics and Rhetoric in Germany c. 1590–1620." *Journal of Ecclesiastical History* 41 (1990): 24–43.

Jenson, Robert W. "You Wonder Where the Spirit Went." *Pro Ecclesia* 2 (1993): 301–302.

Johnson, Roger A. *The Origins of Demythologizing: Philosophy and Historiography in the Theology of Rudolf Bultmann.* Studies in the History of Religions (Supplement to *Numen*), no. 28. Leiden: E. J. Brill, 1974.

Kay, James F. *Christus Praesens: A Reconsideration of Rudolf Bultmann's Christology.* Grand Rapids: William B. Eerdmans Publishing Co., 1994.

Kinkel, Gary Steven. *Our Dear Mother the Spirit: An Investigation of Count Zinzendorf's Theology and Praxis.* Lanham, MD: University Press of America, 1990.

LaCugna, Catherine Mowry. *God for Us: The Trinity and Christian Life.* Harper San Francisco, a division of HarperCollins Publishers, 1993.

Lange, Dietz. "Wahrhaftigkeit als sittliche Forderung und als theologisches Prinzip bei Wilhelm Herrmann." *Zeitschrift für Theologie und Kirche* 66 (1969): 77–97.

Leibniz, Gottfried Wilhelm. *Philosophical Papers and Letters*. Translated and edited by Leroy E. Loemker. 2nd edition. Dordrecht: D. Reidel Publishing Co., 1969.

Textes inédits d'après les manuscrits de la Bibliothèque provinciale de Hanovre. Edited by Gaston Grua. Paris: Presses Universitaires de France, 1958.

Lessing, Eckhard. "Zu Schleiermachers Verständnis der Trinitätslehre." *Zeitschrift für Theologie und Kirche* 76 (1979): 450–488.

Lessing, Gotthold Ephraim. *Gesammelte Werke*. Edited by Paul Rilla. 10 vols. Berlin: Aufbau-Verlag, 1957.

Theological Writings. Translated by Henry Chadwick. Stanford: Stanford University Press, 1957.

Loeschen, John R. *The Divine Community: Trinity, Church, and Ethics in Reformation Theologies*. Kirksville, MO: The Sixteenth Century Journal Publishers, 1981.

Lotz, David W. "Albrecht Ritschl and the Unfinished Reformation." *Harvard Theological Review* 73 (1980): 337–372.

Ritschl & Luther: A Fresh Perspective on Albrecht Ritschl's Theology in the Light of His Luther Study. Nashville: Abingdon Press, 1974.

Luther, Martin. "Against Latomus." Translated by George Lindbeck. In *Luther's Works*, edited by Helmut T. Lehmann. Vol. XXXII, *Career of the Reformer II*, edited by George W. Forell. Philadelphia: Muhlenberg Press, 1958.

"Confession Concerning Christ's Supper." In *Luther's Works*, edited by Helmut T. Lehmann. Vol. XXXVII, *Word and Sacrament III*, edited and translated by Robert H. Fischer. Philadelphia: Muhlenberg Press, 1961.

"Defense and Explanation of All the Articles." In *Luther's Works*, translated by Charles M. Jacobs, edited by Helmut T. Lehmann. Vol. XXXII, *Career of the Reformer II*, edited by George W. Forell. Philadelphia: Muhlenberg Press, 1958.

"The Large Catechism." In Theodore G. Tappert, ed. and trs. *The Book of Concord: The Confessions of the Evangelical Lutheran Church*. Philadelphia: Fortress Press, 1959.

"On the Councils and the Church." In *Luther's Works*, edited by Helmut T. Lehmann. Vol. XLI, *Church and Ministry III*, edited by Eric W. Gritsch, translated by Charles M. Jacobs. Philadelphia: Fortress Press, 1966.

"Preface to the New Testament." In *Luther's Works*, edited by Helmut T. Lehmann. Vol. XXXV, *Word and Sacrament I*, edited by E. Theodore Bachmann. Philadelphia: Muhlenberg Press, 1960.

"Prefaces to Jude and James." In *Luther's Works*, edited by Helmut T. Lehmann. Vol. XXXV, *Word and Sacrament I*, edited by E. Theodore Bachmann. Philadelphia: Muhlenberg Press, 1960.

Sermons of Martin Luther. Edited by John Nicholas Lenker. Translated by John Nicholas Lenker, et al. 8 volumes. Vol. VIII, Sermons on Epistle Texts for Trinity Sunday to Advent. Grand Rapids: Baker Book House, 1983.

"The Smalcald Articles." In Theodore G. Tappert, ed. and trs. *The Book of Concord: The Confessions of the Evangelical Lutheran Church*. Philadelphia: Fortress Press, 1959.

"The Three Symbols or Creeds of the Christian Faith." Translated by Robert R. Heitner. In *Luther's Works*, edited by Helmut T. Lehmann. Volume XXXIV, *Career of the Reformer IV*, edited by Lewis W. Spitz. Philadelphia: Muhlenberg Press, 1960.

"Treatise on the Last Words of David 2 Samuel 23: 1–7." Translated by Martin H. Bertram. In *Luther's Works*, vol. XV, edited by Jaroslav Pelikan. St. Louis: Concordia Publishing, 1972.

Mälzer, Gottfried. *Bengel und Zinzendorf: Zur Biographie und Theologie Johann Albrecht Bengels*. Arbeiten zur Geschichte des Pietismus, vol. III. Witten: Luther-Verlag, 1968.

Meeks, M. Douglas. "Jürgen Moltmann's Systematic Contributions to Theology." *Religious Studies Review* 22 (1996): 95–102.

Mehl, Paul Frederick. "Schleiermacher's Mature Doctrine of God as Found in the Dialektik of 1822 and the Second Edition of the Christian Faith 1830–31." Ph.D. dissertation, Columbia University, 1961.

Meijering, E. P. *Melanchthon and Patristic Thought: The Doctrines of Christ and Grace, the Trinity and the Creation*. Studies in the History of Christian Thought, edited by Heiko Oberman. Leiden: E. J. Brill, 1983.

Melanchthon, Philip. "Apology of the Augsburg Confession." In Theodore G. Tappert, ed. and trs. *The Book of Concord: The Confessions of the Evangelical Lutheran Church*. Philadelphia: Fortress Press, 1959.

Loci Communes Theologici. In Wilhelm Pauck, ed., *Melanchthon and Bucer*. The Library of Christian Classics, edited by John Baillie, et al., vol. XIX. London; SCM Press, 1969.

Melanchthon on Christian Doctrine: Loci Communes 1555. Translated and edited by Clyde L. Manschreck. Library of Protestant Thought. New York: Oxford University Press, 1965.

Opera quae Supersunt Omnia. Edited by Henricus Ernestus Bindseil. *Corpus Reformatorum*. Vol. XXI. New York: Johnson Reprint Corporation, 1963.

"Refutation of Servetus and the Anabaptists' Errors." In *A Melanchthon Reader*, translated by Ralph Keen. American University Studies, series VII: Theology and Religion, vol. XLI. New York: Peter Lang, 1988.

Merklinger, Philip M. *Philosophy, Theology, and Hegel's Berlin Philosophy of Religion, 1821–1827.* Albany: State University of New York Press, 1993.

Meyer, Matthias. "Das 'Mutter-Amt' des Heiligen Geistes in der Theologie Zinzendorfs." *Evangelische Theologie* 43 (1983): 415–430.

Molnar, Paul D. "The Function of the Immanent Trinity in the Theology of Karl Barth: Implications for Today." *Scottish Journal of Theology* 42 (1989): 367–399.

Moltmann, Jürgen. *The Crucified God: The Cross of Christ as the Foundation and Criticism of Christian Theology.* Translated by R. A. Wilson and John Bowden. New York: Harper & Row, 1974.

History and the Triune God: Contributions to Trinitarian Theology. Translated by John Bowden. New York: The Crossroad Publishing Co., 1992.

The Trinity and the Kingdom: The Doctrine of God. Translated by Margaret Kohl. San Francisco: Harper & Row, 1981.

Mueller, David L. *An Introduction to the Theology of Albrecht Ritschl.* Philadelphia: Westminster Press, 1969.

Muller, Richard A. "Scholasticism Protestant and Catholic: Francis Turretin on the Object and Principles of Theology." *Church History* 55 (1986): 193–205.

O'Donnell, John J. "The Doctrine of the Trinity in Recent German Theology." *The Heythrop Journal* 23 (1982): 153–167.

"The Trinity as Divine Community: A Critical Reflection Upon Recent Theological Developments." *Gregorianum* 69 (1988): 5–34.

Oeing-Hanoff, Ludger. "Hegels Trinitätslehre: Zur Aufgabe ihrer Kritik und Rezeption." *Theologie und Philosophie* 52 (1977): 378–407.

Olson, Roger E. "Trinity and Eschatology: The Historical Being of God in Jürgen Moltmann and Wolfhart Pannenberg." *Scottish Journal of Theology* 36 (1983): 213–227.

"Wolfhart Pannenberg's Doctrine of the Trinity." *Scottish Journal of Theology* 43 (1990): 175–206.

Owen, H. P. "Revelation." In Charles W. Kegley, ed., *The Theology of Rudolf Bultmann*, London: SCM Press, 1966.

Pannenberg, Wolfhart. "The Christian Vision of God: The New Discussion on the Trinitarian Doctrine." *The Asbury Theological Journal* 46 (1991): 27–36.

Jesus – God and Man. Translated by Lewis L. Wilkins and Duane A. Priebe. Philadelphia: Westminster Press, 1968.

"Die Subjektivität Gottes und die Trinitätslehre: Ein Beitrag zur Beziehung zwischen Karl Barth und der Philosophie Hegels." *Kerygma und Dogma* 23 (1977): 25–40.

Systematic Theology. Translated by Geoffrey W. Bromiley. 3 vols. Grand Rapids: Wm. B. Eerdmans Publishing Co., 1991–1998.

Theology and the Kingdom of God. Edited by Richard John Neuhaus. Philadelphia: Westminster Press, 1977.

Parsons, Gerald. "Pietism and Liberalism: Some Unexpected Continuities." *Religion* 14 (1984): 223–243.

"Reappraising Ritschl." *Modern Churchman* 22 (1978–1979): 109–117.

Pelikan, Jaroslav. *The Christian Tradition: A History of the Development of Doctrine.* Vol. I, *The Emergence of the Catholic Tradition (100–600).* Chicago: University of Chicago Press, 1971.

Powell, Sam. "The Doctrine of the Trinity in Nineteenth Century American Wesleyanism 1850–1900." *Wesleyan Theological Journal* 18, no. 2 (1983): 33–46.

Prenter, Regin. *Spiritus Creator.* Translated by John M. Jensen. Philadelphia: Muhlenberg Press, 1953.

Preus, Robert D. *The Theology of Post-Reformation Lutheranism.* Vol. II, *God and His Creation.* St. Louis: Concordia Publishing, 1972.

Radlbeck, Regina. *Der Personbegriff in der Trinitätstheologie der Gegenwart – untersucht am Beispiel der Entwürfe Jürgen Moltmanns und Walter Kaspers.* Eichstätter Studien. Neue Folge, vol. XXVII. Regensburg: Verlag Friedrich Pustet, 1989.

Regner, Friedmann. "Lessings Spinozismus." *Zeitschrift für Theologie und Kirche* 68 (1971): 351–375.

Reimarus, Hermann Samuel. *Reimarus: Fragments.* Edited by Charles Talbert. Translated by Ralph S. Fraser. Lives of Jesus Series. Philadelphia: Fortress Press, 1970.

Rendtorff, Trutz. *Church and Theology: The Systematic Function of the Church Concept in Modern Theology.* Translated by Reginald H. Fuller. Philadelphia: Westminster Press, 1971.

Richmond, James. *Ritschl: A Reappraisal. A Study in Systematic Theology.* London: Collins, 1978.

Ritschl, Albrecht. *The Christian Doctrine of Justification and Reconciliation: The Positive Development of the Doctrine.* Edited by H. R. Mackintosh and A. B. Macaulay. New York: Charles Scribner's Sons, 1900.

Three Essays. Translated by Philip Hefner. Philadelphia: Fortress Press, 1972.

Roberts, Richard. "Karl Barth." In *One God in Trinity.* Peter Toon and James D. Spiceland, eds., Westchester, IL: Cornerstone Books, 1980.

Rohls, Jan. "Subjekt, Trinität und Persönlichkeit Gottes: Von der Reformation zur Weimarer Klassik." *Neue Zeitschrift für systematische Theologie* 30 (1988): 40–71.

Rosato, Philip J., S. J. *The Spirit as Lord. The Pneumatology of Karl Barth.* Edinburgh: T. & T. Clark, 1981.

Rosenau, Hartmut. "Philosophie und Christologie." *Neue Zeitschrift für systematische Theologie und Religionsphilosophie* 29 (1987): 39–55.

Ruh, Hans. *Die christologische Begründung des ersten Artikels bei Zinzendorf.* Zurich: EVZ-Verlag, 1963.

Saarinen, Risto. *Gottes Wirken auf uns: die transzendentale Deutung des Gegenwart-Christi-Motivs in der Lutherforschung.* Stuttgart: Franz Steiner Verlag Wiesbaden GMBH, 1989.

Schachten, W. "Die Trinitätslehre Joachims von Fiore im Lichte der Frage nach der Subjektivität Gottes in der neueren Theologie." *Franziskanische Studien* 62 (1980): 39–61.

Schäfer, Rolf. *Ritschl: Grundlinien eines fast verschollenen dogmatischen Systems.* Beiträge zur historischen Theologie, no. 41. Tübingen: J. C. B. Mohr (Paul Siebeck), 1968.

Schaff, Philip, ed. *A Select Library of the Nicene and Post-Nicene Fathers of the Christian Church.* Vol. III, *St. Augustin: On the Holy Trinity, Doctrinal Treatises, Moral Treatises.* Grand Rapids: Wm. B. Eerdmans Publishing Co., 1978.

Schleiermacher, Friedrich. *The Christian Faith.* Edited by H. R. Mackintosh and J. S. Stewart. Philadelphia: Fortress Press, 1976.

Friedrich Schleiermacher und die Trinitätslehre. Edited by Martin Tezt. Texte zur Kirchen- und Theologiegeschichte, vol. XI. Gütersloh: Gütersloher Verlagshaus Gerd Mohn, 1969.

"On the Discrepancy Between the Sabellian and Athanasian Method of Representing the Doctrine of a Trinity in the Godhead." Translated by Moses Stuart. *Biblical Repository and Quarterly Observer,* 1835.

Schlitt, Dale. *Divine Subjectivity: Understanding Hegel's Philosophy of Religion.* Scranton, PA: University of Scranton Press, 1990.

Hegel's Trinitarian Claim: A Critical Reflection. Leiden: E. J. Brill, 1984.

"The Whole Truth: Hegel's Reconceptualization of Trinity." *The Owl of Minerva* 15 (1984): 169–182.

Schmidt, Martin. "Zinzendorf und die Confessio Augustana." *Der Pietismus als theologische Erscheinung.* Arbeiten zur Geschichte des Pietismus, vol. XX. Göttingen: Vandenhoeck & Ruprecht, 1984.

Schmittner, Wolfgang. *Kritik und Apologetik in der Theologie J. S. Semlers.* Theologische Existenz Heute. Munich: Chr. Kaiser Verlag, 1963.

Schultze, Harald. "Religionskritik in der deutschen Aufklärung: Das Hauptwerk der Reimarus im 200. Jahre des Fragmentenstreites." *Theologische Literaturzeitung* 103 (1978): 706–713.

Schwarz, Reinhard. "Lessings 'Spinozismus.'" *Zeitschrift für Theologie und Kirche* 65 (1968): 271–290.

Schwöbel, Christoph. "Wolfhart Pannenberg." In David F. Ford, ed., *The Modern Theologians: An Introduction to Christian Theology in the Twentieth Century.* Vol. I. Oxford: Basil Blackwell, 1990.

Semler, Johann Salomo. *Abhandlung von freier Untersuchung des Canon.* Edited by Heinz Scheible. Texte zur Kirchen- und Theologiegeschichte. Gutersloh: Mohn, 1967.

Apparatus ad Libros Symbolicos Ecclesiae Lutheranae. Halae Magdeburgicae, 1775.

Beantwortung der Fragmente eines Ungenanten [sic] *insbesondere vom Zweck Jesu und seiner Jünger.* Halle, 1779.

"Vorrede" to Samuel Clarke, *Die Schriftlehre von der Dreieinigkeit, worinn jede Stelle des Neuen Testaments, die diese Lehre angeht, besonders betrachtet, und die Gottheit unsers Hochgelobten Heilands nach den Schriften bewiesen und erklärt wird.* Frankfurt, 1774.

Smail, Thomas A. "The Doctrine of the Holy Spirit." In John Thompson, ed., *Theology Beyond Christendom: Essays on the Centenary of the Birth of Karl Barth May 10, 1886.* Princeton Theological Monograph Series, no. 6. Allison Park, PA: Pickwick Publications, 1986.

Smart, James D. *The Divided Mind of Modern Theology: Karl Barth and Rudolf Bultmann, 1908–1933.* Philadelphia: Westminster Press, 1967.

Sockness, Brent W. "Ethics as Fundamental Theology: The Function of Ethics in the Theology of Wilhelm Herrmann." In Harlan Beckley, ed., *The Annual of the Society of Christian Ethics.* Boston: School of Theology, Boston University, 1992: 75–96.

Sommer, Wolfgang. "Die Stellung Semlers und Schleiermachers zu den reformatorischen Bekenntnisschriften: Ein theologiegeschichtlicher Vergleich." *Kerygma und Dogma* 35 (1989): 296–315.

Spiegler, Gerhard. *The Eternal Covenant: Schleiermacher's Experiment in Cultural Theology.* New York: Harper & Row, 1967.

Splett, Jörg. *Die Trinitätslehre G. W. F. Hegels.* Symposion: Philosophische Schriftenreihe. Edited by Max Müller, et al. No. 20. Freiburg: Verlag Karl Alber, 1965.

Stepelevich, Lawrence S. "Hegel and Roman Catholicism." *Journal of the American Academy of Religion* 60/4 (1992): 673–691.

Strauss, David Friedrich. *The Life of Jesus Critically Examined.* Edited by Peter C. Hodgson. Translated by George Eliot. Lives of Jesus Series. Philadelphia: Fortress Press, 1972; repr., Ramsey, NJ: Sigler Press, 1994.

Streetman, Robert Francis. "Friedrich Schleiermacher's Doctrine of the Trinity and Its Significance for Theology Today." Ph.D. dissertation, Drew University, 1975.

Tappert, Theodore G., ed. *The Book of Concord: The Confessions of the Evangelical Lutheran Church.* Philadelphia: Fortress Press, 1959.

Theis, Robert. "Die Lehre von der Dreieinigkeit Gottes bei Karl Barth." *Freiburger Zeitschrift für Philosophie und Theologie* 24 (1977): 251–290.

Thompson, John. "On the Trinity." In John Thompson., ed., *Theology Beyond Christendom: Essays on the Centenary of the Birth of Karl Barth May 10, 1886*. Princeton Theological Monograph Series, no. 6. Allison Park, PA: Pickwick Publications, 1986.

Tillich, Paul. *Systematic Theology*. 3 vols. Chicago: University of Chicago Press, 1951–1963.

Troeltsch, Ernst. *The Christian Faith*. Translated by Garrett E. Paul. Edited by Gertrud von le Fort. Fortress Texts in Modern Theology. Minneapolis: Fortress Press, 1991.

Ernst Troeltsch: Writings on Theology and Religion. Edited and translated by Robert Morgan and Michael Pye. Louisville: Westminster/John Knox Press, paperback edition, 1990.

Religion in History. Translated by James Luther Adams and Walter F. Bense. Fortress Texts in Modern Theology. Minneapolis: Fortress Press, 1991.

The Social Teaching of the Christian Churches. Translated by Olive Wyon. 2 vols. Midway Reprint. Chicago: University of Chicago Press, 1976.

Voelkel, Robert T. *The Shape of the Theological Task*. Philadelphia: Westminster Press, 1968.

Voisin, Carol Jean. "A Reconsideration of Friedrich Schleiermacher's Treatment of the Doctrine of the Trinity." Th.D. dissertation, Graduate Theological Union, 1981.

Vorster, Hans. "Werkzeug oder Täter? Zur Methodik der Christologie Albrecht Ritschls." *Zeitschrift für Theologie und Kirche* 62 (1965): 46–65.

Wagner, Falk. "Religiöser Inhalt und logische Form: Zum Verhältnis von Religionsphilosophie und 'Wissenschaft der Logik' am Beispiel der Trinitätslehre." *Die Flucht in den Begriff: Materialen zu Hegels Religionsphilosophie*. Herausgegeben von Friedrich Wilhelm Graf und Falk Wagner. Deutsche Idealismus: Philosophie und Wirkungsgeschichte in Quellen und Studien. Band VI. Stuttgart, Ernst Klett, 1981.

Wartenberg, Thomas E. "Hegel's Idealism: The Logic of Conceptuality." In Frederick C. Beiser, ed., *The Cambridge Companion to Hegel*. Cambridge Companions to Philosophy. Cambridge: Cambridge University Press, 1993.

Wessel, Leonard P. *G. E. Lessing's Theology: A Reinterpretation. A Study in the Problematic Nature of the Enlightenment*. The Hague: Mouton & Co., 1977.

Williams, R. D. "Barth on the Triune God." In S. W. Sykes, ed., *Karl Barth: Studies of His Theological Method*. Oxford: Clarendon Press, 1979.

Williams, Robert R. *Schleiermacher the Theologian: The Construction of the Doctrine of God*. Philadelphia: Fortress Press, 1978.

Willis, W. Waite, Jr. *Theism, Atheism and the Doctrine of the Trinity: The Trinitarian Theologies of Karl Barth and Jürgen Moltmann in Response to Protest Atheism.* American Academy of Religion Academy Series, no. 53. Atlanta: Scholars Press, 1987.

Willmer, Peter. *Lessing und Zinzendorf: Eine vergleichende Studie zu Lessings Glauben.* American University Studies. Series I: Germanic Languages and Literature, vol. LXXII. New York: Peter Lang, 1989.

Wood, Laurence W. "From Barth's Trinitarian Christology to Moltmann's Trinitarian Pneumatology: A Methodist Perspective." *The Asbury Theological Journal* 48 (1993): 49–80.

Wrzecionko, Paul. *Die Philosophischen Wurzeln der Theologie Albrecht Ritschls. Ein Beitrag zum Problem des Verhältnisses von Theologie und Philosophie im 19. Jahrhundert.* Berlin: A. Töpelmann, 1964.

Zimmerling, Peter. "Zinzendorfs Trinitätslehre: Eine Herausforderung und Bereicherung in systematisch-theologischen Überlegungen der Gegenwart." *Evangelische Theologie* 51 (1991): 224–245.

Zinzendorf, Nicholaus Ludwig Count von. *Hauptschriften.* Edited by Erich Beyreuther and Gerhard Meyer. 6 vols. Hildesheim: Georg Olms Verlagsbuchhandlung, 1963.

Nine Public Lectures on Important Subjects in Religion. Translated by George W. Forell. Iowa City: University of Iowa Press, 1973.

Zscharnack, Leopold. *Lessing und Semler: Ein Beitrag zur Entstehungsgeschichte des Rationalismus und der kritischen Theologie.* Gießen: Verlag von Alfred Töpelmann, 1905.

Index

analogy 5–7, 23, 29, 210
  Barth 184, 186, 189
  Leibniz 32, 46–58
  Lessing 80–87
  Luther 23
  Melanchthon 6, 26–28
  Tillich 212
Aristotle 17
  Hegel 105, 116
  Leibniz 46, 47, 53
  Lessing 82, 85
  Ritschl 149
Augsburg Confession 34
Augustine 5–7, 26–27, 47, 202, 212, 216,
  230–231
Augustinian-Thomistic tradition 5–7, 24,
  47, 48–51, 123, 126, 140, 143, 167, 216,
  218, 220–221, 224–225, 237–238

Barth, Karl 174
  attitude toward dogma 243–244
  contrasted with Leibniz 57–58
  difference from Bultmann 183, 185–191
  difference from Tillich 183, 216–217
  God as person 217–220, 224
  God's freedom 185, 192, 221–222, 248
  God's historicity 246–248
  God's otherness 213, 221–223
  God's selfhood 216–226
  Holy Spirit 188–189, 225
  Jesus Christ 187–190, 222–224
  relation to Hegel 184, 190, 191, 192–193
  relation to liberal theology 164
  relation to Melanchthon 191
  revelation 183–193, 246–247
  Sabellianism 186, 219–220
  subordinationism 223–224
  Trinitarian persons 222–224
Bengel, Johann Albrecht 40

Bible's authority 43
  critique of Zinzendorf's view of the
    Trinity 44–45
  view of the Bible 42–43
Bible 3
  Bengel 42–43
  Lessing 85–86
  Luther's use of 24–26
  Melanchthon 22
  Reimarus 64–67
  Schleiermacher 92–93
  Semler 71–74
  Zinzendorf 43–45
Bultmann, Rudolf 174
  criticism of the Trinity 177–179
  historical criticism of the Trinity
    239–240
  Jesus Christ 176–178
  relation to Barth 176, 185–191
  relation to liberal theology 175, 180, 240
  relation to Melanchthon 13, 178–179,
    190–191
  view of revelation 175–180

Enlightenment and Enlightenment
    theology 58–59, 60–63
  Hegel 104, 105, 107–110, 111, 125–126,
    130
  Lessing 81–82, 83
  liberal theology 171
  Schleiermacher 87–88, 102

Formula of Concord 28

Gadamer, Hans-Georg 174
God the Father
  Leibniz 49–50, 52–53
  Schleiermacher 93, 94–95, 101
  Zinzendorf 36, 39–40, 41–42

276

God the Son (the Word)
  Leibniz 48, 50, 52–53
  Lessing 83–84, 86–87

Harnack, Adolf von 142
  historical criticism of doctrine 161–162,
    163–164
  interpretation of Luther 147–148
Hegel, Georg Wilhelm Friedrich 104
  absolute spirit 113–115, 120
  Begriff (concept) 119, 121–122
  conceptual comprehension 106–113,
    124, 136, 138
  critique of Kant 111–112
  dialectical thinking 112–113, 117
  difference from Melanchthon 139
  economic Trinity 128–134
  faith 120, 124, 136–138
  finitude 123–124, 128–133
  God as spirit 115, 116
  Hegel as a metaphysical thinker
    114–115
  Holy Spirit 120, 134–138
  influence on contemporary theology
    258–259
  Jesus Christ 108–109, 118, 120, 131–137
  knowability of God 105–110
  lectures on the philosophy of religion
    115–116
  love 126–127, 137–138
  ontological Trinity 120–128
  pantheism 129–130, 131
  person 125–127
  representational thinking 108–110,
    120–122, 138
  revelation 106–107, 116–120
  role of God in his system 113–115
  Son 130–133
  system 113–115
  understanding 111–113, 116–117, 124–125
  universality and particularity 117–119,
    120–121, 128–129, 130–131, 133–134,
    136–137
Herrmann, Wilhelm 142
  faith 153–154
  historical criticism of doctrine 160
  influenced by Schleiermacher 157–158,
    160
history
  Moltmann 198–201
  Pannenberg 208–210
historical criticism 60–62, 102
  Barth 243–244

Bultmann 239–240
Moltmann 244–245
Pannenberg 244–245
Reimarus 9, 63–69
Schleiermacher 87–88, 99–100,
  102–103
Semler 70–72, 74–78
Tillich 240–243
historicity of God
  Barth 246–248
  Hegel 128–134, 139–140
  Moltmann 248–253
  Pannenberg 253–258
Holy Spirit
  Barth 188–189, 225
  Hegel 120, 134–138
  Leibniz 48, 50, 51–52
  Lessing 84–85
  Ritschl 144
  Schleiermacher 94–95, 97–101
  Zinzendorf 40, 42

Jesus Christ
  Barth 187–190, 222–224
  Bultmann 176–178
  Hegel 108–109, 118, 120, 131–137
  Lessing 85
  Moltmann 197–199
  Pannenberg 205–210
  Reimarus 67–68
  Ritschl 143–144, 149–151
  Schleiermacher 94–95, 97–101
  Tillich 182–183
  Zinzendorf 36–37, 39–42

Leibniz, Gottfried Wilhelm 32
  faith seeking understanding 46–47
  God as substance 47–48
  God the Father 49–50, 52–53
  God's unity and the Trinity 51–52
  Holy Spirit 48, 50, 51–52
  idea of force 47–48
  idea of substance 47–48
  lack of interest in historical dimension
    of the Trinity 54–55
  modalism 50
  Son 48
  speculative-analogical Trinity
    55–57
  substance and the Trinity 48–49
  Trinity and the divine intellect 52
  Trinity of knower and known 50–53
  Word 50, 52–53

Lessing, Gotthold 62
    attitude toward Enlightenment theology
      81–82
    God's relation to the world 86
    Holy Spirit 84–85
    Jesus Christ 85
    Son 83–84, 86–87
    "The Christianity of Reason" 82–85
    view of Christian doctrine 85–86
    view of the Bible 85–86
Luther, Martin
    importance of the doctrine of the
      Trinity 18–19
    influence on later Protestant thought
      28–29
    influence on liberal theologians 146–155
    subordination of creeds to Bible 22
    Trinity and human reason 23–24
    use of the Bible 24–26
    view of creeds 14–16, 18

Melanchthon, Philip
    affirmation of the Trinity 19–21
    influence on later Protestant thought
      28–30
    relation to Schleiermacher 88, 103
    response to Michael Servetus 21
    subordination of creeds to Bible 21–22
    view of Christian doctrine 16–17
    view of revelation 4–5
Moltmann, Jürgen 174
    attitude toward dogma 244–245
    critique of Augustine 201
    critique of liberal theology 194–196,
      249–250
    critique of monotheism 226–227
    critique of Schleiermacher 194, 197
    divine love 200–201, 229–231, 251–253
    doxological and economic Trinity
      199–200, 250–251
    God's freedom 199, 228, 250–251
    God's historicity 248–253
    God's relation to the world 251–253
    God's selfhood 226–233
    Jesus Christ 197–199
    relation to Barth 193–198, 199, 200,
      220–221, 227–229
    relation to Hegel 193, 195, 200, 230,
      252
    revelation 193–202
    Sabellianism 227
    social analogy 226, 231–233

subordinationism 232
Trinitarian persons 195, 198–199,
    231–233, 250
unity of God 231

Pannenberg, Wolfhart 174
    attitude toward dogma 244–245
    criticism of Schleiermacher 203
    eternal and economic Trinity 207,
      254
    eternity and time 256–258
    God as person 234–236
    God's freedom 207
    God's historicity 253–258
    God's love 234, 235
    God's selfhood 233–239
    history and revelation 253
    incarnation 208
    Jesus Christ 205–210
    Rahner's Rule 207
    relation to Barth 193–194, 202–204,
      220–221, 233–234
    relation to Hegel 193, 203, 233–235
    retroactive power of history 239, 245,
      255–256
    revelation 202–210
    Trinitarian persons 204–205, 208–209,
      236–239, 254
    unity of God 204–205, 235–236
personality 8–9
    Barth 217–220, 224
    liberal theology 163, 166–171
    Pannenberg 234–236
pietism 32, 37, 76
    Hegel's criticism of 105–107

Rahner, Karl 207
rationalism 32, 60–61
Reimarus, Hermann Samuel 62
    historical criticism 9
    intention of Jesus 67–68
    interpretation of New Testament 64–67
    interpretation of the disciples 68–69
revelation (the Word)
    Barth 183–193, 246–247
    Bultmann 175–180
    Hegel 106–107, 116–120, 139
    Luther 4, 18–19, 23
    Melanchthon 4–5
    Moltmann 193–202
    Pannenberg 202–210
    Ritschl 143, 145, 149–152

Schleiermacher 88, 92, 94, 95, 99,
  102–103
Semler 73
Tillich 180–183, 241
Zinzendorf 36–46
Richard of St. Victor 202, 230, 235–236
Ritschl, Albrecht 142
  citation of Spener 152–153
  compared with Barth 150–151
  faith 150–153
  Holy Spirit 144
  influenced by Schleiermacher 157
  Jesus Christ 143–144, 149–151
  personality of God 168–169
  place of the Trinity in theology 144
  revelation 143, 145, 149–152
  similarity to Zinzendorf 146
  soteriology 150–153
  use of Luther's theology 149–153
  view of doctrine 157
  views of Luther 12–13

Sabellius, Sabellianism, modalism 56, 77,
  79, 93
  Barth 186, 219–220, 244
  Leibniz 50
  Moltmann 227, 230, 232
  Schleiermacher 91, 99–101
Schleiermacher, Friedrich 59, 63
  conception of God 89, 94–97
  criticisms of Schleiermacher 88–90
  critique of the doctrine of the Trinity
    90–96
  divine essence 98–100
  divine nature 96
  God the Father 93, 94–95, 101
  God's love 100
  history 10
  influence on liberal theologians 155–159
  Jesus Christ and the Holy Spirit 94–95,
    97–101
  relation to the Enlightenment 87–88,
    102–103
  Sabellius 91, 99–101
  similarity to Melanchthon 88, 103
  view of dogma 102–103, 156
  view of revelation 92, 94, 95, 99,
    102–103
scholastic theology 33, 37–38, 69–70, 72,
  73, 84, 143, 154, 191, 203
Schweitzer, Albert 2
Semler, Johann Salomo 62

critique of Reimarus 78–79
doctrine of the Trinity 73–74, 76–77,
  78–80
inner and outer religion 74–76
interpretation of the creeds 71–72, 77–78
relationship to Luther and
  Melanchthon 69–71
similarity to Zinzendorf 69–70
understanding of the Bible 71–74
view of revelation 73
Socinianism and Arianism 34, 45, 77, 92,
  129, 240
Spinoza, Benedict 46, 80, 82
subordinationism 93, 94
  Barth 222–224
  Moltmann 232
  Pannenberg 208
  Zinzendorf 41–42

Thomas Aquinas 5–7, 18, 20, 47–50, 51–53,
  82, 84, 87, 169, 218
Tillich, Paul 174
  agreement with Schleiermacher
    182–183
  God as spirit 211–212, 214–216
  God's selfhood 211–216
  historical criticism of the Trinity
    240–243
  Jesus Christ 182–183
  life and dialectics 212–213
  relation to Barth 182–183, 213–214
  relation to Hegel 211–212, 214–215
  relation to Schelling 212, 215
  revelation 180–183, 241
  Trinitarian persons 214
  Trinitarian symbols 180–181, 211, 214
Troeltsch, Ernst 142
  critique of traditional theology 162–163
  essence of Christianity 164–165
  influenced by Schleiermacher 158

Zinzendorf, Nicolaus Ludwig von 32
  appropriations 41
  debate with Johann Albrecht Bengel 40,
    42–45
  doctrine of the Trinity based on
    experience of redemption 35
  God the Father 36, 39–40, 41–42
  Holy Spirit 40, 42
  Jesus Christ 36–37, 39–42
  knowledge of the Trinity only through
    revelation 38, 141

Zinzendorf, Nicolaus Ludwig von (*cont.*)
    metaphors for the Trinity 39–40
    place in the Protestant tradition 37–38
    rejection of speculation 35
    similarity to Melanchthon 32–33, 35

subordinationism 41–42
use of Luther 36–37
view of the Augsburg Confession 34
view of the Bible 43–45
view of revelation 36–46